# *Angelology*

# *Angelology*

Recovering Higher-Order Beings as Emblems of
Transcendence, Immanence, and Imagination

Dylan David Potter

*Foreword by David Brown*

CASCADE *Books* · Eugene, Oregon

ANGELOLOGY
Recovering Higher-Order Beings as Emblems of Transcendence, Immanence, and Imagination

Cascade Books
An Imprint of Wipf and Stock Publishers
199 W. 8th Ave., Suite 3
Eugene, OR 97401

www.wipfandstock.com

PAPERBACK ISBN 13: 978-1-4982-2107-8
HARDCOVER ISBN 13: 978-1-4982-2109-2


*Cataloguing-in-Publication Data*

Potter, Dylan David

Angelology : recovering higher-order beings as emblems of transcendence, immanence, and imagination / Dylan David Potter, with a foreword by David Brown.

xiv + 214 p. ; 23 cm. Includes bibliographical references.

ISBN: 978-1-4982-2107-8 (paperback) | ISBN: 978-1-4982-2109-2 (hardback)

1. Angels—History of doctrines. 2. Angels—History. 3. Angels—Biblical teaching. I. Brown, David. II. Title.

BT966.2 P78 2016

Manufactured in the U.S.A.                                              04/05/2016

Dedicated to Jacqueline and Sebastian . . . *sine qua non*

# Contents

# Foreword

AMONG CONTEMPORARY RELIGIOUS BELIEVERS treatment of angels tends to lie at one or other of two extremes: an enthusiastic endorsement in which their presence is detected everywhere, or else relegation of them to a now redundant past worldview, perhaps seen as inspired by Persian mythology. It is one of the great merits of the discussion that follows that Dylan Potter rejects both extremes. Instead, readers are offered a carefully nuanced account of how angels have functioned symbolically at various key points in their development, not, however, with the intention of dismissing them as "mere symbolism" but rather as a way of working through their meaning to a more profound grasp of why their existence might after all be deemed important to religious belief.

Accordingly, three key moments in history are chosen for further examination: at the origins of the Christian tradition in the Hebrew Scriptures, and then subsequently in the writings of two major theologians of later Christian history, St. Thomas Aquinas in the thirteenth century and before him the anonymous sixth-century figure now known as Pseudo-Denys because of his once presumed identification with the Greek Dionysius who heard Paul preach on the Areopagus Hill in Athens (Acts 17:34). In each case Potter offers powerful challenges to any simplistic account of why angels appear so prominently in each of the three cases. His suggestion in the case of the Hebrew Scriptures is that the intention was to augment a growing sense of divine transcendence while with Pseudo-Denys the aim was the exact opposite: to draw God closer in the celebration of the liturgy. Both accounts challenge commonly accepted views, especially in the case of Pseudo-Denys where he is often presented as a Neoplatonist concerned to use angels as a way of enhancing the distance and mystery of God. Equally when Potter turns to Aquinas he insists that interpretation has focused too narrowly on his more philosophical works and that this has resulted in a distorted account that can only be corrected by turning to Aquinas' neglected biblical commentaries.

To the general reader such disputes about the interpretation of past writings may seem of little significance, but in fact what Potter succeeds brilliantly in doing is demonstrating how important it is to note context before commenting on how angels might contribute to Christian theology. That is why his final chapter is of such importance, for there Potter shows how contemporary theology weakens the case for the existence of angels by ignoring those earlier connections, and this is true not only of those with a more liberal agenda, such as New Age theologians, but also even of a theological giant such as Karl Barth. Barth, Potter suggests, actually undermines his claims for a transcendent God by loosening the original Hebrew undergirding of such transcendence through angels.

I was privileged to supervise this work while Dylan was studying at the Divinity School at St. Andrews, and learnt much in the process. Dylan's examiners were also fulsome in their praise. While such esteem can be partly explained by his careful attention to detail and to historical context, no less important was the quality of his chosen theological method which could easily be applied more generally. In an age when Christians so often divide into liberal or conservative Dylan offers an alternative way forward, one in which the contingencies of history are fully accepted but then not used to cast aspersion on the past. Instead, parallels are seen in our own present circumstances that can then be used to deepen theology in our own day, certainly in respect of angels but also potentially much more widely.

*David Brown*
*University of St. Andrews*

# Preface

THE AIM OF THIS book is twofold: to identify the theological purpose underlying the depiction of angels at certain key points in the history of their use, and to explore how far that deeper theological rationale can be reappropriated for our own day.

This study first traces the progression of the angelic motif in the Hebrew Scriptures. By examining numerous pericopes in the Pentateuch, Major Prophets, and Daniel, I demonstrate that the metamorphosis of higher-order beings like the angel of the Lord, cherubim, and seraphim, is directly related to the writers' desire to enhance God's transcendence.

Next, I evaluate pseudo-Denys's hierarchical angelology, which prominent theologians like Luther and Calvin condemned as little more than a Neoplatonic scheme for accessing God through angels. I propose that not only has pseudo-Denys's Neoplatonism been overstated, but that his angelology is particularly noteworthy for the way it accentuates Christ's eucharistic immanence to the church.

Then I maintain that because assessments of Aquinas's angelology are often based upon the *Summa Theologiae*, his views are wrongly portrayed as overtly philosophical, rather than biblical and exegetical. In his lesser-known biblical commentaries, however, Aquinas pushes the semantic range of the word "angel" to include aspects of the physical world, which unveils an imaginative, Christocentric, and scriptural dimension of his angelology that is rarely acknowledged.

The conclusion considers how contemporary figures and movements relate to these three angelologies. Barth emphasizes the transcendent God, but unlike Hebrew Scripture, weakens connections between God and angels. New Ageism affirms the immanent angel, but unlike pseudo-Denys, does so at the expense of Christology and ecclesiology. Contemporary ecological discourse generally lacks Aquinas's appreciation for an imaginative, supernatural approach to the world. Finally, I ground the angels' relationship to transcendence, immanence, and imagination in an experiential, eucharistic context.

# Acknowledgements

THIS BOOK WOULD NOT have been possible without support and guidance from a great number of people. First of all, I wish to express my gratitude to Professor David Brown, my doctoral supervisor, for his generous patience and the valuable insights he provided during my time at the Divinity school at St. Andrews. His expert oversight and broad knowledge of theology, philosophy, and biblical studies steered me in the right direction on numerous occasions. Likewise, I want to recognize Dr. Gavin Hopps and Dr. David Torevell, my examiners, whose helpful recommendations improved my research.

Special thanks are also due to my family for their interest and kind encouragement during the research and writing process: to David, Kathy, Dagan, and Bree Potter, to Darcy and John Melnik, and to Mdm Lee Guat Lean. Also of special note are, Isabella, Gabrielle, Ayla, and Liam.

Most of all, I am ever grateful to my wife, Jacqueline, and my son, Sebastian, who are to be enormously thanked for the countless ways they supported and inspired me. This book is lovingly dedicated to them.

# Introduction

## THE EXISTENTIAL PROBLEM

EVER SINCE GOD PLANTED cherubim outside the eastern entrance to Eden's garden, humanity has grappled with a religion of exile and distance, an estrangement neither desired nor entirely understood. Attempts to recover the paradisiacal have led persons to pursue assurances of salvation, secular enlightenment, psychic catharsis, the establishment of civic justice, and even martyrdom. The mythopoeia of a relinquished, verdant garden is symbolic of humanity's collective sense of separation from the divine, and the tenets of myriad religions, sects, and philosophies, even political ideologies, are faint echoes of the innate desire to recolonize this sacred abode.[1] Whether Paradise is an internal or external phenomenon, a present or a future experience, a realm shrouded behind death's veil or the dark clouds of an eschatological future, the longing for undisrupted tranquillity is evenly distributed across the human spectrum.[2]

However, if Paradise is the dwelling of God and angels then theophanies and angelophanies are nothing less than manifestations of this sacred realm. Once our ancestor's pens first scratched sacred parchment, their records of such epiphanic events offered a reminder that glimpses of felicity also exist east of Eden. Christianity affirms that the Son of God, through the cross, ultimately reconciles the inequality between the eternally-edenic and moribundly-mundane. However, efforts to paint

---

1. The Edenic setting is a common motif in world literature; one example is its role as a *locus amoenus*, described in Curtius, *European Literature and the Latin Middle Ages*, 192–201.

2. Even the atheist may find solace in the idea that life's cessation marks the end of life's struggles and disappointments.

Christ as the one who reconnects the golden chain once severed by the ancient pair must not simultaneously debrush the angels who gilt the biblical panorama. As T. F. Torrance cautioned, "Disregard of the ministry of angels will certainly lead to a serious deficiency in Christian spirituality, bringing many forms of shallowness and instability in its train."[3] Christ's active and passive work provides the definitive solution to the human predicament, but the angels fill numerous lacunae for persons presently absent from his ascended presence. Therefore, the aim of this book is twofold: first, to identify the theological purpose underlying the depiction of angels at certain key points in the history of their use, and, secondly, to explore how far that deeper theological rationale can be re-appropriated for our own day.

## GAPS IN MODERN ANGELOLOGY

Modern Christian angelologies belong under one of three rubrics: reaffirmation, revision, and rediscovery. There are strengths and weaknesses peculiar to each group. The first group of angelologies, those of reaffirmation, is often produced by conservative writers and systematicians. This approach largely involves collating biblical pericopes about angels. The noble motivation of such works is to derive doctrine from Scripture alone. However, the drawback is that the approach tends to promote an exceedingly narrow ribbon of interpretation, eschews critical scholarship, and is generally unsympathetic toward pre-Reformation angelologies.[4] It is easier to commend the group's convictions regarding the reality of angels than it is to uncover how their methodology, which is usually confined to mere reiteration, contributes to the doctrine.

While many reaffirmers punctuate their topical collection of Scripture verses with broad affirmations about the importance of angels to Judeo-Christian history, others emphasize the modern experience of angelic encounters, such as can be found in Billy Graham's book *Angels:*

---

3. Torrance, "The Spiritual Relevance of Angels," 122–39.

4. For instance, Schemm Jr., "The Agents of God: Angels," 293–337. Rhodes, *Angels among Us.* Boa and Bowman, *Sense and Nonsense about Angels and Demons.* Chafer and Walvoord, *Major Bible Themes*, 151–55. Calvin and other Reformed theologians intentionally restrained the scope of their discussion of angels to that which could be affirmed by the Bible itself. See 1:14.3–12; 163–72 in John Calvin, *Institutes Of the Christian Religion*, trans. Henry Beveridge. Also, Hodge, *Systematic Theology* 1:637–43; Berkhof, *Systematic Theology*, 141–48.

*God's Secret Agents*, which was a boon for popular interest in celestial be-ings.[5] Yet when compared to earlier centuries, serious discussions about angels are somewhat thin on the ground, even in conservative, academic circles. Prominent British evangelicals like N. T. Wright and Alister Mc-Grath, for instance, have said little about angels in their works, ostensibly because the subject falls outside their catalog of research interests. Mc-Grath's popular *Christian Theology* does not even retain an index entry for angels, nor does Reformed theologian Robert Reymond's textbook of theology. Similarly, even collaborative works of mainline scholarship, like *The Oxford Handbook of Systematic Theology*, fail to broach the subject.[6]

Although Karl Barth's discussion of angelology in his *Church Dog-matics* represents an exception to the uncritical and sparse treatment angels typically receive in modern systematics, he reasserts with the Reformers the stifling proposition that angelic *function* is all-important, deeming superfluous all discussions of the angel's form.[7] Needless to say, this approach undermines centuries of theological reflection by Chris-tian theologians who believed otherwise. My final chapter addresses this flaw in greater detail, arguing that Barth exalts God to such an extent that he needlessly marginalizes the angel's function and role. Even in Barth's admirable attempt to relate angelology to Christology, like Calvin and Luther before him, he minimizes the contributions of earlier luminaries like pseudo-Dionysius and Aquinas, to whom I have dedicated chapters in this work. So by ignoring angelology, limiting it to the reiteration of biblical verses or invalidating the benefits of earlier models, the reaffirmer unavoidably quashes the motive for further study and inquiry.[8]

Those fitting the second category, the revisers, are characterized by a willingness to embrace critical scholarship. However, unlike the reaffirm-ing group, these individuals normally shy away from the idea of angels

5. Modern systematicians like Wayne Grudem and Millard Erickson have chosen simply to reassert biblical support for literal angels without entertaining personal accounts. See Grudem, *Systematic Theology*, 397–411. Erickson, *Christian Theology*, 457–78.

6. Similarly, Migliore, *Faith Seeking Understanding: An Introduction to Christian Theology*. There are less than a dozen uses of the word "angel," most of which are part of quoted biblical verse. Reymond, *A New Systematic Theology of the Christian Faith*.

7. See *CD* III/3, 369–418. Pannenberg criticized him for this oblique emphasis. See Pannenberg, *Systematic Theology*, 2:102–8. Also, Osborn, "Entertaining Angels: Their Place in Contemporary Theology," 273–94.

8. There are also scant references to angels in the writings of Thielicke and Moltmann.

as literal beings.[9] For instance, Schleiermacher, Bultmann, and Rahner emphasized the influence of the biblical writer's mythological milieu over against divine inspiration, surmising that angels are essentially relics of an archaic *Weltanschauung*.[10]

Bultmann wrote, "It is impossible to use electric light and the wireless and to avail ourselves of modern medical and surgical discoveries, and at the same time to believe in the New Testament world of daemons and spirits."[11] Schleiermacher was slightly more charitable, admitting that angelology might be valuable for "private and liturgical use," but argued that "for the province of Dogmatics the subject remains wholly problematic."[12] His conclusion was based upon the premise that angelophanies "occurred in that primitive period when the interdependence of man with nature was not yet settled and he himself was undeveloped."[13] Rather than ascribing the same naiveté to Jesus' teaching about angels, however, Schleiermacher reframed it in terms of his own view, recruiting Christ as something of a theological colleague: "Christ and the Apostles might have said all these things [concerning angels] without having had any real conviction of the existence of such beings or any desire to communicate it . . . as, for example, we might talk of ghosts and fairies, although these ideas had no definite sort of relation to our actual convictions."[14]

Schleiermacher was reluctant to censure language about angels in hymnody or liturgy, even though he rejected them as actual, spiritual

---

9. For example, Tigchelaar, *Prophets of Old and The Day of the End: Zechariah, the Book of Watchers and Apocalyptic*, 69. Also see Harrington's work, where angels are described as "symbols of God's variegated communication with this creation" and "literary mediators in the dramatic unfolding of God's plan for his world." Harrington and Harrington, *Revelation*, 16:29.

10. Rahner, *Theological Investigations*, 19:250–65. Even Marcus Borg, hardly a traditionalist, acknowledges that "modern biblical scholarship has sought to understand its subject matter in accord with the root image of reality that dominates the modern mind"; and since this root image tends to value the observable, physical world over the imperceptible world of angels, "the aggressive denial of the two-foldness [sic] of reality" has largely been replaced by a "bracketing" or ignoring of the question. Borg, *Jesus in Contemporary Scholarship*, 133–34.

11. Bultmann, "The New Testament and Mythology," 5.

12. Schleiermacher, *The Christian Faith*, 160.

13. Ibid.

14. Ibid., 158.

guardians.[15] Yet more recently, the English theologian J. G. Davies cautioned against liturgical settings that promote a dichotomy between transcendent and immanent realms. Purporting to interact with "another, sacred, world" where congregants imagine themselves singing "praises in company with the heavenly choir of angels, archangels and saints," threatens to reduce "God to the status of a tribal deity," presumably because it removes the tincture of celestial presence within the world.[16] Although revisers attempt to offer scientifically credible and liturgically sensitive angelologies, their angels are religious artefacts whose relationship to the present world and the individual remains uncertain, if not meaningless.[17]

Finally, one encounters in the third category a small assortment of scholars whose research is geared toward the rediscovery of particular facets of angelology, including: studies of the variegated traditions associated with the *mal'ak YHWH*;[18] the role of angels in apocryphal books or ancient enclaves;[19] the roots of angelomorphic Christology;[20] exegetical considerations;[21] or the question of how diverse cultures understood

---

15. His rationale was that the angel "belongs to a time when our knowledge of the forces of nature was very limited, and our power over them at its lowest stage." Ibid., 159.

16. See, Davies, *Everyday God*, 243–45, 51.

17. The nineteenth-century educator, theologian, and church historian Karl von Hase and his contemporary, D. F. Strauss, echoed Schleiermacher's angelology. Strauss dismissed angels as "simply the ideal of created perfection: which, as it was formed from the subordinate point of view of a fanciful imagination, disappears from the higher and more comprehensive observation of the intellect." Strauss, *The Life of Jesus, Critically Examined*, 82.

18. Fossum, *The Name of God and the Angel of the Lord*; White, "Angel of the Lord: Messenger or Euphemism?"; MacDonald, "Current Issues in Biblical and Patristic Interpretation."

19. Davidson, *Angels at Qumran*; Frennesson, *In a Common Rejoicing*.

20. Foster, *Angelomorphic Christology and the Exegesis of Psalm 8*; Gieschen, *Angelomorphic Christology*; Hoffmann, *The Destroyer and the Lamb*; Hannah, *Michael and Christ*; Fletcher-Louis, *Luke-Acts*. This is not to suggest that their efforts are unimportant; for example, when modern theological discussions of angelomorphic Christology were in vogue, one learns that despite differences in approach to the subject, nearly all scholars rejected Werner's earlier theories that the first Christians thought of Christ as an angel by nature and that Christianity is essentially a faith built around an angel Christology.

21. McGarry, "The Ambidextrous Angel (Daniel 12:7 and Deuteronomy 32:40)," 211–28.

angelic beings throughout history.[22] This group's strength lies in its ability to analyze and integrate particularly obscure, complex swaths of literature. What one discovers in such volumes, though, is a closed form of conversation between specialists, which is largely inaccessible to the church. It is theology in service of the academy. While there is nothing inherently wrong with the rediscoverer's rationale, tone, or content, their conclusions are generally limited to the exploration of esoteric points of view. Yet in an age of dwindling institutional resources (especially for the humanities), it is questionable whether such a rarefied community will be able to support itself much longer without first demonstrating its value to both the academy and the church.

Consequently, I have attempted to position the present work in the crosscurrents of these three groups by interacting with angelology on a critical level, but without losing sight of the primacy of Scripture, the usefulness of imagination, or the traditions and needs of the church.

While disinclined to separate from those who reaffirm angels as literal beings, the scholarly prospects of the group are hindered by hermeneutical rigidity, a polemical stance toward pre-modern Christian angelologies, and a reluctance to interact meaningfully with ancient Near Eastern influences. Although sympathetic toward those in the second group who wish to revise the doctrine to account for philosophical differences between our era and the biblical age, I find their approach no less reductive than the reaffirming group, albeit for different reasons.

In fact, both camps share several faults. First, each group uses evidence selectively, creating an unnecessary dialectic that caricatures the angel as either pure myth or exclusively real. This law of the excluded middle plays upon the assumption that the mythology and historicity surrounding the angel figure are mutually exclusive, not congruous. Secondly, both groups tend to desacralize the angel by undermining its role as a mediator; the affirmer tends to associate mediation exclusively with either the Second or Third Person of the Trinity, while the reviser pursues a comparatively anthropocentric and Pelagian approach. Finally, both appear unsure what to make of the angels' role beyond the reach of theology or liturgy.

This brings us back to the third and final category of angelologies, which are bent upon neither reaffirmation nor revision, but rediscovery.

22. Tuschling, *Angels and Orthodoxy*; Olyan, *A Thousand Thousands Served Him*; Sullivan, *Wrestling with Angels*; Keck, *Angels & Angelology in the Middle Ages*. Also, see Bucur, *Angelomorphic Pneumatology*.

Unlike the other groups, one can hardly fault their scholarship or desire to follow truth wherever it leads. Yet just as the affirmer is perhaps too focused upon the church and the reviser is too focused upon the *Zeitgeist*, one wonders if in this last group, the study of angels sometimes tips too far in service of the academy. My goal, naturally, is to accommodate and synthesize the strengths of all three positions, while attempting to avoid their weaknesses.

## A DIFFERENT APPROACH

In light of these conceptual gaps, and because of a nagging sense that the doctrine is presently out of step with its eclectic origins and subsequent history, I have sought answers along more ancient byways. Therefore, my response to the modern paradigm emerges from the respective angelologies of the Hebrew Scriptures, pseudo-Denys, and Thomas Aquinas. There are several ways to interpret this approach. Since the following chapters stress three defining epochs in the evolution of angelology, they may be read as historical theology, although the chapter on Old Testament angelology is a form of biblical theology. This book is also compatible with the objectives of systematic theology, because each chapter profiles one distinct theme related to the doctrine itself. A third alternative would be to interpret the work as an ecumenical theology, attempting to reconcile what may be described as a broad representation of Jewish, Orthodox, Catholic, and Protestant angelologies. The work's primary objective, however, is to illustrate and contextualize a theological apparatus whereby the angel becomes a means of enhancing divine transcendence and immanence as well as human imagination—ideas absent in much of the current literature on the subject.

My first chapter focuses upon the Hebrew Scriptures, where I argue the angelic motif was a form of theological shorthand used by biblical authors to promote monotheism and Y*HWH*'s transcendence. By positioning the angels as celestial intermediaries, these writers—particularly in the Pentateuch, Major Prophets, and Daniel—indirectly emphasized God's otherness while simultaneously polemicizing the pantheon of the ancient Near East. Higher-order beings were conceived as actual entities throughout the region, and biblical writers transformed and shaped them in specific ways by the power of the narrative. Various patterns within the Old Testament demonstrate how the theological use and significance of angels intensified over time.[23] Despite their often-overlooked reliance upon the angel-motif, these writers did not feel an angelic aegis, so closely tied to pagan lore, posed a threat to monotheism. Instead, their literary revolution exalted Yhwh, identified patriarchs and prophets as his spokespersons, and provide a means of comfort to a nation in flux.

In chapter 2, I maintain that pseudo-Dionysius's angelology takes seriously the idea that an emphasis upon God's transcendence, like the one seen throughout the Old Testament, must also be complemented by a theology of immanence. My contention is that Denys's angelology was misunderstood by the Reformers and others as a Neoplatonic statement about accessing God's transcendence through angels. It was actually a means of mediating and accentuating divine immanence in light of Christ's physical absence and eucharistic presence. Thus angels, sacraments, liturgy, symbolism, and church offices become a statement of God's unifying activity among his people, serving to bridge all ontological and experiential gaps from a human perspective. Such a conception is often far removed from modern forms of worship, which may appear disjointed as a result. I conclude that the concept of an angelic hierarchy, even as a metaphor, helps to illustrate the sacred value of subtle forms of immanence within the church today. Yet, because pseudo-Denys tends to limit the experience of divine immanence to worship itself, one must look elsewhere in order to appreciate the angel's role within the natural world.

This point leads me to discuss a third approach to angelology in the penultimate chapter, gleaned from Thomas Aquinas's biblical commentaries. Providing glimpses of a forgotten thirteenth-century hermeneutic, these works illustrate how angelology may preserve Christocentric and scriptural dimensions without sacrificing imaginative creativity. Aquinas pushes the semantic range of the word "angel" to include aspects of the physical world itself, which allows him to use the angel to stress the

---

23. One does not need to be as skeptical about these details as David Jones is in his recent work on angels. Jones' main defence for his rejection of the idea that angels represent "a compromise with polytheism" is that it "is hard to know exactly what people believed in ancient Israel." However, one need not have comprehensive access to an era before advancing hypotheses about it. In fact, the correlation I defend in chapter 1 emerges from a numerous resources: biblical texts, secular histories, the lore of the ancient Near East and archaeological discoveries. Oddly enough, Jones sees no such pattern despite his recognition that "at the same time the Jews were asserting their monotheism, they were also becoming more interested in angels." Jones, *Angels*, 38.

presence of God throughout creation. Theologians during the sixteenth and nineteenth centuries severely limited the angel and criticized Aquinas's angelology, branding him as more of a dry academic than a pastoral theologian; but none, to my knowledge, interacted with his vibrant biblical commentaries, the majority of which remain untranslated. I conclude that by revisiting Aquinas's broad interpretation of what constitutes an angel, the church may again learn to see the physical world as a sacred place that ultimately points to God.

Each of the chapters examines monumental themes in the history of angelology, and my hope is that these issues will continue to cast long shadows down the corridors of theological reflection. Yet the angel's relationship to divine transcendence, immanence, and creativity must also be brought to bear upon more contemporary issues in order to be a compelling model for future theological orientation. This leads me in my final chapter to use the angelologies of the Old Testament, pseudo-Dionysius, and Aquinas to appraise several contemporary approaches. Accordingly, I contrast the relationship between angels and transcendence in the Old Testament with Karl Barth's version, arguing that Barth's emphasis upon divine transcendence does not always reflect the biblical witness about the importance of angels, and risks alienating an already skeptical, modern society. Next, the quality of immanence in pseudo-Denys's angelology is set against that of the New Age movement, which places an emphasis upon angels at the expense of God-ordained means of grace. Thirdly, I propose that modern ecology would be more animated if it maintained Aquinas's creative relationship between angels and the natural world. Finally, I offer a new perspective on angelology that harmonizes the peculiarities of transcendence, immanence, and imagination in the form of eucharistic experience.

Like the seeds of ancient date palms that still retain their fecundity after lying dormant for centuries, these ancient approaches to angelology remain equally potent for the needs of today's church. For that reason, my intention is for these chapters to constitute a series of stepping-stones that allow the reader to ford, perhaps in a new and unfamiliar way, a vast river of angel-related literature. The most critical rediscovery for the present day, however, is that the intricate history of angelology revealed herein is a product of the fluidity that was written into this doctrine from its inception. It is my hope that by reflecting upon the deeper theological purpose of angelology, the church will interpret life outside Eden's garden in a divine and supernatural light.

# Chapter I

# Angels in the Hebrew Scriptures
## *Means of Enhanced Transcendence*

## INTRODUCTION

Two premises explain the thrust of this chapter. First, angelophanies function as a form of theological shorthand in the Hebrew Scriptures. Secondly, these epiphanic events have more to do with the being and worship of God than with the angels themselves. This is neither to discount the reality of angelic beings, nor to take away from their necessary role within the continuum of being; it is simply to suggest the biblical writers employed angelic figures as a stylistic marker.

Since biblical accounts of celestial beings appear similar to earlier models found in the ancient Near East, it appears authors and redactors subjected the region's oral history to a sophisticated process of theological reflection and interpretation before committing their pericopes to parchment. Like sailors harnessing the wind in order to propel their craft, these writers built upon familiar regional mythology without compromising their theology of God in the process. Through the formation of their particular narratives, the authors captured, concretized, and historicized the ubiquitous angelic imagery of the ancient Near East so that higher-order beings might act as foils with respect to God's presence and transcendence.

The metamorphosis of angelology since the biblical era is partially explained by the evolving discretion of theologians. However, in order to evaluate their influence on Christian thought, one must first establish whether their views reflect the biblical record itself. In other words, if doctrinal metamorphosis is endemic to the Scriptures, perhaps greater latitude ought to be given to subsequent angelologies. I believe the use of the angelic motif in the Hebrew Scriptures reveals prominent patterns that are best explained by the underlying theological concerns and motivations of the biblical writers. Theologians reluctant to venture more than an angelology of biblical reaffirmations may oppose such a proposal;[1] however, their disinclination is problematic in that it overlooks primary human and contextual elements written into the origins of angelology.[2]

Angelic narratives demonstrate that higher order beings played a supporting role in the author's diachronous emphasis upon God's transcendence, the relegation of local pagan deities (many of whom were worshipped by practitioners of folk Judaism), and the ascent of monotheism. While the intercalation of angels allowed later writers and redactors to build a case for monotheism by re-mythologizing the pagan gods in the form of angels (despite their palpable disdain for pluralism and polytheism), one must also bear in mind that the writer's phenomenological and cultural views were not *entirely* dissimilar to those of the populace. Angel narratives are deliberately loaded with theological insinuations designed to extol the magnificence and transcendence of Israel's God, yet the Hebrew Scriptures also reflect the belief that angelic encounters were valid experiences in a world where the veil between heaven and earth remained permeable.

While the broad concern of this chapter is to demonstrate the overarching progression of the angelic motif as a way of emphasizing the otherness of God, the following pages are anchored at two major points. First, I consider the versatile angelic image with respect to God and humanity in the book of Genesis. In this section, I pay special attention to the use of cherubim and the *mal'ak YHWH/Elohim* as means

1. For examples of this rudimentary approach see: Thiessen and Doerksen, *Lectures in Systematic Theology*, 131–48; Chafer and Walvoord, *Major Bible Themes*, 151–5; Barackman, *Practical Christian Theology*, 231–50.

2. Few conservative theologians connect biblical angels with the lore of surrounding cultures. Berkhof denies the Hebrews borrowed from Persian angelology, Berkhof, *Systematic Theology*, 143. Neither Grudem nor Reymond entertain the concept. Stanley Grenz, however, represents an exception to this rule; Grenz, *Theology for the Community of God*, 228–35.

of illustrating either God's otherness or his accessibility in what is essentially a semi-coordinated theological wrestling match between J, E, and P. Although I follow the general assumptions of the documentary hypothesis throughout, I am aware of its alternatives and the fact that it is not universally advocated.[3] However, this book does not rely entirely upon how one delineates the writers.[4] It is sufficient to accept that much of the language in Genesis, especially in the case of the *mal'ak* YHWH/ *Elohim*, is representative of more than one tradition.

Since each of Genesis's authors had a somewhat unique agenda, it is preferable to speak of the *angelologies* in Genesis rather than *an* angelology in Genesis. Therefore, I argue that Genesis contains one angelology that bears traces of pagan mythology, and another that reveals an original pre-exilic concept of hypostasis. Both angelologies, however, ultimately gave way to one that emphasized the encroaching reign of divine transcendence, where transcendence is identified as God's "otherness." Thus, I argue that following the micro-narrative of angelic accounts at this primeval stage allows one to gain insights into the author's broader theological rationale.

In the second section, I contend that in addition to establishing the authority of the Major Prophets, the angelophanies in Isaiah and Ezekiel played a symbolic role in the furtherance of YHWH monotheism. Later apocalyptic literature, like the book of Daniel, exhibits similar hallmarks. These angelologies demonstrate that while subsequent authors revisited themes found in earlier angel narratives, they share P's aversion to the image of the *mal'ak* YHWH and his concern for the temple and worship. While angels continue to appear alongside God in this literature, they begin to assume prophetic profiles of their own, often functioning as dispensers of mysteries and portents of judgment. At points during this section, I interject and entertain controversial passages that have, for better or worse, been interpreted and debated in either Midrash or popular Christian theology as angelophanies, theophanies, or Christophanies. While these brief excursions are less pivotal than the major themes, they

---

3. For instance, see Cassuto, *The Documentary Hypothesis and the Composition of the Pentateuch*; Rendtorff, *Problem of the Process of Transmission in the Pentateuch*; Van Seters, *The Pentateuch*.

4. For a recent defence of the documentary hypothesis, see Nicholson, *The Pentateuch in the Twentieth Century*. Also, the Anchor Bible Commentary series follows the hypothesis in William Propp, *Exodus 1–18*, and Propp, *Exodus 19–40*.

help to illustrate the influence, range, and texture of the angelic motif in the Hebrew Scriptures as well as subsequent theological reflection.

The reason biblical texts portray angels in a vastly different light from the supple-skinned figures found in Renaissance art has as much to do with the development of theology as it does with any particular angelophany. Indeed, both literary and artistic depictions of angels illustrate attempts to concretize the intangible, as if ink or paint could establish the angel's existence and relevance at a point in time. Artistic renditions of celestial beings have been theologically misleading at times, a point of particular concern to Barth, but it may still be helpful to conceive of these beings as portraits painted by various biblical artists throughout the history of revelation.[5]

Nevertheless, if the Old Testament gallery contains a particular collection dedicated to the portrayal angels, why do some author-artists render them as fierce creatures who unleash devastating plagues upon the firstborn of Egypt, the rebels in the wilderness, the people of Israel during King David's rule, and the forces of Sennacherib;[6] yet others represent them as revealers of mysteries and resolute-yet-compassionate forces in the lives of individuals?[7] Angelic portraits are manifold: Michael and Gabriel are rendered as named, titled beings, but others are purely anonymous; certain angels speak in visions, but others appear in person; additionally, particular classes of angels, like cherubim, are described differently depending upon the author. Perhaps angels are better conceived of as motion pictures rather than static photographs: they are dynamic beings who, while moving through time and space, are perennially re-adapted to accentuate the peculiarities of the narrative, historical milieu, and authorial disposition. The following sections explore several of these theological undulations in detail, with an eye toward the kaleidoscopic use of cherubs as symbols of divine transcendence.

5. Barth scoffed at what he called "Raphael's little darlings," insisting that Christian art is "responsible for so much that is inappropriate" in the popular concept of angels; he rails against depictions of angels at the Nativity as "a veritable kindergarten of prancing babies amusing themselves in different ways and yet all contriving in some way to look pious." *CD, III*:3, 492.

6. Exod 12:23; Heb 11:28; 1 Cor 10:10; 2 Sam 24:16; 1 Chr 21:16; 2 Kgs 19:35. Centuries later, an angel would strike Herod dead for his impiety in Acts 12:23.

7. Dan 9:20–27; Gen 16:7—18:23.

## CHERUBIM

## Guardians of the Sacred

Although biblical authors offer no information about when angels were created, celestial beings are treated as well-known figures from the earliest canonical layers, beginning with Adam and Eve's deportation from Eden.[8] The cherubim are introduced abruptly in Genesis 3:24 with no explanation about their form, only their function. We are merely told that God stationed them outside the entrance to Eden, to guard it along with a flaming sword. This conspicuous absence of detail suggests that early readers and hearers were so conversant with such beings that no authorial elaboration was necessary. Yet since this community's perspective is so far removed from that of the modern reader, it is not readily apparent whether higher-order beings like cherubim were intentionally used as a leitmotif for accentuating divine otherness.

Therefore, one must attempt to decipher authorial intent by searching for linguistic modalities related to cherubim. In other words, what additional insights can be gained by studying the themes, imagery, and words that regularly emerge alongside cherubim? These supplementary features should allow us to evaluate the correlation between cherubim in Gen 3:24 and the transcendence of God. I maintain that if the author is using cherubim in a manner consistent with biblical literature, their appearance in Gen 3:24 depicts Eden in a new light: as God's earthly garden sanctuary and throne. This reading also shifts the focus of the passage from interpretations fixated upon the act of human disobedience and places it instead upon the splendor of the transcendent YHWH.

In Genesis 3, the Jahwist provides insights into the divine rationale by implying that YHWH stations cherubim at the garden's entrance to prevent Adam and Eve from regaining access to the fruit of immortality.[9] J conscripts language with militaristic overtones when describing the scene: "[God] *drove out* the man; and at the east of the Garden of Eden he placed the cherubim, and a *sword* flaming and turning to *guard* the

---

8. As Keck notes, medieval theologians were bothered by the lack of information in Genesis concerning the creation of angels. For an overview of different opinions: see his discussion of Bonaventure's *Breviloquium,* 2.5.8–9 in *Angels & Angelology in the Middle Ages,* 19–24; Cf. Jubilees 2:1–2; Augustine, *City of God* 11.9; Aquinas's *ST* 1.61.1; Rapaport, *Tales and Maxims from the Midrash,* 1; Matt, *The Zohar,* 253.

9. Gunkel, *Genesis,* 1–40. Also, Von Rad, *Genesis,* 73–101.

way to the tree of life."[10] Whether this is meant to emphasize the obsti-
nacy and furtiveness of sinful humanity, the fierceness of the cherubim,
or the sacredness of the garden is unclear, but what is apparent is that
the cherubim are Yʜᴡʜ's loyal subordinates. However, the account fails
to provide the reader with either an explanation of what the cherubim
*are* or a description of their appearance (unlike the author of Ezekiel,
who, as we shall see later, seems fascinated by their form). Nonetheless,
that cherubim could be identified as such suggests that by the time the
Genesis account was written, early Jewish angelology had already evolved
to the point that celestial beings could be differentiated via an official,
albeit arcane, taxonomy.

While the cherub appears spontaneously to emerge at this em-
bryonic stage of the biblical narrative, archaeological evidence has long
supported the idea that the Hebrews received a thorough education in
cherubic imagery through prior interaction with surrounding cultures.
In fact, the relationship between such beings and sacred trees is a well-
documented motif in the mythology of the ancient Near East.[11] Gunkel
is slightly too conservative in maintaining that little can be "said with
precision concerning the origin and history of the cherubim, although it
seems likely that this particular concept found in Ezekiel is of Babylonian
origins."[12] In fact, the description of cherubim in Ezek 1:6 as winged beings with an eagle's face bears a striking likeness to the primitive shamans
who wore vulture-like vestments in the region south of Tabriz, Iran, an
area that may have served as the model for Eden. Perhaps oral narratives
about this human ritual directly influenced the description of cherubim
in Gen 3:24 and elsewhere. What is more certain is that the Hebrew *kerub*
either derives from the Akkadian *karibu*, having to do with praise and
adoration, or *kuribi*, who were winged creatures thought to guard Mesopotamia's royal and sacred buildings, more specifically, their doorways
and gates.[13] In either case, such beings have long been used in the ancient
Near East to invoke strong, venerative overtones.

10. Though I will not pursue an evaluation of the flaming sword (*lahat hahereb*)
itself, some scholars believe the image is related to Ugaritic mythology and refers to a
supernatural being in its own right. See Miller, "Fire in the Mythology of Canaan and
Israel."

11. Kitto and Taylor, "Cherubim," 192–95. Giovino, *The Assyrian Sacred Tree*.

12. Gunkel, *Genesis*, 24.

13. See Rohl, *From Eden to Exile*; Ebeling, "Cherubim," 233.

As for cherubim as sacred sentinels, there is an additional connection with earlier Sumerian deities Ig-galla and Ig-alima, who acted as doorkeepers between the holy and the common.[14] In fact, cherub-like imagery appears throughout the religious symbolism of the ancient Near East in the form of winged sphinxes and winged lions with human heads in Egypt, not to mention the magnificent winged bulls of Assyria. Many well-preserved examples of these Assyrian *shedu* or *lamassu*, from the palace of Sargon II (721–705 BCE), are currently housed in the Louvre.[15] Thus, the mysterious figures in Gen 3:24 are also conjoined with a far-reaching legend about humanity's origin, sanctified embellishments emerging from the region's mythology, and then shaped by biblical authors to signify guardianship of the sacred.[16]

Yet in order to establish a meaningful link between the cherubim of Gen 3:24 and the transcendence of YHWH, one must bear in mind that the biblical literature differs from regional lore in that it never mentions angelic beings without also relating them to the sacred person or presence of God. Where there are cherubim, God is. Thus, in Gen 3:24, it is YHWH who "places" (*shakan*) the cherubim (lit. causes to dwell) at the entrance to Eden; interestingly, *shakan* is typically associated with YHWH's abiding glory, tabernacling amongst his people.[17] The following sections suggest that given the cherub's close relationship to God's throne and the divine presence in the sanctuary elsewhere in Scripture, their presence outside the sacred orchard may imply that the writer was hinting that God remained present *within* Eden indefinitely.

14. Kapelrud, "The Gates of Hell and the Guardian Angels of Paradise."

15. They first appear in Nimrud under the reign of Ashurbanipal II (883–859 BCE). Pauline, *Le palais de Sargon d'Assyrie*. Also, "Human-headed winged lion (lamassu) [Excavated at Nimrud (ancient Kalhu), northern Mesopotamia] (32.143.2)." "Human-headed winged lion (lamassu) [Excavated at Nimrud (ancient Kalhu), northern Mesopotamia] (32.143.2)," in *Heilbrunn Timeline of Art History*, n.p. [cited 5 May 2009]. Online: http://www.metmuseum.org/toah/ho/04/wam/ho_32.143.2.htm.

16. For instance, consider how the Enoch legend of Gen 21:24 evolved into an elaborate tale of heavenly ascent in 1–3 Enoch, and his ultimate transformation into the angel Metatron.

17. Exod 24:16; 25:8; 29:45; Num 5:3; 9:18; Deut 14:23; 26:2

## Cherubim and Sanctuary Imagery

Whether or not the edenic description of primeval history belongs to the Jahwist, it is impossible to extrapolate theories about the significance of cherubim in Gen 3:24 without consulting additional sources. For instance, P's focus upon the Aaronic priesthood features cherubim as inanimate beings contributing to the aesthetics of tabernacle worship. P records God's commission to fashion golden cherubim to "overshadow" the mercy seat atop the ark of the Covenant;[18] their likeness was also to be embroidered into the tabernacle's innermost curtain.[19] In Hebrew, the word for overshadow, *sakak*, is often used to describe a protective act. The word is used in Exod 33:22 to describe God shielding Moses after hiding him in the cleft, and in passages like Ps 91, where God protects the faithful under his wings. Similarly, the Hebrew for the inner curtain of the tabernacle is *paroketh*, which has etymological connections to the Assyrian *paraku*, meaning to "shut off."[20] Thus, both *sakak* and *paraku* suggest that the cherub's relationship to sacred architecture was to protect and delineate the holy from the pedestrian.

Although it is possible the artisan's cherubim were merely representational and ornamental, one cannot rule out a talismanic interpretation. Were these cherubim considered as actual tabernacle sentries just as their spiritual counterparts guarded the entrance to Eden? The evidence is circumstantial, but this interpretation was integral to the regional mythology, and is strengthened by the Deuteronomist's description of the sanctuary within Solomon's Temple. Dominated by enormous statues of cherubim guarding the ark, and covered in carvings of cherubim upon the doors that led to the inner sanctuary, one wonders why such an emphasis might have been placed upon these peculiar beings if they were not thought to have some mystical agency:

> In the inner sanctuary he made two cherubim of olivewood, each ten cubits high. . . . He placed the cherubim inside the innermost room of the temple, with their wings spread out. The wing of one cherub touched one wall, while the wing of the other

18. Exod 25:13; 37:7 "The conception underlying this designation is well illustrated by representations of a king seated on a throne supported on each side by cherubim, which have been found at Byblus, Hamath, and Megiddo, all dating between 1200 and 800 B.C." Albright, "What Were the Cherubim?" 2.

19. Exod 26:31.

20. Cf. Driver, *The Book of Exodus*, 289, n. 31.

touched the other wall, and their wings touched each other in
the middle of the room. He overlaid the cherubim with gold.
. . . For the entrance to the inner sanctuary he made doors of
olivewood; the lintel and the doorposts were five-sided. . . . He
covered the two doors of olivewood with carvings of cherubim,
palm trees, and open flowers; he overlaid them with gold, and
spread gold on the cherubim and on the palm trees.[21]

Unmistakably related to God's glorious and heavily-restricted presence, Hebrew craftspersons purposely depict cherubim (*keruvim*), not
simply angels (*malakim*), as indispensable components of Israel's sacred
architecture.

For instance, in Exodus 25, P describes cherubim as paired golden
figures that protect the mercy seat atop the ark of the covenant, and in
Num 7:89 Moses hears God's voice above this mercy seat "from between
the two cherubim." Here, Yhwh's presence is enhanced by a portable,
cherub-adorned throne, enclosed behind two sets of curtains with embroidered images of cherubim, and located within a wider arrangement
of ten outer, cherubim-embroidered curtains.[22] Modern ecclesiastical
architecture may emphasize function over form, and clergy might treat
God as a chummy deity—"God wants to be your best friend," emotes
pastor and bestselling author, Rick Warren—but imagery of cherubim as
restrictive images were the *sine qua non* for generations of Hebrew worshippers.[23] The depiction of supernatural guardians in relation to sacred
places suggests that cherubim were used to signify the otherness of God,
which enhances our understanding of their purpose in Gen 3:24.

So far, we have seen that just as J introduces the cherubim in relation
to Eden as a sacred garden, so both P and D relate them to holy places of
worship as a further gesture to the transcendence of God. One must probe
additional manifestations of cherubim in the Bible and the surrounding
region, however, especially when trying to understand why later biblical
authors appear more comfortable with the idea of affiliating them directly with God than J, E, or D did. In fact, one only observes a particular
interest in the cherubim as beings-in-themselves when contrasting the
faceless creatures of Gen 3:24 with meticulous descriptions of cherubim

21. 1 Kgs 6:23, 27–28, 31–32. Also, see 2 Chr 3:7–14

22. Exod 25:13; 37:7. The irony is that cherubim were fashioned atop a box which
held the Decalogue, since the Second Commandment is cautious about handmade
imagery. Exod 26:1, 31.

23. Warren, *The Purpose-Driven Life*, 85.

during the exilic and post-exilic period. Once passages like Ezek 1:10 were written, cherubim became chimeras with the faces of a man, lion, eagle, and ox, though in the vision of the temple in Ezek 41:18–20, they were carved in the wall with only two faces, human and lion.[24] Either the artisans were not able to render such complicated versions as found in visions or, more probably, the visions were embellishments of the sanctuary imagery that inspired them.

Appearances aside, note how the text describes the orientation of the cherubim: just as God planted Eden in the east (with respect to Jerusalem), so he places the cherubim at the east of the Garden itself. Based upon the role of the eastern gates as a portal to the sacred, especially in the visions of Ezekiel, I believe that J intends for us to interpret Eden as more than an early domicile, but as a sanctuary where YHWH dwells.[25] Similarly, Solomon's Temple was constructed on the easternmost mountain in Jerusalem, Mt. Moriah (1 Chr 3:1), and faced east like the tabernacle before it. Thus, the cherubim within the tabernacle and temple guarded the eastern entrance there as well. If the cherubim are J's way of hinting about this relationship, it explains why Eden and its accoutrements (tree of life) must be protected from unworthy intruders. In fact, later authors describe Eden as a blissful garden sanctuary that belongs to YHWH; Isa 51:3 is one example,

> For the Lord will comfort Zion;
> he will comfort all her waste places,
> and will make her wilderness *like Eden*,
> her desert like the *garden of the Lord*;
> joy and gladness will be found in her,
> thanksgiving and the voice of song.

Ezekiel 28 also endorses this view, calling Eden "the garden of God" (v. 13) and the "holy mountain of God" (vv. 14, 16) from which "the guardian cherub [singular] drove" out the hubristic King of Tyre.

I maintain that the relationship between the cherubim, the presence of God, and the place of worship appears frequently enough throughout the Hebrew Scriptures to allow for the suggestion that in the case of the Garden of Eden, the author is intentionally depicting cherubim as guardians of the *first* earthly sanctuary of YHWH, and that it must be fortified,

---

24. For more about the role these symbols played in Jewish and Christian theology, see Eskola, *Messiah and the Throne*.

25. Ezek 10:19; 11:1–2; 42:15; 43:1–2, 4; 44:1; 46:1, 12.

not for YHWH's sake, but for the sake of those who might encroach upon the resplendence of divine glory. Similarly, as an example of life imitating art, Victor Hamilton notes that just as cherubim protected the eastern entrance to the Garden of Eden so the Levites were posted around the eastern side of the tabernacle with instructions to put to death anyone who "encroaches upon the forbidden sancta."[26] Thus, while J's depiction of the cherubim in Gen 3:24 is tame compared to Ezekiel's composite beings by the same name, his imagery is in line with the broader culture and the rest of the Old Testament. The cherub's chief duty is to defend that which is regal and holy, or in the case of the Garden of Eden, that which is forbidden to sinful humanity. Without the cherubim to stand guard, an unwitting or overweening person might mistakenly saunter into the overwhelming presence of divine transcendence. Although the cherub's form and function is not peculiar to the biblical text, biblical authors and artisans translated the regional mythology into written and physical form in order to emphasize not only holy *places* (Garden of Eden, tabernacle, Solomon's Temple, etc.), but the holiness of *God*.

## Cherubim and Thrones

Further evidence supports the idea that J conceived of Eden as more than a primeval sanctuary where YHWH dwelt, but as the very throne of God. Bronze Age ivories dating from the thirteenth century BCE were excavated at the Canaanite town of Megiddo that portray a regal figure enthroned upon composite winged beings; remarkably similar depictions of winged cherubim in relation to YHWH's throne appear in the Hebrew Bible.

While it cannot be proven, this compatible symbolism corroborates Finklestein's theory that the Hebrews arose as a subculture from within Canaanite society around the twelfth century BCE.[27] Since these relics predate their biblical counterparts, it is almost certain that the writers adopted and adapted this widely accessible motif as a means of communicating a specific message about their God. In fact, there are numerous examples of ancient Near East iconography dating from 4500–2900 BCE that feature storm gods atop bulls, lions, lion-headed birds, and dragons.[28]

---

26. Hamilton, *The Book of Genesis*, 210. See 1 Chr 9:17–18; Num 1:50–51.

27. See Finkelstein and Silberman, *The Bible, Unearthed*.

28. Green, *The Storm-God in the Ancient Near East*, 13ff.

The concept of depicting deities enthroned upon chimera was also popular in ancient Egypt, Phoenicia, and Northern Mesopotamia between 2000 and 700 BCE.[29] In Babylonia, the deity was occasionally symbolized by a winged shrine and later by a thunderbolt, but in Israelite symbolism the glorious God was conceived as enthroned upon golden cherubim.[30] Again, the imagery of Gen 3:24 suggests that Eden represents the earliest biblical setting of YHWH's enthronement upon the cherubim, even though it is not as explicit as what one finds in comparative mythology and numerous passages throughout the Old Testament (2 Sam 22:11; Ps 18:10, 80:1, 99:1; Isa 37:16; and Ezek 10:1–22). In fact, if it is not, then it represents the single exception of cherubim without a relationship to the divine sanctuary or throne.

Yet, while the message that YHWH is a holy and heavenly king with powerful courtiers is clear from later texts, what is missing in the Gen 3 account is a statement about the divine throne. Again, because the preponderance of evidence suggests such a correlation, I believe that we may be missing implications that the original readers (and culture) would have understood. There is an allusion to this idea in 1 En. 24:3–5, which describes angels leading Enoch to an Eden-like mountain throne:

> And the seventh mountain was in the midst of these, and it excelled them in height, resembling the seat of a throne: and fragrant trees encircled the throne. And amongst them was a tree such as I had never yet smelt, neither was any amongst them nor were others like it: it had a fragrance beyond all fragrance, and its leaves and blooms and wood wither not for ever: and its fruit is beautiful, and its fruit resembles the dates of a palm.[31]

---

29. Tomb 19 at Thebes contains an image of Amenhotep shielded by Horus' wings while being carried upon a golden, ark-like throne. Kitchen, *Pharaoh Triumphant, the Life and Times of Ramesses II, King of Egypt*, 166–67. See the winged Sphinx throne from Phoenicia which dates from the Hellenistic period (fourth to first century BCE) in Keller and Kaiser, *The Bible as History*, 198. Also, the wooden side-panel from Thutmose IV's (c. 1419–1386 BCE) throne in Smith, *Ancient Egypt, as Represented in the Museum of Fine Arts, Boston*, 123. For more examples, see Metzger, "Der Thron Als Manifestation Der Herrschermacht in Der Ikonographie Des Vorderen Orients Und Im Alten Testament."

30. Albright, "What Were the Cherubim?" 2–3.

31. Artefacts dating from the ninth century BCE depict an Assyrian image of a winged lion with human head protecting a sacred palm tree. See Demisch, *Die Sphinx*, 62. Also, 1 Kgs 6:31–32.

Then after Enoch asks the archangel Michael for clarification concerning the mountain throne in 25:3–4, Michael answers:

> This high mountain which thou hast seen, whose summit is like the throne of God, *is* His throne, where the Holy Great One, the Lord of Glory, the Eternal King, will sit, when He shall come down to visit the earth with goodness.

Admittedly, the scene in 1 Enoch fails to tick *all* the boxes: it has an archangel, but no cherubim; and while it describes Eden as the location of God's throne, the throne itself has been abdicated and will only be filled when God returns to judge the world. 1 Enoch also recognizes that Eden does not suffer the effects of sin, but it fails to explain how the garden sanctuary could remain a paradise without the presence of God in its midst since his being is the *source* of its fecundity.

Instead, we find a better example of Eden as Yhwh's throne room in the twenty-second chapter of the Apocalypse of Moses, where in vv. 3–4, Eve describes the fall to Seth, her son:

> And when God appeared in paradise, mounted on the chariot of his cherubim with the angels proceeding before him and singing hymns of praises, all the plants of paradise, both of your father's lot and mine, broke out into flowers. And the throne of God was fixed where the Tree of Life was.

Here we have all the variables: the abiding presence of God, a chariot, a throne, Eden as a sanctuary, and of course, cherubim. Thus, the cherub's seemingly innocuous role in Gen 3:24 was understood by certain Christian communities as an essential part of a larger picture, namely the depiction of Eden as a garden sanctuary where the transcendent God was enthroned.

So if the image of cherubim at the Garden of Eden is truly connected with the larger idea of the divine throne and the transcendent God, then it is not surprising that we also find similar ideas in the Psalms and Ezekiel (which I will address later) as well as at the conclusion of the New Testament. There, the writer of the Apocalypse resurrects the imagery of Eden—now reopened—complete with the sacred tree and garden imagery, and within its midst, surrounding the throne of God and Christ, he reintroduces the cherubim. Yet now these chimeras are engaged in worship, and the believer is *welcomed* into a heavenly Eden, and more importantly, into the presence of God. I shall briefly revisit these figures and their relationship to the divine throne later in the respective angelologies of pseudo-Dionysius and Aquinas where they enjoy a similar degree of attention and admiration.

## Summary

In spite of conventional views of Israel's monotheism, I argued that early biblical authors appropriated pagan images like cherubim in order to articulate YHWH's transcendence. This suggests that the writers were not only aware of competing theologies from surrounding cultures, but took an assertive approach to the Hebrew narrative by associating such imagery with YHWH himself. As Hebrew artisans defined sacred boundaries by producing cherubim-themed statuary and tapestries, so scribes affirmed God's otherness through the literary reconstruction of cherubim. Such writings allowed the Jahwist to station cherubim at Eden's entrance, transforming Gen 3 into a dramatic description of Eden as a holy of holies and God's symbolic, earthly throne-room. The cherubim of Gen 3 also set the stage for hamartiology by stressing humanity's subsequent distance from this transcendent God. J's depiction is noteworthy given the close association between divine figures, sacred places, and winged sub-deities in adjacent cultures. However, one may also conclude that the cherubic motif is universal because it points to something altogether real and astonishing—beyond myth and symbol—signifying that God himself adopted pagan archetypes in his progressive self-revelation as a way of accommodating and fostering the burgeoning concept of his transcendence and of monotheism itself.

## MAL'AK YHWH: IMAGE OF PROGRESSIVE TRANSCENDENCE IN JEP

Cherubim are not unique to the Hebrew Scriptures. The writers described them in a manner consistent with the regional mythology: composite denizens of sacred *places* and preternatural associates of revered *persons* (YHWH, storm gods, or ancient rulers). While I have argued that the appearance of higher-order beings in Gen 3:24 and elsewhere is an indication that a biblical author or artisan was making an unambiguous statement about the otherness of God, I believe it is also possible to trace a subtle evolution of this larger theme by turning our attention to a different angelic figure also introduced in Genesis.

God occasionally revealed himself to people in various guises during the early layers of the biblical text in a voice from heaven or a burning bush. However, numerous epiphanic events, which were generally limited to the pre-monarchic period, equate a figure known as the "Angel of the Lord" (mal'ak YHWH) with God himself. At first glance, the presence of the genitive case suggests that the angel is subordinate to YHWH, similar perhaps to the messengers of gods in regional mythologies.[32] However, the Angel of the Lord is a more complex figure for several reasons: he identifies himself as God, the biblical writers refer to him as YHWH, and those to whom he appears often treat him as a divine being.[33] To understand how various biblical writers may have used this provisional figure for theological effect, I shall explore the discontinuity between their descriptions of this extraordinary being.

While the appearance of the mal'ak YHWH eventually loses its theophanic overtones in later texts like Zechariah, his presence within the concise framework of Genesis helps to illustrate the important relationship between angelology and an emerging appreciation for the transcendence of God. In addition, this section provides a unique scheme through which to view the documentary hypothesis that J, the earliest literary source, tends to anthropomorphize God, while E and to a greater extent P are predisposed to maintain his transcendence.

In the Jahwist's storyline, for instance, theophanies are typically described as *visual* experiences: "The Lord appeared to Abraham. . . . He [Abraham] looked up and saw three men standing near him."[34] Likewise, in his initial appearance, the mal'ak YHWH finds Hagar by a spring of

---

32. For example, in the Sumerian poems "Enki and Ninhursaga" and "Inana and Enki," Isimud (Akkadian Usmu) is a messenger for the god of the subterranean freshwater ocean, Enki. In Mesopotamian lore, Dzakar was the messenger of the god Sin, who relayed messages to humans through dreams. Namtar was the messenger and minister of Ereskigal, the Sumerian goddess of the underworld. Papsukkal (who was formerly known as Ninshubar, a *sukkal*—faithful messenger—in Sumerian myth), was the messenger god for the Akkadian pantheon. He is referred to as one of "the fifteen gods of E-dubba' in BM 32516, Text no. 4, MS a, line 24. George, "Four Temple Rituals from Babylon," 295.

33. The appearance of the mal'ak YHWH or mal'ak Elohim is found almost exclusively in the Pentateuch: Gen 16:7; 18:1–33; 22:11; 31:11–13; 32:24–30; 48:15–16; Exod 3 (cf. Acts 7:30); 13:21; 14:19 (cf. Num 20:16); 23:20; 32:34; Judg 2:1–5; 6:11–26. Comparing these passages reveals examples when YHWH is distinguished from mal'ak YHWH or mal'ak Elohim (2 Sam 24:16; Ps 34:7), but there are also instances when the two are interchangeable (Gen 16:13; 31:11, 13; Exod 3:2, 6).

34. Gen 18:1–2. Gen 19 reveals that at least two of these "men" are angels.

water in the wilderness, and after he informs her that she is pregnant with a son, he commands her to return to Sarah.[35] J records Hagar's theologically astute reaction to this visible phenomenon: "You are El-roi"; for she said, "Have I really seen God and remained alive after seeing him?"[36] There is little doubt that J asks the reader to assume that both accounts involved a face-to-face meeting with God, but later authors and the final redactor were not as generous with God's image.

For example, E's narration of a second encounter between Hagar and the angel of YHWH introduces a subtle theological shift. Rather than the close-and-personal figure of Gen 16, the *mal'ak Elohim*—a title synonymous with *mal'ak YHWH*—merely speaks to Hagar "from heaven."[37] There is no trace of J's visible phenomena. Juxtaposing these two Hagar stories helps to support the angel's identity as a divine figure; however, it does not explain the significance of the respective emphases upon visible and audible revelation. I believe the two stories possibly depict a micro-evolution in the *mal'ak YHWH's* interaction with humans at different points in Hebrew theology, thus demonstrating a growing appreciation for the aseity of God.

There are also examples where influences from *both* J and E appear to converge in order to form a single story. In Gen 22:11 the *mal'ak YHWH*, normally a visible being in biblical narratives, calls to Abraham "from heaven" and in v. 15 calls "a second time from heaven." Why does the *mal'ak YHWH* speak twice, and more importantly, why does he remain in heaven, which, as we see in Hagar's example, is a trademark of Elohist literature? Gunkel believes both questions can be answered by assuming the existence of an earlier recension where YHWH, rather than an angel, spoke.[38] If his theory is correct, this raises the possibility that a redactor may have simply inserted *mal'ak* out of reverence for God much in the same that Matthew's Gospel tends to use reverential circumlocutions like *basileia ton ouranon* (kingdom of heaven) instead of *basileia tou theou* (kingdom of God).

More recently, James Davila suggested another alternative. Instead of inserting "*mal'ak*," a scribe may have simply altered the divine names (from Elohim to YHWH) in order to harmonize the text. He writes, "The

---

35. Gen 16:7.

36. Gen 16:13.

37. Gen 21:17.

38. Gunkel, *Genesis*, 236.

Vorlage of the Syriac Peshitta seems to have read *mal'ak elohim*, and it has been argued that this reading is original and that Yahweh crept into the verse by assimilation to the *mal'ak YHWH* in the secondary addition of v. 15, who is presented as calling to Abraham *shanyth*, 'again.'"[39]

Whether siding with Gunkel or Davila, one begins to sense the redactor's uncertainty about how to make neat distinctions between the transcendent God and the Angel of the LORD, especially when different authors use different motifs to tell similar stories. Not only does the redactor feel the need to harmonize such accounts, but appears to have reconciled the issue by blending J's propensity to present God in rather concrete, immanent terms, as in the wider Abrahamic narrative, with E's discrete "angel of Elohim" who calls from heaven and reveals himself to Abraham's grandson Jacob in a dream (Gen 31:11), a form of self-disclosure that is even less sensory-dependent.[40]

Another classical partition in Pentateuchal authorship involves the later Priestly source. P supplements the epic approach of J and E with discussions about the priesthood and regulations of worship, and his Genesis narratives cluster around four events: the creation, the flood, the covenant with Abraham, and the purchase of the cave of Machpela. Generally comfortable with the Tetragrammaton, he often renders God as an omnipotent, disembodied spirit who reveals himself to patriarchs like Abraham and Noah, but otherwise deals only with the Levitical priesthood. P's divine appearance accounts in Genesis are vague, as illustrated by Gen 17:1,[41] "When Abram was ninety-nine years old, the LORD appeared to Abram, and said to him, 'I am God Almighty (*El Shaddai*);

---

39. Davila, "The Name of God at Moriah," 579.

40. In Gen 31:11–13 Jacob is said to have wrestled with a man [*iysh*] on his return to his childhood home, but he seems to associate him with *Elohim* in 32:30, "So Jacob called the place Peniel, saying, 'For I have seen God [*Elohim*] face to face, and yet my life is preserved.'" However, later interpretations (Hos 12:4) say that it was a *mal'ak*, perhaps representing a growing emphasis upon the transcendence of God and an embarrassment over anthropomorphisms. This is especially likely considering v. 5, "The LORD the God of hosts, the LORD is his name!" refers not to the account at Peniel, but to the author's of YHWH in vv. 1–3. YHWH, he states in v. 5, is the *Elohe ha'sabbaoth*; he is the God of the angels, but he is not a *mal'ak*. Also interesting, in Gen 48:15–16 Jacob describes *Elohim* as an angel, "He blessed Joseph, and said, 'The God [*Elohim*] before whom my ancestors Abraham and Isaac walked, the God [*Elohim*] who has been my shepherd all my life to this day, the angel [*mal'ak*] who has redeemed me from all harm, bless the boys.'"

41. Though J also suggests a non-visible YHWH appearances at 12:7; 26:2; they are not God's typical form of revelation in his writing.

walk before me, and be blameless.'" The theophanies in P lack angelic language and salient details like J's earthy accounts of patriarchs feeding freshly baked bread to a visible God and his angels, but what this suggests is that P's sensitivity to Yhwh's otherness surpasses even the Elohist's *mal'ak Elohim* who speaks from heaven and in dreams. Furthermore, it is P who introduces the cosmic significance of Yhwh as the creator of all things; so while God may have *fashioned* the angels in 2:1, as far as P is concerned, an angel-figure he is not.

## YHWH'S APPEARANCE WITH *MAL'AKIM* IN GENESIS 18

God's appearance in the likeness of an angel or in close proximity to angels presents a unique view of divine activity before it was obscured behind tabernacle curtains. However, given the early date of these accounts, whether such appearances ought to be interpreted as theophanies is not as troublesome as the proposal that they represent Christophanies. This point brings us to what is perhaps the most notable and disputed description of divine self-disclosure in the Hebrew Scriptures. Recorded in Gen 18 is an account of the day when Yhwh and his angelic entourage visited Abraham and Sarah. While decidedly Christian interpretations of this event were more fashionable during earlier eras, the theory that the pre-incarnate Christ was the principal figure among the trio remains popular with many traditionalist exegetes.[42]

For example, Barth argues that "we may adopt the explanation of early exegesis that these are not appearances of angels but of the Holy Trinity in which the Logos is obviously the spokesman."[43] Calvin also maintained that the principal angel in Gen 18 was a preincarnate Christ, but unlike Barth, he disagreed with the trinitarian interpretations of "some of the ancient writers," whom he felt were mistaken in their view that Abraham "perceived by faith, that there are three persons in one God."[44] Others have interpreted the passage as an oblique reference to the

---

42. See Hengstenberg, *Christology of the Old Testament*, 1:119–22. On p. 61 of their book, *Sense and Nonsense about Angels and Demons*, Boa and Bowman write, "So then, it appears that the Angel of the Lord in the Old Testament was actually the Son of God, coming to earth in visible form before he became the physical, human being known as Jesus." Also, cf. Funderburk, "Angel," 162–63.

43. Barth, *CD III/3*, 490.

44. Calvin, *A Commentary on Genesis*, 470.

*mal'ak YHWH*, and although three figures are mentioned, the text itself only speaks of two angels.[45] For example, Thiessen cites Gen 18, among other passages, to support his view that "the oft-recurring phrase 'the Angel of the Lord' found in the Old Testament has special reference to the preincarnate second person of the trinity."[46]

Although a precedent exists within the New Testament and Christian theology for typological readings of the Hebrew Scriptures with respect to Christology, I find christological interpretations of this particular event to be anachronistic and historically implausible.[47] This has long been a matter of debate within the faith, and though figures like Augustine, Aquinas, and Gregory the Great did not identify the most prominent figure of this heavenly trio with Christ, Justin Martyr, Irenaeus, Tertullian, and Eusebius did.[48] On one hand, there is a legitimate need for the church to grapple with the Hebrew Scriptures in light of Jesus' statement in John 5:39 that they testify of him, but one must concede that a purely christological interpretation of the angel of YHWH overlooks the relationship between the biblical authors and their original audience.[49]

Turning theophanies into Christophanies is not without biblical precedence, but I find it curious that such a supposedly prominent Christophany in Gen 18 was not mentioned by the author of Hebrews, given his fondness for Old Testament archetypes that corroborate his high Christology. However, the description of Abraham's visitors in 18:2 as "three men" has also been construed by some as a figurative statement about the trio's equivalence of being: since one of the visitors is clearly YHWH, the others may be understood as the Son and the Spirit, a concept Rublev illustrated in his famed Icon of the Holy Trinity. Yet I will

45. Rembrandt's etching from 1656, *Abraham Entertaining the Angels*, may be the only major work of art that depicts God and two angels, rather than three angels, though other interpretations are possible such that the servant-figure is Abraham.

46. Thiessen, *Lectures in Systematic Theology*, 91.

47. See France, *Jesus and the Old Testament*.

48. Justin, *Dialogue with Trypho* 76; Irenaeus, *Against Heresies* 4.10.1; Tertullian, *Against Marcion* 3.9.1; Eusebius, *Church History* 1.2.1–13.

49. John 5:39. See Dunn's excellent discussion demonstrating how foreign such a concept was, even to New Testament writers: Dunn, *Christology in the Making*, 149–62. For a linguistic angle on the angel, see W. G. MacDonald, "Current Issues in Biblical and Patristic Interpretation," 324–35. However, MacDonald's controversial argument that the phrase should be interpreted in both Testaments as "an angel of the Lord" has not been influential. Hurtado argues convincingly for one distinct angel in *One God,* 71–92.

demonstrate throughout this chapter that there is no need to turn Gen 18 into a Christophany or a divine dress rehearsal where all members of the Trinity are present. The use of two angels is a common device in the Hebrew Scriptures to accentuate the importance of the central, divine being whom they serve.

At the other end of the interpretive spectrum is Brueggemann's rather understated discussion of the pair of angels in Gen 18 as "strange men," and Westermann's view that the *mal'ak YHWH* was simply another created angel rather than a divine being; both alternatives hardly do justice to the enigmatic overtones of this passage or others that are similar.[50] Letellier's view is more convincing; he argues that the Gen 18 pericope is indeed an example of a theophany that differs somewhat from YHWH's appearance to Abraham in Gen 12, 15, and 17, "The situation in Gen 18 is different because YHWH appears here as a man (either with two companions or in the form of three men; the details of 18:16 suggest that he was accompanied by two angels)."[51]

The extraordinary language and imagery of the narrative ensures that the identity of the travellers in the passage will continue to be a source of much theological speculation within Jewish and Christian circles alike, but for now, my concern is that trinitarian or christological readings of the Genesis angel narratives may perpetuate predetermined assessments of what the *text* itself says.[52]

Christian theologians are not the only group that takes interpretive liberties with angel narratives, however. Rabbinical speculation about the subject of angels eventually fuelled debates about their physical composition. Midrashic stories show how these discussions occasionally led to peculiar opinions, with one rabbi suggesting that angels are unable to turn their heads round.[53] Similar but less trivial disputes also plagued the interpretation of Gen 18 in Jewish circles, such as the belief that God never sends more than one angel to perform the same duty.[54] This tradi-

---

50. Brueggemann, *Genesis*, 162; Westermann, *God's Angels Need No Wings*, 69.

51. Letellier, *Day in Mamre, Night in Sodom*, 89.

52. See, White, "Angel of the Lord: Messenger or Euphemism?"; Fossum, *The Name of God and the Angel of the Lord*, 192–220; other sources simply hold that Abraham welcomed "a mysterious Guest into his tent," Bordwell, ed., *Catechism of the Catholic Church*, 547. Hobbes suggests it was the Lord who appeared "by an apparition of three Angels" in Hobbes, *Leviathan*, 251.

53. Rapaport, *Tales and Maxims from the Midrash*, 49.

54. Ibid., 50.

tion helps to explain the rationale behind the Midrash interpretation of Gen 18 that identifies the three men who visited Abraham, not as YHWH, but as angels with three separate errands (one to announce the birth of Isaac, one to destroy Sodom and Gomorrah, and one to save Lot).[55]

Finicky theological quibbles like these may appear strange to the modern reader, especially when they betray the natural sense of the text in chapter 19 that clearly states *two* angels visited and rescued Lot (vv. 12–17). One sees from this simple example how hermeneutical and theological assumptions have shaped the doctrine of angelology for good or ill. Is it unlikely that the authors and redactors of Genesis faced similar deliberations?[56] This would certainly explain why the Angel of the LORD seems more divine at times than others. Nevertheless, by imputing personal religious opinions to Old Testament writers and redactors, Jewish and Christian commentators alike have inadvertently obscured the unique role of angels and the *mal'ak YHWH* in JEP's early struggle to find language that would communicate the otherness of an omnipresent God.

In general, the role of cherubim in the biblical and archaeological record, as well as the imagery of seraphim in passages such as Isa 6, reveals that paired angelic beings were employed as icons to illustrate YHWH's transcendence in theophanies much in the same way that two outer panels of a triptych are designed to emphasize the central panel. This proposal may seem to conflict with J's general accent upon the immanence of YHWH in passages like Gen 18 where two angels accompany him. Yet one should not conclude that J's anthropomorphic language required God to divest himself of his otherness; the very fact that the Almighty journeyed from heaven accompanied by angels simply to visit Abraham's tent is precisely what makes the event noteworthy.[57] Dyrness, however, overstates the account, "When the angel of the Lord is present, God's protecting or fearful presence can be felt, while his transcendence

55. Genesis Rabbah 50:2. Also, Josephus' *Antiquities* has "Then they concealed themselves no longer, but declared that they were angels of God; and that one of them was sent to inform them about the child, and two about the overthrow of Sodom."

56. If similar preoccupations with angels continued into the early first century CE, the writer of Hebrews may have chosen not to comment upon the angelology of Gen 18–19 simply because it would have detracted from his main contention that all beings are subordinate to Christ.

57. Centuries after Abraham met angelic beings in Gen 18, Homer reflected a similar belief in the Odyssey that such divine visits were entirely plausible, "The Gods may look like strangers from far off. They take on every shape and move through our cities." Homer, *The Odyssey*, 257.

is not questioned."[58] It would be better to say that while the paired angels suggest that the presence of God's transcendence in the Angel of the LORD is not meant to be questioned by the reader, Abraham is unaware of the identity of the man until it is revealed to him at the end of the story, and Sarah would have only learned of it later through Abraham's witness.

In Gen 18 and elsewhere, YHWH's manifestation in relation to angels presupposes eagerness on his part to interact and even identify with the creation itself. While these appearances were temporary, there are significant theological implications to consider if the authors are depicting God in divine/angel/human form. These theophanic narratives provide us with a unique insight into the competing and complementary views of deity during the nascent stages of Hebrew theology; they also illustrate the evolution of the concept of God's presence in relation to terrestrial and celestial beings.

God's willingness to occupy the world he created is often portrayed by biblical authors in objective, rather than metaphysical, terms. Unfortunately, the language usage presents its share of problems, not least of which is the anthropomorphism of God's presence. This may explain why P, as the latest source in the Pentateuch and the one most concerned with divine transcendence, eschews the term *mal'ak YHWH*. However, it would be incorrect to assume that any of the biblical writers conceived of God as being circumscribed by space. Quite the contrary, by also allowing the *mal'ak YHWH* to speak from heaven or in a dream, E and the redactors ensured that the motif did not ultimately compromise God's omnipresence or otherness.

Whether Gen 18 asks the reader to assume an appearance of God as the angel of YHWH or not, this mysterious being speaks to Abraham for the last time in Gen 22:11, where the *mal'ak YHWH* speaks "from heaven" in order to prevent him from sacrificing the very son that was promised to him in Gen 18. Earlier, I mentioned Gunkel's theory that a later redactor may have inserted the qualifying noun *mal'ak* into passages like Gen 22:11 in order to disassociate God with certain activities like direct interaction with humans, but what he overlooks is that this use of angelic imagery also helps to circumvent what would otherwise be certain death for the person who caught a glimpse of the Almighty's *panim* (face).[59]

58. Dyrness, *Themes in Old Testament Theology*, 42.

59. See Exod 33:20. This is apparent by Hagar's stunned reaction to the *mal'ak YHWH* in Gen 16:13, "You are El-roi"; for she said, "Have I really seen God and remained alive after seeing him?" Also noteworthy is Jacob's statement in Gen 32:21

Like the relationship between God and the cloud in Exod 19:9; 24:16; 34:5, the presence of the *mal'ak YHWH* is more than a statement about divine immanence: it is a mollification of the otherwise consuming glory of God. So while Moses sees the *mal'ak YHWH* in the burning bush, when he asks for an unrestricted view of the divine glory, YHWH gives him an austere warning, "you cannot see my face; for no one shall see me and live" (Exod 33:20).[60] As Michael Widmer points out, one must interpret God's subsequent concession to "pass by" Moses in light of the fact that: "YHWH's presence cannot be restricted to the sensory or visual sphere. . . . His presence also has clear moral dimensions. Thus YHWH's consuming holiness, His moral demand, and His transcending presence are brought together into Moses' experience of God . . . the visual aspect of Moses' request has been subordinated to the proclamation of the moral aspects of God's nature."[61]

The *mal'ak YHWH* was never intended to project the beatific vision, but he prefigures the hypostasis of divine condescension and grace, symbolizing the threshold of supernatural revelation prior to the incarnation.

What appears to be the author's progression toward the transcendence of God may also indicate a growing appreciation for the individual's need for genuine doubt and authentic faith. Placing one's faith in God as a transcendent Spirit is a far more complex proposition than to suggest that God may spontaneously appear to certain human beings on an *ad hoc* basis. Thus, the disappearance of the Angel of the LORD allows for a God who is *other*, yet, universally accessible. However, I do not suggest that theo/angelo-phanies are merely metaphorical, nor do I believe they have ceased altogether since one only needs to look to other cultures in the global south in order to see that visions of spiritual beings are still common.[62]

---

where he named the land "Peniel" because after wrestling with the "man," he claims to have seen Elohim "*panim el-panim.*" Hosea 12:4 insists it was merely a *mal'ak.*

60. For a good representation of early Christian exegesis on the issue, see Munk, *The Devil's Mousetrap.* Munk discusses Jonathan Edwards' interpretation of the Moses passage—the angel is not really an angel as much as a typological figure, with the burning bush acting as a sort of non-lethal crucifixion, demonstrating that Christ was crucified but not consumed. Though most modern scholars do not follow this explanation, Edwards follows on the heels of christocentric, patristic interpretations of the Hebrew Scriptures from the likes of Justin, Chrysostom, and Melito.

61. Widmer, *Moses, God, and the Dynamics of Intercessory Prayer,* 168. (*N.B.* Widmer appears to have inadvertently duplicated the same phrase on p. 336).

62. See Jędrej and Shaw, *Dreaming, Religion, and Society in Africa.* More broadly,

The lack of such miraculous events in the Western world today says as much about the presuppositions of our culture as it does about those in biblical times. Yet while the visions described in Genesis and elsewhere are undoubtedly influenced by cultural conditioning and personal expectations, it would be unfair to suggest that the experiences were not also indicative of a heightened sensitivity to supernatural forces. God's proclivity for self-disclosure through extraordinary means, whether it involves appearing in the form of the *mal'ak YHWH* or with paired angels, prefaces the incarnation itself. Theophanies are gestures of divine generosity accommodating human limitation and longing, but in order for humanity to apprehend such sentiments the gesture must be conspicuous. Yet, because epiphanic events are also transitory by design, the *locus* of one's assurance lies not in sight, but in faith.

## Summary

The writers of Genesis reveal their struggle with YHWH's immanence and transcendence at the level of their angelo/theo-phanic narratives. Paying special attention to different accounts of the *mal'ak YHWH* allowed me to pursue a diachronic and comparative approach to the use of angelic language and imagery as it relates to the being of God. This supports my general thesis that angelology provides cues about the divine nature. Moreover, I have illustrated that while J and E often chose to describe God's presence in angelomorphic terms, like P, they neither abandoned his transcendence nor did they reduce him to an exalted mortal.

Nonetheless, the difference between the narratives presented makes it clear that Genesis's authors and redactors occupied different places upon the theological spectrum with respect to theophanic and angelophanic accounts. For example, J's preference for anthropomorphic theophanies is evident in his presentation of YHWH as a mysterious figure accompanied by two angels and in his account of the *mal'ak YHWH* who appears to Hagar. On the other hand, Elohist literature cloaks theophanies in the form of a reserved angel who speaks from heaven and in dreams. Finally, P's early depiction of God as the sovereign creator of angels seems to transform theophanic appearances into thoroughly abstract events that permit God to retain his full transcendence and cosmic spatiality.

---

Cox, *Fire from Heaven.*

Secondly, I argued that while the third figure at the center of the Gen 18 narrative has been the subject of much debate and speculation, the identity of the trio is threatened by the overriding tendency to manipulate the story to conform to one's own theology. Interpretive precedents that read Christology into the passage are not sympathetic enough to the biblical author's view, often revealing more about the psychological needs of the interpreter and his or her readership than they do the text itself.

Ironically, deliberations about which member of the Godhead visited Abraham in Gen 18 retards the theological momentum behind the account itself. Instead, J simply asks the reader to assume that the central figure is YHWH who is somehow related to his entourage of paired *mal'akim*. Saying anything beyond this obscures his subtext, which is concerned with God's *character* rather than his form. I argued that the appearances of God in Genesis, whether with the *mal'akim* or as the *mal'ak YHWH*, are kenotic modes of revelation, designed to accommodate humanity's epistemological frailties. This led me to conclude that while the epiphanic events of Genesis reveal much about the tension between divine transcendence and immanence, they are best interpreted as examples of God's love in action.[63]

## THE FUNCTION OF ANGELS IN PROPHETIC AND APOCALYPTIC LITERATURE

In the book of Genesis, angelic figures are typically paired on earth;[64] in visions, angels appear in large groups.[65] Moreover, when an *individual* angel does appear, he is *always* described as the angel of YHWH/Elohim, a being generally treated as God himself.[66] Outside Genesis, however, angels emerge as individual messengers or participants in a divine council that acts as YHWH's liaison between heaven and earth.[67] These angels alleviate or introduce tension in the narrative itself because their interac-

63. This is especially true where love is demonstrated as compassion for the weak, since many appearances of the *mal'ak YHWH* are related to the birth and welfare of children. One may even argue that the *mal'ak YHWH* is also a form of guardian angel.

64. Gen 3:24; 18:1–9, 16–22; 19:1–22; possibly 32:1.

65. Gen 28:12.

66. Gen 16:7; 18:1–33; 22:11; 31:11–13; 32:24–30; 48:15–16. Cf. Gen 16:13; 31:11, 13; Exod 3:2, 6.

67. Job 1:6–12; 1 Kgs 22:19–22; 2 Chr 18:18–22; Pss 29:1–2; 89:6–9; 95:3; 96:4; 97:7, 9; 148:2.

tions with humans are meant to function as a pivotal point in the person's life and the plot of salvation history. In the following section I argue that angelophanies in prophetic and apocalyptic literature not only highlight God's unique ontology, but that they foster the development of monotheism and establish the authority of the person to whom the literature is attributed (i.e., Isaiah, Ezekiel, and Daniel).

I contend, for example, that Michael and Gabriel appear in the book of Daniel in order to identify Daniel as Israel's spokesperson, just as angelophanies illustrated the significance of the patriarchs. It is no coincidence that an angelic being meets Abraham in Gen 18 to foretell Isaac's birth, then appears again in Gen 22 in order to prevent him from sacrificing Isaac upon Mount Moriah;[68] similarly, Isaac's opportunistic son, Jacob, meets the angel of Elohim in a dream, and is instructed to return to his native land, where he is reunited with his estranged family; likewise, in Exod 3:2 Moses spots the same angel in the flaming bush and hears YHWH's voice commissioning him to travel to Egypt in order to deliver Jacob's descendents from the clutches of slavery.

Of course, one danger with this line of reasoning is that it appears to employ angelology as a way of setting an honored patriarch apart from the rest of humanity. Taken to its extreme, it implies a range of transcendence (in addition to the distinction between God and humanity) between humans. However, angelic imprimaturs never result in an ontological change for patriarchs or prophets, but simply functioned to authenticate their role as spokespersons for God.

The subsequent sections follow the premise that while angels consistently draw attention to certain persons and positions (in this section, the prophetic office) throughout the Bible, their *primary* function is to exalt God. Furthermore, I am not implying that only prominent male figures experienced angelic visitations or that their lives are more noteworthy than those of Hagar, Sarah, Mary, or others; my intent is simply to explore the implications of angelic appearances to later Old Testament figures such as Isaiah, Ezekiel, and Daniel.

## Angels as Advocates of Monotheism

Earlier I explored differences between the angelology of J and that of E and P by illustrating the degree to which they used angelic language

---

68. Gen 22:11.

to anthropomorphize YHWH. Although continuing to interact with the Israelites during their formative period, the distance between God and the created order appears to increase as one journeys into the world of exilic and postexilic authors. During this period, the growing gulf between heaven and earth is reflected in the absence of the *mal'ak YHWH* and God's reluctance to chastise the wayward, often erring on the side of longsuffering and mercy over wrath.[69]

Taking a step away from depictions of the *mal'ak YWHW* allows one to see conventional angels within the prophetic and apocalyptic oeuvre as beings-in-motion between paradise and the world. Their popularity increases in proportion to Israel's years of captivity as verified by Isaiah, Ezekiel, and Daniel, where they emerge full-force to fill the vacuum left by the progressively evaporating presence of the *mal'ak YHWH*, a transition not unlike the coming of the Holy Spirit to compensate for the ascended Christ. During this period, holy angels convey perplexing prophetic messages to biblical figures while baleful angels (albeit by different names) act as their adversaries in the background.[70]

During the sixth century BCE the Jewish people were exiles in the land of Babylon; in the midst of their intractable cluster of circumstances, it appears they found more consolation in the concept of angels as forecasters of future events and national guardians rather than as Eden's wardens and heralds of miraculous births. Not coincidentally, this transition occurred during a significant point in the consolidation of Israel's understanding of the being of God. As Robert Gnuse argues, Hebrew monotheism "arose in the exile to explain the reasons for Israel's destruction" and "to give hope to despairing people."[71]

Yehezkel Kaufmann challenged this proposition that monotheism had evolved from polytheism, henotheism, or monolotry. Kaufmann

---

69. The angel of YHWH only appears once in the Major Prophets (Isa 37:36) and twice in the Minor Prophets (Zech 1:11–12; 3:1–6). In the mid-second century CE, the recognition of what seemed like a split personality in the heavens led to Marcionism. However, even during the exile, God's punishments were never separated from his promises of hope and restoration. This is not as evident in the Pentateuch.

70. I am alluding to the "princes" in Dan 10:13, 20.

71. Gnuse, *No Other Gods*, 90. It is possible for monotheism, or at least henotheism, to have arisen much earlier in Israel, as testified to by the influence of Akhenaten's/ Amenhotep IV's cult of the sun god Aten (Heliotheism) during the fourteenth century BCE. See Hornung, *Akhenaten and the Religion of Light*. Also, in *Moses and Monotheism*, Freud styled Moses as a transitional figure between the two cultures: an Egyptian who introduced Akhenaten's religion to Israel.

argued that Hebrew monotheism was fundamentally different from other forms of theism on a number of levels, most significantly, because it posits a moral God who is transcendent and uncreated. He maintained that unlike other gods in the ancient world, YHWH is an eternal being who is exempt from the laws of a meta-divine realm (i.e., fate, etc.).[72] Yet, since he cannot but be truthful, just, and holy, it appears YHWH *is* subject to a set of defining attributes.

Despite real differences between YHWH and other gods of the ancient Near East, one must still accept that passages like Josh 24:14 portray the Israelites as the product of *generations* of polytheistic worship even prior to the exile: "Now therefore revere the LORD, and serve him in sincerity and in faithfulness; put away the gods that your ancestors served beyond the River and in Egypt, and serve the LORD."[73] Though Kaufmann suggests that Israelite worship was distinctly different from that of neighboring tribes (despite the fact that both maintain a sacrificial system and temple worship), the Hebrew Scriptures testify that YHWH's uniqueness failed to deter the general population from syncretistic and idolatrous practices. Furthermore, excavations of Israelite homes dating from the tenth to the sixth century (like the one at Tel Rehov that produced a goddess figurine dating to around 850 BCE) confirms that many Israelites were not particularly dedicated to the Abrahamic and Mosaic covenants.[74]

Alternatively, if Gnuse is correct that Jewish monotheism is essentially a modification of polytheism, then the noticeable increase in angelic activity during the exilic era could be explained as a sanctified "makeover" of the Babylonian deities or as an affirmation of Zoroastrian influences. For whatever reason, the Babylonian exile had an enormous impact upon Jewish angelology; in fact, the Jerusalem Talmud (Rosh Ha-Shana 1:2) acknowledges that just like the names of the Jewish months, "[t]he names of the angels were brought by the Jews from Babylonia." As I have suggested, the escalating profile of angels during this period can be explained as an orthodox response to Babylonian polytheism. Such a theological campaign would allow the authors to emasculate pagan gods and triumph over their oppressors via non-violent means.[75] It

72. Kaufmann and Greenberg, *The Religion of Israel*, 21–59.

73. Cf. Gen 31:34–36; Exod 15:11; Ps 82:1, etc.

74. Mazar, "To What God? Altars and a House Shrine from Tel Rehov Puzzle Archaeologists."

75. That syncretism continued to flourish in Hebrew culture during the latter

hardly seems coincidental that during this time *mal'akim* began to play a dominant role in the revelation of Y<small>HWH</small> and his mysterious foreknowledge of future events (information and activity that would typically be restricted to the ancient Near Eastern pantheon).

If such a theological movement existed, it was so effective in disguising pagan influences upon Hebrew angelology that many Jews and Christians now interpret even pre-exilic references to sons of the god (*b'ney ha-elohim*) without any appreciation for the backstory. Again, Gnuse explains that such views still helps to "preserve the monotheistic identity of Yahweh . . . [b]ut pre-exilic Israelites would have understood these messengers, angels or *aides-de-camp* as gods, as the frequently used Hebrew word in such instances, *elohim*, truly implies."[76] Nevertheless, while the development in angelology during this period represents something akin to a Cambrian explosion in the doctrine's grand evolutionary record, Jewish angelology (outside the mystical traditions) resists neat systemization due to the complex relationship between the motivation of biblical authors, the *Zeitgeist*, the religions of the ancient Near East, and the nature of midrash.

Prophetic and apocalyptic literature depicts angels as inhabitants of a heavenly assembly, a belief that leans heavily upon ancient Near Eastern fables about the celestial sphere. As we have noted, the metamorphosis of Hebrew angelology appears to be contemporaneous with their exposure to the cultural and theological milieu of Babylon, a region rich with lore and imagery related to spiritual beings.[77] It was here that the Israelites likely came in contact with new theological constructs such as Zoroastrianism's angels (*yazatas* and *amesha spentas*) and the grander fable of a cosmic battle between Ahura Mazda and Angra Mainyu, the good and evil deities, respectively.[78] However, the Hebrew Scriptures also reflect

---

stages of the monarchy is testified to by the prophetic literature as well as archaeology: Israelites worshipped other gods alongside Y<small>HWH</small>. William Dever postulates that the inscription he found at Khirbet el-Kom, near Hebron, which reads "Y<small>HWH</small> and his Asherah," indicates some early Israelites believed God was married. See his book, Dever, *Did God Have a Wife?*

76. Gnuse, *No Other Gods*, 180.

77. See McIntosh, *Ancient Mesopotamia*, 209–19. It is noteworthy that angels are mentioned far more frequently in the Babylonian Talmud than the Palestinian version. Compare Corré, *Understanding the Talmud*, 48–49. Rubenstein, *The Culture of the Babylonian Talmud*, 28–29.

78. Luhrmann, "Evil in the Sands of Time: Theology and Identity Politics among the Zoroastrian Parsis," 861–89; Johnston, *Religions of the Ancient World*, 199–204.

Canaanite cosmology that portrays the relationship between the divine and earthly realm as if it was governed by a formal court of sub-deities; this idea reappears in the post-exilic concept of an angelic community.

## The Angelic Deposition of Canaanite and Babylonian Pantheons

Passages like Ps 82, for example, depict a reinterpretation of pre-exilic Canaanite monolotry. The third book of Psalms is generally thought to belong to the exilic or early post-exilic period, but dating Ps 82 is problematic because the eclectic language carries the residue of a myth that was common to many ancient Near Eastern cultures.[79] The psalm reveals El, the chief deity, in the midst of a divine council meeting along with other members of the pantheon.[80] "God [*elohim*] has taken his place in the divine council," writes Asaph, "in the midst of the gods [*elohim*] he holds judgment." The context of vv. 2–4 suggests that the other gods were unethical subordinates who had shirked their earthly responsibilities toward humanity: "How long will you judge unjustly and show partiality to the wicked?" demands God; "Give justice to the weak and the orphan; maintain the right of the lowly and the destitute. Rescue the weak and the needy; deliver them from the hand of the wicked." Later, the celestial trial concludes as El triumphantly condemns the sub-deities to death in v. 6: "I say, 'You are gods [*elohim*], children of the Most High [*elyon*], all of you; nevertheless, you shall die like mortals, and fall like any prince.'" It is uncertain whether Asaph was lampooning the concept of a divine council or unwittingly demonstrating the influence of mythical language upon the Jewish worldview.[81]

Mullen explains the dynamics within the Canaanite pantheon, "All the gods, even the highest in the pantheon, were subject to the decisions of the council," but "the god El is equivalent to the entire council. The

---

Also, Coudert, "Angels," 283.

79. See Goulder, *The Psalms of Asaph and the Pentateuch*.

80. For examples in the Psalms: Pss 29:1–2; 89:6–9; 95:3; 96:4; 97:7, 9; 148:2.

81. While interpretations abound concerning the identity of the *elohim* on trial, Lowell K. Handy, echoes the majority view (Bertholet, Budde, Gunkel, and Peters, for example) that the passages "refers to 'gods' . . . not 'angels,' 'rulers,' 'judges,' or 'tenured professors.'" See Handy, "The Appearance of Pantheon in Judah," 40. Though the Targum translates it as "You are reckoned as angels, and all of you are like angels of the height." However, there is no conceivable reason why Israel's God would condemn the angels to perish in v. 6, since, as created beings, they pose no actual threat to his rule.

decree of El is the decree of the gods."[82] Handy's distinctions are more explicit, he separates this assembly into four tiers: there are "authoritative" deities like El and Ashera who own the cosmos and act as parental figures for the gods; "active" deities like Baal, Anat, and Mot who are territorial deities not unlike the description of "princes" in Daniel; "artisan" deities who perform skills for their superiors; and the final level of "messenger" deities who were rather commonplace.[83] Given that these gods play a hefty role in early Near Eastern beliefs, it is only logical that they would disappear or be redefined as the twelve tribes inched toward monotheism. The Psalms provide numerous examples of God's supervisory role among other heavenly beings; this alone would have reinforced the imagery to the Israelites during worship.[84] While Ps 82 expresses a desire to annihilate other gods, other early exilic rhetoric indicates the move toward monotheism was gradual, as God reasons with the exiles, "How can I pardon you? Your children have forsaken me, and have sworn by those who are not gods" (Jer 5:7).

David Freedman affirms the value of the ongoing tension between Hebrew monotheism and the Near Eastern pantheon, "But there are other gods, that is clear. Otherwise, there can be no comparison to demonstrate the incomparability of Yahweh."[85] Unlike the author of Ps 82, the author of Daniel employed a subtler approach to affirming YHWH's uniqueness, though he shared the same desire to move beyond monolotry to monotheism. Rather than deriding the gods directly, Daniel elevates angelic beings to function in a similar fashion by endowing them with personalities, jurisdictions of influence, titles, and names. It appears that the greater emphasis he places upon angelic function was his way of enfeebling the pantheon. So while their theology of higher order beings differed from that of the surrounding culture, some Hebrew authors retained the language of the *elohim* even as others began to appraise angels with greater value.

As early as the eighth century, groups of Israelite scholars imposed a monotheistic structure upon biblical texts, projecting this imagery back upon an earlier era. The prophetic literature attempts to move the faith beyond the family cult of Genesis (Abraham, Isaac, Jacob) by articulating

82. Mullen, *The Assembly of the Gods*, 115.

83. See chs. 4–6 in Handy, *Among the Host of Heaven*.

84. Pss 29:1–2; 89:6–9; 95:3; 96:4; 97:7,9; 148:2.

85. Freedman, "Who Is Like Thee Among the Gods?" 328.

the religion of the fathers in a new way. Even the contributions to angelology read as a veiled push for monotheism by the community's theological elite. One reason why their angelology was so effective is that it was familiar, in a sense; their descriptions of angels combine the anthropomorphic language of J with the emphasis upon divine transcendence found in E and P.

Unlike earlier reactions to Canaanite mythology, the prophetic and apocalyptic literature seems to posit an alternative to the Babylonian pantheon without ascribing personhood to their gods. Thus, these prophets launched a second wave of theophanic and angelophanic language similar to what we have already seen in Genesis. Though the accounts are extraordinary, I do not dismiss the idea that the writers were sharing their genuine experience. Cultures with a supernatural worldview may tend to see angels where others may not, simply because it falls within the realm of their expectations.

My premise that regional gods were transformed into angels would allow the Hebrews to maintain reverence for a category of higher-order beings without transgressing the first two Commandments, but the suggestion is not without difficulties. There is no direct evidence in the Old Testament that angel worship was ever a problem, something one might expect to see during an era when such a transformation was taking place. However, searching the text for polemics against angel worship inevitably leads to two fallacious conclusions about the evolution of angelology. First, it may imply the absence of evidence is evidence for the absence of such a switch. Secondly, it assumes that the Scriptures themselves are like a magic window through which one can see glimpse every detail of theological history.

However, beyond the Old Testament itself, one *does* find just the sort of evidence they would expect to discover if a theological transition between gods and angelic figures occurred. In portions of extant Judeo-Christian literature there are warnings against sacrificing to angels, prohibitions against angelic iconography, injunctions against prayers directed to angels, rejections of dualism between God and angels, and accusations of early Christian apologists directed toward angel-worshipping Jews.[86] Might this support the idea that angels became substitutes for the pagan gods that the biblical writers were attempting to overthrow? If so, does it also suggest the program had unintended consequences?

---

86. Goodenough, *The Archaeological Evidence from the Diaspora*, 145–46.

Goodenough comments, "The rabbis consistently opposed any type of angel worship, and their prohibitions are usually naively quoted to prove that Jews did not practice it . . . their very protest also bears witness to its practice."[87] Stuckenbruck also concludes, "While there is a lack of data that supports any general or widespread existence of cultic organization around a heavenly angel (or angels), the polemical texts seem to suggest that attitudes and devotional practices relating to them were not only a hypothetical possibility but also posed a practical problem that was subject to internal debate."[88]

In fact, it appears, however anecdotally, the transition period from gods to angels may have lasted much longer than generally assumed. This theological merger may have continued into the ascent of Christianity.[89] In fact, warnings against angel worship in the Epistle to the Colossians certainly indicate that an angel cult was a perceived threat until as late as the mid-first century CE.[90]

Is it possible that biblical writers and redactors made a minor concession when it came to undermining the pantheon? In what appears to be a moderate validation of Canaanite and Babylonian mythology, the Hebrew Scriptures portray YHWH as presiding over an administration of spiritual beings comprised of *elohim, bene ha' elohim, qedoshim,* and *mal'akim*; yet, such a notion needed to change if Israel was to differentiate itself from the surrounding cultures in matters of worship.[91] Just as I demonstrated the apparent evolution of the *mal'ak YHWH* in JEP, as the emphasis upon monotheism developed after the Second Iron Age, it seems that writers and redactors elevated the *mal'akim* to play roles previously held by *elohim* and *bene ha' elohim*. They also made it clear that the

87. Ibid. However, Stuckenbruck maintains that early Jewish sources "could tolerate language of prayer and praise as directed towards angels" without undermining a "resilient" monotheistic framework. Stuckenbruck, "'Angels' and 'God'" 70.

88. Ibid., 52.

89. The Christian Scriptures resolutely condemn the practice of angel worship: cf. Col 2:18; Rev 19:10.

90. See Col 2:18 where the Greek "*thraeskeia*" likely refers to cultic worship. There is a long history of mystical angelology in the *Merkabah* tradition. Also, Metatron is called a "lesser Yahweh" 3 En. 12:5 and the Melchizedek fragment from Qumran describe Melchizedek as an angel who establishes freedom for the righteous. See 11QMelch. Furthermore, the Council of Laodicea condemns angelolatry.

91. For *elohim*: Pss 95:3; 96:4; Dan 2:47; *bene ha' elohim*: Gen 6:2, 4; *qedoshim*: Job 1:6; 2:1; 38:7; Pss 29:1–2; 89:6–9; 97:7, 9; *mal'akim* Job 5:1; 15:8; 16:19–21; Zech 14:5; Dan 8:13, 23.

intervention of Yʜᴡʜ's angels was quite dissimilar to the capriciousness of Babylonian and Canaanite gods and goddesses.[92] So by the New Testament era, the *elohim* were entirely reduced to either benevolent *angeloi* or wicked *daimonia*.[93]

It may appear inconceivable that orthodox authors of prophetic and apocalyptic literature like Isaiah and Daniel would essentially reassign pagan deities to Yʜᴡʜ's service rather than simply condemning them as false gods.[94] However, I propose that two parallel, and mutually influential, theological movements were in motion as these books were being written. The first group comprised the majority of Israelites, many of whom were entrenched in superstition and largely syncretistic in their personal devotion. If these individuals were eventually to think of the pagan gods as angels, it would not be without the influence of a second group: the elites who transcribed the official account of Israel's theology.

In what Mark Smith refers to as the "telescoping of the pantheon and the collapse of its middle tiers," these authors leveraged the prevailing superstition by reinterpreting polytheistic beliefs to conform to the orthodox religion of the elites (just as the church may have used Saturnalia and *Sol Invictus* to assimilate pagans via a new holiday called "Christmas").[95] Furthermore, given their observation of the Babylonian's stratified system of government, the exilic and post-exilic writers may have thought that a similar celestial retinue would do more to increase Yʜᴡʜ's glory than simply positing him as the only inhabitant of the spiritual realm.

If Hebrew monotheism took shape as a redefinition of regional polytheism, then angelology would have functioned as the most logical image through which to depict ideas about hierarchy, transcendence, and revelation, without conceding orthodoxy.[96] Since orthodoxy is par-

92. The gods in the *Enuma Elish* are referred to as "ungracious," Speiser, "The Creation Epic." Cf. Livingston, *The Pentateuch in Its Cultural Environment*, 134.

93. 2 Cor 8 provides a possible exception, but the passage is likely intended to be read tongue-in-cheek.

94. The Major Prophets clearly distinguished between Israel's God and pagan gods: Cf. Isa 21:9; 36:18–20; 37:19; as did apocalyptic literature like Dan 2:47; 3:12–18; 5:23.

95. Smith, *The Origins of Biblical Monotheism*, 50. "Christianity did not destroy paganism," observed Will Durant, "it adopted it . . . ." Durant, *The Story of Civilization*, 3:595.

96. For works on the relationship between polytheism and legend, see Kaufmann and Greenberg, *The Religion of Israel*; and Hanson, *The People Called*; Oden, *The Bible*

tially the result of a group's degree of influence within the historical and theological dialectic, one can say that Hebrew monotheism, inasmuch as it is defined by the status of intermediaries between heaven and earth, was also deemed superior to competing pantheistic views of the world because it allowed YHWH to defeat his opportunistic, divine rivals by way of *his* faithful intermediaries, otherwise known as angels. Given that this crescendo in angelology occurs in literature associated with the humiliation of the exile, it is also possible that the new scheme served as a veiled portent of eschatological destruction to be visited on Israel's enemies.

Whether or not the emergence of a distinctly Hebrew angelology helps to demonstrate the disproportionate influence of certain motifs in the ascendance/overthrow of unorthodox beliefs and doctrines, it remains probable that the writers were extraordinarily gifted and devout pragmatists who accommodated popular opinion by redefining gods as angels without compromising the holiness of YHWH or committing the sin of idolatry in the process. Again, I am not suggesting that one should disregard the accounts of angels in the prophetic and apocalyptic books as a genuine form of history. Nevertheless, it would be careless to overlook the way the angelic theme also augmented the prophet's influence within their community or, in Daniel's case, secured reputations as one "who is endowed with a spirit of the holy gods" among the Babylonian nobility.[97]

Like the patriarchs, these prominent figures are supposed to have interacted directly with the angels as recipients of divine guidance in a relay between heaven and earth. Yet since the *angels* were often the harbingers and enforcers of YHWH's explicit hostility toward polytheism, they, rather than Daniel or the Major Prophets, conveniently bore the brunt of responsibility for the contents and consequences of the message.[98] I shall

---

*without Theology.* For a defense of the conventional view of biblical narrative and monotheism, see Alter, *The Art of Biblical Narrative.*

97. Dan 4:8.

98. See the angel's role in the slaughter of idolaters in Ezek 9:1, 5, 7; note Dan 11:8, where Gabriel foretells a battle that will involve the captivity of gods and idols. However, there is no Old Testament parallel to Paul's wariness of angelic communication, "But even if we or an angel from heaven should proclaim to you a gospel contrary to what we proclaimed to you, let that one be accursed!" Gal 1:8. Cf. Mafico, *Yahweh's Emergence as "Judge" among the Gods.* Mafico suggests Israel's move toward monotheism was related to the political advantages of having a united kingdom. This adds further justification for the prophets' demotion of the gods of Israel's forebears and neighbors.

now turn to various pericopes in the books of Isaiah, Ezekiel, and Daniel to detail how temple-related angelophanies were used in the campaign to quash the pantheon.

## ANGELS AND THE TEMPLE: RELOCATING THE DIVINE COUNCIL

### Introduction

That the exile symbolizes an essential turning point in Israel's monotheism is further testified by the fact that archaeologists have unearthed scores of idols in Israelite settlements dating before the exile, but few in locations associated with later periods.[99] According to Ephraim Stern of the Hebrew University of Jerusalem, the pagan figurines and shrines that are commonly found in pre-exilic strata are virtually nonexistent in locations connected to dates after 586 BCE.[100] This leads me to believe that the trauma of the exile and the grace symbolized by the temple were catalysts for a period of profound theological reflection and creativity that refined the tenets of ethical monotheism.

The biblical texts reveal that idolatry continued to be a thorn in Israel's paw for years to come, but I propose its gangrenous effects were largely curtailed by the literary efforts revealed in Isaiah, Ezekiel, and Daniel. While the genres and dates of these books differ, the works advance a similar message by re-imagining the beings that governed the affairs of the cosmos. Specifically, their temple-focused angelology helped foster a theological revolution. Through their efforts, the council of El slowly gave way to YHWH and his team of angelic courtiers. However, it is necessary to demonstrate similarities between epiphanic accounts within these later books in order to advance the idea that, despite the different dates and circumstances involved, the authors accomplished their mission by using remarkably similar imagery.

---

99. Concerning those discovered in Samaria and Lachish, see Knowles, *Centrality Practiced: Jerusalem in the Religious Practice of Yehud and the Diaspora in the Persian Period*, 72–73.

100. Stern, *What Happened to the Cult Figurines?*, 22–29, 53–55.

## Seraphim as YHWH's Temple Attendants

The book of Isaiah depicts one of the more prominent examples of angel-human contact in the prophetic literature. In a highly evocative account in the sixth chapter, one finds Isaiah standing spellbound inside the temple as God—flanked by ministering seraphim—all but engulfs him with an overwhelming exhibition of regal authority. The imagery in the pericope of an enthroned, robed deity acknowledges God's status as *the* sovereign in contrast to the presumptuous Uzziah, Israel's late ruler (6:1).

This vision of the enthroned God, accompanied by supernatural courtiers recollects descriptions of the innermost sanctum of the tabernacle and temple where the ark of the covenant (YHWH's throne) was protected by cherubic statuary. It also reveals a different layer to Israel's emerging concept of God. Although theophanies are common to the Old Testament, during the time of proto-Isaiah God was "conceived of as dwelling in heaven," thus explaining the contrast between this scene and the anthropomorphic God who strolled within Eden and ate with Abraham.[101]

The appearance of God in Isa 6 strikes me as an obvious allusion to divine council imagery, which played a large role in the regional mythopoeia. However, rather than positioning God as the judge of opportunistic and reluctant sub-deities, as in Ps 82, proto-Isaiah substitutes a pair of six-winged seraphs who carry out YHWH's commands flawlessly, praising him for his glory.[102] If my hypothesis is correct that angels gradually replaced sub-deities during the era of the prophets as a way of promoting monotheism and God's transcendence, the significance of this exchange in Isa 6 is not immaterial. The paired angel motif discussed in the section on Gen 3:24 and 18–19 also appears here, demonstrating continuity with earlier theophanic settings.[103] It may also have served as a model for subsequent throne/temple theophanies in Ezekiel, as I will discuss later.

Isaiah's theophany, however, introduces *seraphim*, rather than the conventional cherubim. This appears counterproductive since cherubim

---

101. Morgenstern, "The Mythological Background of Psalm 82," 52.

102. Note the similar description of angelic courtiers in Rev 8:2–3 "And I saw the seven angels who stand before God, and seven trumpets were given to them. Another angel with a golden censer came and stood at the altar; he was given a great quantity of incense to offer with the prayers of all the saints on the golden altar that is before the throne."

103. Gen 18; 2 Kgs 19:15; Ps 80:1.

were employed as a means of redefining regional iconography in light of Hebrew theology. Why introduce another angelic category, especially with a word typically reserved for poisonous serpents, when cherubim already enjoyed considerable standing in Hebrew legend? Morgenstern suggests the choice may relate to the seraph's functional resemblance to the "the sons of God" (*ben ha elohim*) in Job 1:6; 2:1, the "army of heaven" (*tsaba shamayim*) of 1 Kgs 22:19–23, and "the standing ones" (*ha omedim*) of Zech 3:1–7.[104] Although this alignment positions the seraph as symbolic of strength and proximity to the divine, there is another explanation.

Like earlier writers (cf. Num 21:6; Deut 8:15), Isaiah typically uses the term *seraph* to describe poisonous serpents; but his *saraph* is also capable of flight. For example, in 14:29 he prophesies "from the serpent's root a viper will come out, and its fruit will be a flying serpent [*saraph*]," and 30:6 describes a land of "trouble and distress, of lioness and roaring lion, of viper and flying serpent [*saraph*]." We also know from 2 Kgs 18:4 that Moses' bronze serpent (*Nehustan*) was a feature in Israelite cultic veneration in Jerusalem before being destroyed during Hezekiah's iconoclasm campaign, approximately one generation after Isaiah.

In addition, archaeology reveals that since the exodus, serpent fertility cults were familiar elements in pagan worship in nearby Megiddo, Gezer, Hazor, and Shechem.[105] What had originally been an artifact of healing and deliverance became an idolatrous token, which reintroduces the question as to what extent familiar cultural icons may have influenced such visions. Could the seraphim of Isaiah's vision be related to cultic worship rituals that featured serpent-idols?[106] It is possible that *Nehustan* had been in the temple in Isaiah's day, providing inspiration for the vision. So might Isa 6 be attempt to recapture the meaning of the original image by relating it to the life-giving mercy of God just as Jesus does in John 3:14–15? At the least, it seems plausible that such visions were subconsciously tethered to the regional mythology; as with the cherub, this would identify the seraph as another icon adapted by ancient Hebrew authors as they struggled to transcend their polytheistic milieu.

104. Morgenstern, "The Mythological Background of Psalm 82," 56.

105. Joiner, "The Bronze Serpent in the Israelite Cult."

106. My position is that it was essentially a borrowed image from Canaanite worship, but for a summary of alternative origins for Nehustan, see Fabry, "Nechosheth," 378–80.

Returning again to the passage, one notices that given the economy of being, Isaiah's seraphim have too many wings.[107] However, he explains that they use one pair to protect their eyes from God's resplendent glory, another to fly, and one to conceal their feet—possibly euphemistic for sexual organs.[108] The author's first-person message is clear, despite their proximity to YHWH, the seraphic splendor is only derivative; they need four extra wings in order to curve in upon themselves while in God's sacred presence. To quote from Barth, though they may indeed enjoy "primary and original knowledge of what He says and does,"[109] the six-winged seraphim are not to be confused with YHWH, nor can they "replace the prophetic and apostolic witness, or the witness of the community."[110]

Nevertheless, these divine attendants are indispensable to God's revelation of himself as they speak their words of praise while flanking YHWH's throne, as humanity, in the form of the prophet Isaiah, instinctively falls to the ground in abject terror. Wieringen observes that the emotional overtones of the vision *depend* upon the seraphim as characters who construct their own transcendent domain within the narrative space by their speech and activity in vv. 2–4, 6–7.[111] Though never called *mal'akim*, perhaps to suggest that they are not primarily messengers, their message is one of unending worship as testified to by the foundations that reverberate with their stentorian trishagion.[112] In 6:3 the trishagion of the seraphim becomes a model of orthodox temple worship, a stark contrast to the idolatrous worship of Nehustan and especially poignant when juxtaposed against the impending destruction of Ashera poles, sacred pillars, and trees from the land in v. 13.

107. Marvin Pope adds, "Coins of Byblos represent El in the form of a man with six wings, one pair hanging down." Pope, *El in the Ugaritic Texts*, 46.

108. The depiction of seraphim as winged beings symbolizes their ability to travel between YHWH and humanity. Also, God is often described figuratively as a winged being, presumably because the heavens are his abode (Pss 17:8; 36:8; 57:2; 61:5; 63:8; 91:4; Deut 32:11; Exod 19:4).

109. Barth, CD, III.3, 497.

110. Ibid., 498.

111. Van Wieringen, *The Implied Reader in Isaiah 6–12*, 36.

112. Brevard Childs adds, "Holiness in the Old Testament is not an ethical quality, but the essence of God's nature as separate and utterly removed from the profane. Holiness, the 'glory and majesty' strikes terror in the unholy and proud (Isa 2:19), but to his attendants awe and reverence . . . the Seraphim offer worship and praise." Childs, *Isaiah*, 55.

Isaiah comes undone at the otherworldly specter, instinctively interjecting his angst—literally, "*Oy!*" Immediately, one seraphic attendant leaves Yhwh's side in order to cauterize Isaiah's lips with a hot stone, absolving his sin.[113] Only then does God invite the freshly-consecrated prophet into the divine council in order to speak an authoritative message to the "stiff-necked" people of Judah. Mullen observes,

> The prophet is the herald of the divine council. He delivers the decree of Yahweh, which is the decree of the council. The authority of the prophet as the herald/messenger of the assembly is that of the power which sent him. He is the vocal manifestation of the deity who dispatched him. The parallel position of the prophet and the messenger-deity in Canaanite literature makes this fact undeniable. . . . The Hebrew prophets, like the messenger-deities described in the Ugaritic myths, are clearly envoys who carry both the message and authority of the divinity who dispatched them. In the case of the prophets, this was Yahweh, and ultimately the council that surrounded him.[114]

While one does not need to go as far as Hayman, who argues that Jewish monotheism was not truly practiced until the medieval period, the author(s) of Isaiah introduce the idea that Yhwh was *the* transcendent being by portraying theo/angel-ophanies within the temple, corroborated by a prophetic figure who, in turn, is commissioned to speak a divinely-revealed oracle to the rest of humanity.[115] Aside from the paired angel motif, visions of this type reflect little of the Jahwist's terrestrial God. Instead, they are much closer to the later Priestly testimony of a cosmic Creator whom higher-order beings praise and mortals fear. Rather than working through the indifferent gods of the ancient Near Eastern pantheon, God now seems to relate to the world via a system of benign celestial (and occasionally human) intermediaries whose presence accen-

---

113. Angelic beings are often presented as priests of the heavenly temple, as shown in; 1 Kgs 22:19, "I saw the Lord sitting on his throne, with all the host of heaven standing beside him to the right and to the left of him"; Dan 7:9–10, "As I watched, thrones were set in place, and an Ancient One took his throne. . . . A thousand thousands served him, and ten thousand times ten thousand stood attending him. The court sat in judgment, and the books were opened"; and Rev 5:11 "I heard the voice of many angels surrounding the throne and the living creatures and the elders; they numbered myriads of myriads and thousands of thousands. . . ."

114. Mullen, *Assembly of the Gods*, 228. I explore this idea of angel-preachers further in the chapter on Aquinas's angelology.

115. Hayman, "Monotheism—A Misused Word in Jewish Studies?"

tuates his glory as they accompany his travels between heaven and the temple sanctuary.[116]

Isa 6 helped to establish a relationship between the angelic council and the temple by surrounding Yhwh's chariot-throne with seraphim within the sanctuary; the writers of Ezek 8–10 and Dan 7:9–10 employ similar imagery. Out of this motif arose Merkabah mysticism, a branch of theology that focused upon analogical interpretations of God as an enthroned, transcendent deity surrounded by angelic courtiers, a movement that illustrates the resilience of the underlying metaphors.[117] In order to demonstrate the marriage between angels and temple imagery as a semi-coordinated means of establishing the divine council within the temple, the following sections briefly detail the relationships between Isa 6, Ezek 8–10, and Dan 7 by focusing upon three concepts common to each passage: the liturgical setting of the vision, the angelic attendants, and the imagery of burning coals/fire.

## The Liturgical Setting

Ezek 8–10, like Isa 6, envisions the angelic council within the midst of the temple. However, God and his celestial retinue depart from the structure due to rampant idolatry among the priests, only returning again in chapters 40–43 to take possession of a newly built, undefiled temple. The vision of the angelic court in Dan 7 is situated not in an earthly temple, but in the grandest venue possible, heaven. The writer of Rev 4–5, in his heavy reliance upon Dan 7, appears to reinterpret it, as do I, in terms of a cosmic sanctuary. Lacocque observes that while Daniel's vision "has the temple as its framework," it is absent because it "had been profaned by Antiochus IV and was temporarily unfit for a theophany."[118] Nonetheless,

116. Note Paul's insistence that women cover their heads during worship "because of the angels" (1 Cor 11:10).

117. See Halperin, *Faces of the Chariot*. Because of the tradition that the giving of the Torah on Sinai is related to the Merkavah, many of these passages are read every year in the synagogue on Shavuot. For a well-documented treatment of the cherubim in rabbinical literature, see Heschel, *Heavenly Torah as Reflected through the Generations*, 100–103. Also, Davila, *Descenders to the Chariot*. Davila refers to the essence of Merkavah mysticism and its heavy reliance upon angelic motifs as an esoteric form of Jewish shamanism that "must be read on its own terms as the literary residue of a quasi-shamanic intermediary movement, not on the terms of the earlier and quite different apocalyptic literature." Ibid., 308.

118. Lacocque, *The Book of Daniel*, 125.

the common theme in all three pericopes is that the visions effectively transport the recipient to a consecrated setting where the enthroned God is worshipped and attended to by angels.

## Angelic Attendants

As in the Isa 6 passage, God is accompanied by an angelic court in the visions of Ezekiel and Daniel. For example, Dan 7:9–10 reads,

> As I watched, thrones were set in place, and an Ancient One took his throne; his clothing was white as snow, and the hair of his head like pure wool. . . . A thousand thousands served him, and ten thousand times ten thousand stood attending him. The court sat in judgment, and the books were opened.[119]

The imagery may have been based upon bureaucracies in the ancient Near East.[120] Yet, while the concept of a deity surrounded by an assembly of gods was widespread in the region, the writer radically modifies the image by replacing gods with angels.[121] Unlike Isaiah and Ezekiel, Daniel stresses the number of courtiers rather than their peculiarities, but all three texts make it clear that the angels are subordinate to God.

In each instance, the beings show deference to YHWH and do his bidding. Ezekiel's throne scene reintroduces the more conventional image of cherubim in relation to the divine presence that we examined at the beginning of this chapter, and as in Isaiah's description of the seraphim, he elaborates upon their appearance in chapters 1 and 10, depicting them

---

119. Daniel could possibly be drawing upon older traditions here, echoing imagery found in Deut 33:2 where YHWH is accompanied by angels in a holy war. Also, Jude 1:14; Rev 5:11.

120. Handy argues the pantheon in ancient Syria-Palestine reflects the social structure; it was a bureaucratic hierarchy. See Handy, *Among the Host of Heaven*. Also, Teixidor, "Review of The Genesis Apocryphon of Qumran Cave I." Teixidor argues convincingly that the "watchers" (angelic figures in Dan 4:10, 14, 20 and Enochian literature) are a "reminiscence of the officers who kept the Achaemenid kings informed of all the events that happened in the empire."

121. For example, the tenth-century building inscription that reads "A house built by Yehimilk, king of Byblos, who also has restored all the ruins of the houses here. May Baalshamem and the Lord of Byblos and the Assembly of the Holy Gods of Byblos prolong the days and years of Yehimilk in Byblos, for [he is] a righteous king and an upright king before the Holy Gods of Byblos!" Pritchard, *The Ancient Near East*, 215.

with four faces and four wings (two of which shield their body) and covering them in eyes.[122] They support and attend to the throne itself.[123]

## Coal/fire and Wheel Imagery

Although remarkably similar, rather than using coals as a symbol for purification and forgiveness, as in Isa 6, God instructs an angelic being in Ezek 10 to use burning coals as a portent of judgment against unrepentant idolaters: "Go between the wheelwork underneath the cherubim. Fill your hands with burning coals from among the cherubim and scatter them over the city." Analogously, the chariot-throne scene in Dan 7:9 retains the wheels of the Ezek 10 vision, but substitutes fire in place of the altar of burning coals found in both Isa 6 and Ezek 10, stating that God's chariot-throne "was fiery flames, and its wheels were burning fire" and that a "stream of fire issued and flowed out from his presence."

While Isaiah and Ezekiel alone preserve the ember imagery, all three authors associate combustible elements with the throne of God and his angels. Only Ezekiel and Daniel emphasize the throne's chariot-like characteristics, however. Yet, taken together, the scenes are redolent of the ark and the bronze altar used in tabernacle and temple worship.

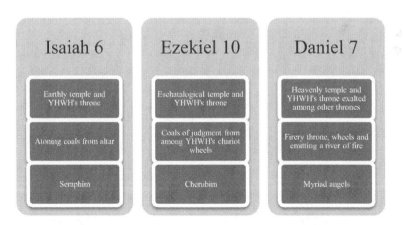

Fig. 1. Angels, thrones, and temples in Hebrew Scripture

122. Ezekiel typically uses "four" (*arba*) in connection with the temple (41:5), and the altar (43:14, 15, 17, 23; 45:19), so I propose the author's association of "four" with the number of cherubim, their faces and wings, carries priestly overtones.

123. Ezek 1:12–21; 10.

To summarize, both Isa 6 and Ezek 8–10 represent a throne/altar scene in the temple, burning coals, angelic beings, and a prophet. While much of the imagery in the Dan 7 vision is similar, it is less detailed; though it is no less compelling given that Dan 7–12 is an especially late composition, dating well after the exile.[124] Was Daniel's angelic court a necessary reminder to Israel because of a theological relapse into superstitions about the divine council? Possibly, but it is equally likely that the writer chose the imagery to express the heavenly character of temple worship, as something in which angels participate. Nonetheless, it is apparent that theo/angel-ophanies follow similar patterns in passages featuring prominent biblical personalities like Isaiah, Ezekiel, and Daniel.

Aside from the remarkable degree of correspondence between these accounts, what do they say about the function of angelology as a disguise for fundamental doctrines? One way to reconcile the differences between the three narratives is to imagine that each writer is emphasizing particular elements of the tabernacle/temple into a single prototype. However, there are other alternatives; earlier I maintained that the prophets employed angels in order to supplement their emphasis upon monotheism and divine otherness, but the recurrent angelic presence in temple visions also suggests their metaphorical role as an ideal community engaged in the purity of YHWH-exclusive worship.

Rather than simply delivering bespoke messages (Gen 16–19; Judg 6), angels are now organized, and appear to be concerned with a divine liturgy complete with choreography and antiphonal song (Isa 6:3; Ezek 10:6–7; Dan 10:7), and with broader matters of worship (Ezek 40–47:12).[125] This broadening of mission may indicate the angelic council was conceived of as a body of sacerdotal intermediaries between humanity and God, which seems especially likely given the altar and atonement imagery connected with angelic appearances in Isa 6, Ezek 10, and Dan 7–10.[126]

Ezekiel's reliance upon angels in sanctuary settings plus his reluctance to use "*elohim*" to describe pagan gods is undoubtedly a statement about YHWH-exclusive worship, but what is most intriguing is his

---

124. W. Sibley Towner proposes a date of 167–64 BCE in Towner, *Daniel*, 115, 136, 165.

125. As well as politics (cf. Dan 7–12).

126. The Babylonian Talmud, Tractate Sanhedrin 38b interprets Dan 4:17a, ("The sentence is rendered by decree of the watchers, the decision is given by order of the holy ones"), as proof that God does nothing "without first consulting the family above."

meticulous description of the angels.[127] In fact, their distinctive appearance is equally significant to Isaiah and Daniel. Together, these authors render higher order beings with an array of attributes: radiant bodies, thunderous voices, multiple wings, eyes, and faces. It appears the prophets lean to the flamboyant side of angelology, whereas Genesis often depicts angels as featureless cherubim, male visitors or voices in a dream. However, the new profile is not gratuitous, because it reflects obliquely the newfound glory of temple worship and Israel's *one* God who is other.[128] While the authors are attempting to dissuade the reader from polytheism and idolatry, the colorful accounts they penned are the most detailed pictures of God and angels in the biblical record. These vignettes also present angels as representatives of the post-exilic ideal, embodying worship and service within the sanctuary, and looking hopefully toward the eschatological temple's design and future. Thus, I believe the divine and angelic presence in the temple visions indicates that the building itself became the new locus for the divine council, if only figuratively.

## DANIEL'S PERSONAL ANGEL

Knibb's point that the book of Daniel is *sui generis* is true about the book as a whole, but it is especially pertinent at the level of angelology.[129] The first half of the text features narratives about a handful of noble, Jewish adolescents who rise to prominent positions in the Babylon court via allegiance to YHWH. Although the youths face certain death at numerous points because of their unwillingness to participate in Babylonian worship rituals, they are always rescued in dramatic fashion thanks to well-timed angelic interventions: Shadrach, Meshack, and Abednego were cast into a furnace for refusing to bow to the icon of Nebuchadnezzar, but are delivered by an angel, or as Nebuchadnezzar's minister described him, "a son of the gods."[130] When Daniel himself is thrown to the lions for his worship of Israel's God, he emerges unscathed due to the

127. Also note the use of gem imagery in Ezek 1:22–26 and Dan 10:6. For some reason, Isa 6 does not echo this theme in relation to the theophany, though gems appear later in the description Zion's restoration in 54:11–12.

128. In fact, the interaction between these fantastic beings and a representative of humanity is a trademark of pre-exilic (Isaiah), exilic (Ezekiel and Daniel), and post-exilic (Zechariah) figures.

129. Knibb, "The Book of Daniel in Its Context," 34.

130. Referred to as *mal'ak* in v. 28.

actions of an angel, presumably sent because the prophet "had trusted in his God."[131] Daniel's angels are emblems of an everlasting relationship between the spiritual and physical realms. There is almost a formulaic pattern of heaven vindicating persecuted persons for their devotion to Israel's God, while those who worship other gods experience terrifying visions.[132] Some go mad.[133] Others suffer death.[134]

What makes the book of Daniel exceptional, however, is that individual angels are often the means of vindication and deliverance rather than God himself, though at times the Babylonian king attributes a miraculous deliverance to God, rather than the angel.[135] Daniel presents angels as personal and somewhat autonomous figures; they liberate captives, encourage the prophet, maintain cosmic order, and protect God's people. This emphasis upon individualization marks a notable departure from the austere, nameless angels of earlier biblical accounts (i.e., Gen 3; Isa 6; Ezek 1; 10), who guard Eden and YHWH's throne rather than people. In the second half of the book, and for the first time in Scripture, angels bear royal titles like "prince" and even acquire evocative names such as Gabriel ("strong man of God") and Michael ("who is like God?").[136] Like Daniel ("God is my Judge"), their names contain a form of the divine name El, lending support to my argument for their growing role as replacements for the pantheon and surrogates for the transcendent God.[137] The Scriptures portray Michael and Gabriel as the personification of benevolent care, concern, and guardianship—companions of Israel and her people—the very extension of YHWH's right hand. Before concluding this

131. Dan 6:23b. Also see Bel and the Dragon (vv. 33–39), where an angel carries Habakkuk by his hair from Judea to the lion's den in Babylon in order to feed and encourage Daniel during a six-day stint in the lion's den.

132. 4:5; some involving angels 4:23.

133. 4:31–37.

134. 2:12; 3:22–23; 5:4, 30; 6:24.

135. 6:25–27.

136. The archangels Michael and Gabriel also play important roles in the Qur'an. See Al-Baqara 2:97–98, "Say: Whoever is an enemy to Gabriel—for he brings down the (revelation) to thy heart by Allah's will, a confirmation of what went before, and guidance and glad tidings for those who believe. Whosoever is an enemy of God and His angels and His message-bearers, including Gabriel and Michael, [should know that,] verily, God is the enemy of all who deny the truth."

137. Gabriel would make clear the fact that he was a unique representative of God when speaking to Zechariah in Luke 1:19. "I am Gabriel. I stand in the presence of God, and I have been sent to speak to you and to bring you this good news."

section, I shall now turn to Daniel's image of personal angels with respect to guardianship.

## Guardians of Heavenly Wisdom

Daniel's angelology has hearty sapiential overtones. As revealers of divine mysteries to select individuals, the angels act as guardians of YHWH's wisdom and understanding in the second half of the book.[138] Beginning with chapter 8, Daniel enters a series of dialogues with angels; they impart wisdom to him and instruct him in divine mysteries about the distant future. While Daniel is said to possess ten times the understanding (*binah*) of the court magicians (1:20), he falls short of being able to understand (*binah*) a heavenly vision in 8:16–26.[139] In the midst of this pericope, the first of three visions involving the angel Gabriel, Daniel falls prostrate in terror and enters a deep sleep/trance as the angel attempts to clarify the vision; even after Gabriel rouses him and sets him on his feet again before finishing the explanation, Daniel remains uncharacteristically bemused, "So I, Daniel, was overcome and lay sick for some days; then I arose and went about the king's business. But I was dismayed by the vision and did not understand (*mebin*) it" (v. 27).

In the second vision in chapter 9, Gabriel appears again and proclaims in v. 22, "I have now come out to give you wisdom and understanding (*binah*)."[140] Whether this "giving" indicates the explanation of the vision or the impartation of a gift is not clear, but immediately after Gabriel announces the reason for his arrival, he exhorts Daniel to "know therefore and understand" the significance of the vision. That the seer in the story makes no statements to the contrary allows the audience to assume that he has finally comprehended these heavenly secrets.

138. Handy notes this was also a characteristic of El, who's "wisdom was in knowing how the cosmos ought to function and how to facilitate this end . . . suggested by El's appointment of gods and kings to their offices. Mot, Yam, Baal, and human rulers owed their positions to El." *Among the Host of Heaven*, 80.

139. Also, the queen reminds Belshazzar in 5:11 "There is a man in your kingdom who is endowed with a spirit of the holy gods. In the days of your father he was found to have enlightenment, understanding, and wisdom like the wisdom of the gods."

140. The Akkadian for Nebuchadnezzar is Nabu-kudurri-usur, which translated, means "O Nabu, protect my lineage." Nabu was the god of wisdom and the son of Marduk. See Wiseman, "Babylonia 605–539 B.C.," 229. The irony is that Nebuchadnezzar often did not understand dreams/visions, while Daniel was given the wisdom by Gabriel to interpret them.

The third vision confirms that Daniel is now capable of understanding the genre of heavenly visions. It begins in 10:1, "In the third year of King Cyrus of Persia a word was revealed to Daniel, who was named Belteshazzar. The word was true, and it concerned a great conflict. He understood (*ubin*) the word, having received understanding (*ubinah*) in the vision." What is peculiar is Daniel's confession at the end of the vision in 12:8 that he still lacks sufficient insight: "I heard but could not understand (*abin*)," he says, to which the angel responds enigmatically, "Go your way, Daniel, for the words are to remain secret and sealed until the time of the end. . . . None of the wicked shall understand (*yabinu*), but those who are wise shall understand (*yabinu*)."

What is intriguing about these three pericopes is that they represent the marriage of angelic revelation and human wisdom, implying that an angel's wisdom and insight are so imposing that even the most sagacious human struggles fully to comprehend their cryptic form of communication. The visions are typical of the genre in that they are highly symbolic, stylized, and almost riddle-like in their construction, but they are dissimilar to visions involving angels from later apocalyptic authors such as 1 and 2 Enoch in that Daniel is neither escorted into heaven itself nor told intricate details of the angelic hierarchy. Instead, a member of the angelic council entrusts him with mysterious details concerning God's ordained plan for the world and the Jewish people, some of which he understands.

## Guardians of Israel

Gabriel's magnificent wisdom and understanding are amplified in 10:5–6 by his imposing physical appearance, which Daniel expresses in radiant terms,

> I looked up and saw a man clothed in linen, with a belt of gold from Uphaz around his waist. His body was like beryl, his face like lightning, his eyes like flaming torches, his arms and legs like the gleam of burnished bronze, and the sound of his words like the roar of a multitude.

Daniel may have in mind the linen-clothed scribe of Ezek 9:2, or since priests wore sacred linen garments (Lev 16:32), he may be making a sacerdotal allusion as if the angel was a heavenly priest. Though the text does not specifically name this figure, the fact that he compares himself to Michael in v. 21, and that he addresses Daniel as "greatly beloved" in vv. 11 and 19, the same words Gabriel uses in 9:23, leads me to believe that it is Gabriel. In addition, given that Gabriel is a heavenly, non-corporeal being, it is slightly odd that we are given details as to the earthly origin of his gold belt, though it may simply be a metaphor for purity.[141] Nevertheless, the mere presence of the phenomenon triggers extreme reactions—each vision produces a greater degree of anxiety than the previous one. Daniel, himself a man of celebrated dimensions, is so terrified by the specter and the sound of the angel's voice that he loses consciousness just as Isaiah did in the temple. The fear eventually gives way to a comforting word as the "strong man of God" rouses Daniel: "Do not fear, Daniel, for from the first day that you set your mind to gain understanding and to humble yourself before your God, your words have been heard, and I have come because of your words."[142]

While there are extraordinary similarities, both in description and demeanor, between Gabriel and the man "whose appearance was like bronze" in Ezek 40:3, both interactions are distinct in tone not only from the worship of inanimate representations of Canaanite idols, but from the earliest human experiences with angelic beings, such as in Adam and Eve's expulsion from Eden, Abraham's awkward encounter with the three visitors, and Jacob's fierce wrestling match with the man/god/angel who stubbornly refused to disclose his name. Angels in the book of Daniel are depicted as more than disinterested members of the divine council or anonymous, heavenly couriers and enforcers of Yhwh's law upon disobedient humans; they are guardians of heavenly mysteries and Israel's well-being, a point that the angel later discloses to the prophet. The angels of Yhwh are locked in a cosmic battle with what sounds like deposed members of the pantheon, mysterious forces such as "the prince of the kingdom of Persia" and the "prince of Greece."[143] This celestial skirmish integrates the book, as Reinhard Kratz notes,

> The notion of the fight of the national angel in chapters 10 and
> 12 transfers the historical drama of chapter 11 to heaven and

---

141. The only other appearance of Uphaz gold in the Old Testament is in Jer 8:9, which the pagan nations use to make idols.

142. Dan 10:12. Cf. 4 Esd 5:14–15, "Then I woke up, and my body shuddered violently, and my soul was so troubled that it fainted. But the angel who had come and talked with me held me and strengthened me and set me on my feet."

143. Dan 10:20. Whether this battle is legal or physical is not clear. Cf. warfare imagery in 2 Mac 5:1–4.

> thereby agrees with additions in chapters 7 and 8 . . . which, being dependent upon chapter 11, blend mundane and celestial elements. Not only Antiochus IV but also the combined world powers wage war on two levels: in heaven and on earth, against God and against the people of God.[144]

Daniel expands the role of angels by introducing such elements as conflict between good and evil spiritual beings, a heavenly courtroom, lengthy angelic dialogues, and hierarchical titles (Michael is described as "the chief" [*ha sarim*] prince in 10:13 and 12:1).

One can only speculate what sort of positive, psychological effects this emphasis upon spiritual guardians might have had upon his early hearers. Though Daniel portrays them as real beings, the larger, figurative interpretation of their presence in the book is that the angels came to assist Israel in their captivity for two reasons: in order to reframe their predicament in terms of a celestial battle, and to reveal themselves as national guardians. The author appears to be resurrecting and modifying the ancient idea of territorial gods from Deut 32:8–9: "When the Most High apportioned the nations, when he divided humankind, he fixed the boundaries of the peoples according to the number of the gods; the Lord's own portion was his people, Jacob his allotted share."[145] The gods of the pantheon have not only been dethroned and replaced by the angels, but in a figurative sense, they have come to earth to protect those whom Yhwh has chosen.[146]

---

144. Kratz, "The Visions of Daniel," 107.

145. This is a controversial text, because while the NRS follows a reading of 4QDeutj Dead Sea scroll, the MT has "*bene yisra'el*" and the LXX reads "*angelon theou*," perhaps as an eschewal of the pantheon. I believe the NRS is correct in following 4QDeutj which seems to maintain the older idea of supernatural guardians. In Judg 11:24, Jephthah asks, "Should you not possess what your god Chemosh gives you to possess? And should we not be the ones to possess everything that the Lord our God has conquered for our benefit?" See Wevers, *Notes on the Greek Text of Deuteronomy*, 513.

146. The angelic motif in Daniel can be understood as an orthodox correction of 2:11, where the court magicians protest that they cannot interpret the king's dream, stating "no one can reveal it to the king except the gods, whose dwelling is not with mortals." Also interesting is that after Daniel interprets the dream, the king exclaims "Certainly your God is a *God of gods* and Lord of kings and revealer of mysteries, for you were able to reveal this mystery!" (v. 47). As a result of the interpretation, Nebuchadnezzar exalts Daniel to a similar position in the Babylonian court as Michael, the "chief prince" has in the celestial court.

Aside from acting as an obvious caution to polytheistic people who may have had hopes of currying protective favor with neighboring gods, adding this cosmic variable to the Israelite's dilemma allowed angels to symbolize the faithfulness of YHWH toward his chosen people regardless of their geographical location or the complexity of their circumstances (a point made obvious by the angelic rescues associated with the furnace/lion's den pericopes). Undoubtedly, this imagery also had an immense influence upon intertestamental literature as well as the authors of Ephesians and Revelation as they wrote about angels who were still warring against supernatural adversaries.[147] This leads me to conclude that, regardless of their form or underlying identity, angels came to be understood after the exile as allies who manifest themselves in order to reinforce the always-present *dunamis* and transcendence of God.

Regardless of whether angels actually exist as we imagine them, the tradition of Daniel's celestial guardians still elicits the phenomenal idea that one is never far from heaven. Michael and Gabriel symbolize the presence of benign, supernatural intervention when the human mind becomes overwhelmed by situations beyond its ability to cope. Nonetheless, just as Gabriel differentiates between the symbolism and the reality behind Daniel's visions in Dan 10–12, the authors were careful not to give the impression that their encounters with angels were entirely symbolic. Instead, they seem to suggest that the angelophanies that involved visual appearances, audible speech, and even physical contact were no less authentic than those involving dreams or visions. Thus, while elements within the dream or vision were designed to be interpreted metaphorically, the angel-figure was not.

## Summary

In an effort to demonstrate the existence of a coordinated movement toward monotheism during this period, I have argued that the writers used

147. Pss 34:7 and 91:11 are further examples of an emerging belief in angelic guardianship, undoubtedly bolstered by Israel's experience of the protection of God's angel in the desert. The concept of regional angels and territorial battles does not come to full fruition until the books of Daniel and Revelation appear. However, the sabre rattling of nefarious angels can be heard as early as Gen 6:1–4 and Ps 82. Also, it is crucial to maintain that good angels act as instruments of God's wrath in passages such as 2 Sam 24:16; 2 Kgs 19:35; and Ps 78:49, having a similar effect upon humans as one would expect to receive from the evil angels.

angelology as a polemic against the syncretism of folk Judaism by restyling the pantheon as an angelic court. I have also noted the similarities between several temple visions with respect to angelic imagery in order to suggest corroboration existed, however informally, at the elite level. As pious spokespersons for the national religion, the writers felt a duty to communicate divine truths in order to ennoble Hebrew distinctives, while simultaneously undermining the pantheon that threatened them. While their writings are thick with examples of Yʜwʜ's superiority to other deities and idols, the angelology of visionaries like Isaiah, Ezekiel, and Daniel also functioned to emphasize monotheism, authenticate the writer's authority, establish angels in relation to temple worship, and provide a source of comfort to the faithful.[148] In addition, I shed light upon cultural factors contributing to the use of certain images and settings in these epiphanic accounts. While there is no reason to doubt the authenticity of such visions, it is essential to remember that mystical experiences were conditioned by cultural factors, more specifically, by earlier motifs in Hebrew legend and religious imagery common to the ancient Near East.

## CONCLUSION

This chapter explores the overarching progression of the angelic motif as a way of speaking about God. Initially, I gave attention to the depiction of cherubim and the *mal'ak Yʜwʜ* in Genesis as examples of the theological evolution of angels in J, E, and P. I argued that while Genesis contains traces of pagan mythology as well as an original pre-exilic concept of hypostasis, it ultimately points to the gradual development of divine transcendence within early Israelite theology. Next, I demonstrated that the prophets also used angelic imagery from the surrounding culture in order to build upon P's platform of divine transcendence; however, their concern for monotheism moved angelology in a new direction. I stated that the angelic motif takes different forms throughout the Hebrew Scriptures because each writer and redactor had specific beliefs about God that colored their angelology. While the angel became a pliable figure and interlocutor who accompanied God during his varied modes of

148. Among the most prominent examples are passages from Isa 2:8, 18–20; 19:1–3; 40:18–20; 41:6–7; 44:9–20; 46:1–13; 48:3–8; Jer 8:19; 10; Ezek 6:4–13; 14:1–7; 20:7–39; Dan 2:11–47; 3:12–30; 5:4–28.

self-disclosure, neither writer nor reactor allowed them to intrude upon God's uniqueness.

Angels are part of a literary motif that allowed authors and redactors to provide etiologies for God's presence in light of his transcendence. They are also explanations for the pantheon's extinction, defenses for monotheism, and the assurance of God's never-ending protection of his chosen people. Although biblical authors developed a unique angelology by adapting themes from surrounding cultures in order to elevate Yʜᴡʜ, they were still writing as outsiders to these cultures, and wrestling with imagery that they may not have fully understood in the same way as the other nations did. This leads me to be cautious about suggesting non-provisional relationships between Hebrew angelology and its antecedents, since synthetic connections between two cultures risks jeopardizing the originality of both. Instead, it is wiser to accept the evidence that a mysterious, but effective, process of theological evolution was at work within this doctrine, despite the fact that it may not always yield neat, transitional forms.

# Chapter II

# Pseudo-Denys's Angelology as an Emblem of Divine Immanence

## INTRODUCTION

Five works are credited to pseudo-Denys: *The Celestial Hierarchy*, *The Ecclesiastical Hierarchy*, *The Divine Names*, *The Mystical Theology*, and his *Epistles*. Taken together, they outline a dynamic theology that emphasizes the descent of divine illumination through a maze of angels, clergy, liturgy, sacraments, and apophatic theology, as well as humanity's divinized ascent to God through the same. Pseudo-Dionysius's *Celestial Hierarchy* is perhaps the most developed, if not imaginative, angelology apart from Thomas Aquinas's treatment in the *Summa Theologiae* and biblical commentaries.[1] Embraced by the church for millennia, Denys's influence waned after the Reformers questioned the authenticity of his Christian faith and depicted his angelology as fanciful.[2] Questions surrounding

1. Aquinas quotes pseudo-Denys approximately 1,700 times in the *ST*. See Jaroslav Pelikan's section in Pseudo-Dionysius, *Pseudo-Dionysius*, 21.

2. For the Reformation's general response to earlier angelologies, see Grenz, *Theology for the Community of God*, 215–16; Rorem, *Pseudo-Dionysius*, 77. More broadly, see Phillips, *The Reformation of Images*. Also, an entry in Firth and Rait, eds., *Acts and Ordinances of the Interregnum, 1642–1660*, 425–26; entitled "An Ordinance for the Further Demolishing of Monuments of Idolatry and Superstition" from 1644 includes the opening lines: "The Lords and Commons assembled in Parliament, the better to accomplish the blessed Reformation so happily begun, and to remove all offences and

pseudo-Denys's identity were also an issue for them, as was the fact that his theology, which stressed the correlation of angelic and ecclesiastical hierarchies, appeared to validate Rome's ecclesiology.[3] This chapter concludes that by attacking Denys and his celestial hierarchy, Protestantism's earliest theologians censured an elegant theory that accentuates both the glory of God and Christ's mediatorial presence in the sacrament.

Apart from early citations, little is known about Denys's identity and background. No references exist prior to a work by Severus of Antioch dating from 519, entitled *Adversus apologiam Juliani*, wherein Severus cites the fourth in a series of ten letters pseudo-Denys penned to various monks, deacons, priests, and bishops.[4] Later, he is referred to in an unflattering light during a conference in Constantinople in 533, where Orthodox and Monophysites locked horns.[5] His *nom de plume*, Dionysius the Areopagite, misled readers for centuries to believe his works were that of St. Paul's convert mentioned in Acts 17:34. However, he was in all probability an early-sixth-century Syrian monk with a gift for applying Neoplatonic thought to Christianity.[6] Although it is not uncommon for ancient writers to assume the identity of prominent individuals (a practice known as *declamatio*), pseudo-Denys's writings achieved almost apostolic authority as a result of his supposed relationship to Paul.[7]

---

things illegal in the worship of God, do Ordain, That all Representations of any of the Persons of the Trinity, or of any Angel or Saint, in or about any Cathedral, Collegiate or Parish Church, or Chappel, or in any open place within this Kingdome, shall be taken away, defaced, and utterly demolished; And that no such shall hereafter be set up."

3. Consequently, Protestant theologies of worship have never valued the role of celestial or ecclesiastical hierarchies to the extent found in Jewish, Catholic, and Orthodox spirituality. See *Forms of Prayer for Jewish Worship.*, 2:341; Stern, *Paths of Faith*, 9; Kadushin, *Worship and Ethics*, 145–51; David Bordwell, ed., *Catechism of the Catholic Church*, 203–8, 312; Cabasilas and McNulty, *A Commentary on the Divine Liturgy*, 12, 16, 52; Fortescue, *The Orthodox Eastern Church*, 338–60.

4. See Hathaway, *Hierarchy and the Definition of Order in the Letters of Pseudo-Dionysius*, 4. Also see Rorem, *Pseudo-Dionysius*, 3–38.

5. The second Council of Constantinople was held in order to demonstrate to the Monophysites that the Council of Chalcedon had not fallen into Nestorianism. It anathematized Theodore of Mopsuestia and his works, the writings of Theodoret, Bishop of Cyrrhus, and a letter from Ibas, Bishop of Edessa. Pseudo-Denys's writings were rejected as forgeries by the bishop of Ephesus, but not anathematized.

6. Neoplatonism also influenced Christian theologians prior to Denys, such as: Clement (160–220), Basil (330–79), Gregory Nazianzus (329–89), Gregory of Nyssa (ca. 331–95), Synesius of Cyrene (ca. 373–414), Ambrose (354–450), Augustine (354–430), and Boethius (ca. 460–524).

7. See Berry and Heath, "Handbook of Classical Rhetoric in the Hellenistic

Known for their refulgent language, his writings circulated among religious and civil authorities like Pope Paul I (d. 767) and Pepin, King of the Franks (714–768).[8] Furthermore, Hildin's *History of Saint Dionysius*, written in Latin during the mid-ninth century, coupled with subsequent commentaries by Maximus the Confessor, Hugh of Saint-Victor, Albert the Great, and Thomas Aquinas established Denys as an authority in systematic, philosophical, and symbolic theology in the Western church for centuries to come.[9] As early as the sixth century, Hypatius of Ephesus began questioning the validity of Denys's relationship to Paul, but the popularity of Denys's purportedly apostolic-era works continued into the Early Middle Ages despite their uncanny and anachronistic familiarity with the thought of the fifth-century Neoplatonist, Proclus.

Denys's identity was not strenuously debated until Erasmus aired statements made by Lorenzo Valla in 1457, where Valla, who specialized in exposing historical hoaxes, observed that neither Latin nor Greek fathers had quoted Denys prior to Gregory the Great.[10] Valla's doubts, combined with the speculative tone of the *Celestial Hierarchy*, took a considerable toll upon Denys's reputation during the Reformation era. Calvin and Luther perceived his ideology as unorthodox and threatening to their burgeoning movement, which emphasized the sufficiency of Scripture and the believer's relationship to Christ as the sole mediator between God and humanity. Despite Valla's initial protests over four hundred years earlier it was only after Hugo Koch and Joseph Stiglmayr published definitive proof in 1895 that this pseudonymous individual had indeed poached phrases from Proclus that the pejorative term *pseudo-Dionysius* entered popular use. Fortunately, as demonstrated by the resurgence of scholarly interest in pseudo-Denys during the twentieth and twenty-first centuries, pseudonymity need not invalidate one's contribution to theology.

His writing is notoriously abstruse at times, a fact not unnoticed even by his adroit devotee, Thomas Aquinas:

---

Period," 393–420, esp. 406ff.

8. Ibid., 16.

9. Dionysius' works were standard canonical reading for medieval clerics-in-training. See Gilson, *Elements of Christian Philosophy*, 159–63. Rorem, *Pseudo-Dionysius*, 16. The Western church gained access to Denys's work after Erigena translated them into Latin at the request of Charles the Bald.

10. Rorem, *Pseudo-Dionysius*, 15.

> One must consider that the Blessed Dionysius used an obscure style in all his books. He did this not from inexperience but rather from diligence so that the sacred and divine teachings might be hidden from the ridicule of the unbelievers. . . . [Of the many difficulties] first, he frequently used a style and manner of speaking which the Platonists used, which is unfamiliar to modern readers. . . . The second difficulty in his comments is that he frequently uses effective arguments to make his point but then often refers [back] to them with a few words or even just one word. The third difficulty is that he often multiplies words, which may seem superfluous, but nevertheless will be found to contain a great depth of meaning by those who consider them diligently.[11]

Comprised of fifteen chapters, the *Celestial Hierarchy* hints at a Neoplatonic understanding concerning God's procession into creation and the creation's return to God, albeit with heavier Christian overtones than conceded by the Reformers.

Like early biblical authors, Denys appreciates the role of angelology as a theological device to commend the being and activity of God. The previous chapter suggested that Old Testament writers juxtaposed angels with Yhwh as a way of augmenting God's transcendence over against the Canaanite and Babylonian pantheons; so it may seem that pseudo-Denys's hierarchical angelology, which also highlights God's ineffability, merely reasserts divine transcendence in a different way. However, Old Testament angelology leans heavily upon anecdotes, dreams, and visions to promote God's otherness, whereas Denys's model not only eschews episodic, angelophanic approaches, but establishes the angels' relationship to the church and sacraments.

Thus, since the angelic hierarchy moves in relation to the ecclesiastical hierarchy, every time the celebrant "offers Jesus Christ to our view" in the Eucharist, it is both an assertion of divine immanence and an invitation to join the angels in their contemplation of the God who is beyond being.[12] "The heavenly beings, because of their intelligence, have their own permitted conceptions of God," writes Denys, but it is the "perceptible images" of the Eucharist that raises believers "to the contemplation of what is divine."[13] Before unfolding my case for the significance and

---

11. Aquinas, *In Librum Beati Dionysii De Divinis Nominibus Expositio*, 1–2.

12. *EH* 444C.

13. *EH* 373B.

recovery of pseudo-Denys's angelology within the church, however, one must first hear the Reformers' objections.

## DENYS'S DETRACTORS

### Martin Luther

Venerated as sacred at the Lateran Synod of 649, the *Areopagitical Corpus* was considered by many as a lifeboat that made the vast ocean between heaven and earth more navigable, but an undercurrent of unfavorable reactions during the sixteenth century prevented it from berthing within Protestant harbors.[14] Luther first interacted with pseudo-Denys's works while training to become a monk, but eventually disavowed this component of his education.[15] His discomfort began in 1516 after reading of Valla's suspicions in a footnote in Erasmus's Greek New Testament.[16] Three years later, while in Leipzig, Luther dismissed John Eck's arguments for papal supremacy, which Eck had partially drawn from his reading of the *Celestial Hierarchy* and *Ecclesiastical Hierarchy*. Luther did not formally denounce pseudo-Denys until slightly later, but during his twenty-three-day disputation at Leipzig, he argued that the Dionysian hierarchies supplied no justification for the Catholic Church's ecclesiastical hierarchy and sacramentology.[17]

Luther continued to find fault with Denys after the Leipzig debates, more for his theology than his pseudonymity. As stated in the introduction, the identity question had largely been solved by Valla in 1457, and after Erasmus lost interest in the Dionysian corpus, there was little reason why works like the *Celestial Hierarchy* would appeal to the Reformers. So they began to characterize Denys as a philosopher whose teachings were incompatible with Christian orthodoxy, partially because they felt Denys

14. The synod erroneously considered Denys's writings as authoritative, and quoted them against the Monothelites. Cross, *The Oxford Dictionary of the Christian Church*, 488.

15. See Oberman, *The Dawn of the Reformation*, 133 nn. 23, 24.

16. Malysz, "Luther and Dionysius: Beyond Mere Negations," 150.

17. Although Eck's best efforts failed to persuade Luther, the claim by Marius that Eck's "use of Dionysius was probably disingenuous" is problematic given that Eck had not only published a new edition of Denys's *Mystical Theology* with a commentary just prior to the debate in Leipzig, but continued to defend Denys as Paul's disciple until later in life, and edited a rejoinder in 1526 entitled "Epistle in Defence of Dionysius," written in response to Valla and Erasmus. Marius, *Martin Luther*, 173.

was an impostor, but mostly because they thought he misrepresented Christ and had pushed angelology beyond justifiable limits.[18]

Luther's denouncements were based upon first-hand knowledge of Denys's works, and he was as characteristically critical of Denys as he was of Erasmus and the Pope.[19] For example, after first denouncing Bonaventure and the scholastics during an informal discussion with his students, Luther aired his grievances toward the supposed Areopagite, cautioning his listeners:

> The right, practical divinity is this: Believe in Christ, and do thy duty in that state of life to which God has called thee. In like manner, the mystical divinity of Dionysius is a mere fable and lie. With Plato he chatters: *Omnia sunt non ens, et omnia sunt ens*—(all things are not one, and all things are one)—and so leaves things hanging.[20]

Denys is known for his emphasis upon unity and oneness, but Luther sees him as a conflicted figure, torn between the mutually-exclusive teachings of Christ and Plato.[21]

It is clear that Luther considered Denys's entire catalog to be puerile and unfaithful to Scripture.[22] Elsewhere, he warns that Denys's ideas are so virulent that contact with his writings will cause readers to lose their understanding of Christ:

> But in his [pseudo-Denys's] *Theology*, which is rightly called *Mystical*, of which certain very ignorant theologians make so much, he is downright dangerous, for he is more of a Platonist than a Christian. So if I had my way, no believing soul would give the least attention to these books. So far, indeed, from learning Christ in them, you will lose even what you already know of him. I speak from experience. Let us rather hear Paul,

18. Melanchthon called him a "new and fictitious author" in his 1537 work, "Treatise on the Power and the Primacy of the Pope."

19. Luther was known to call papal decretals "decraptals" (*Dreketalen*), he renamed the Farnese pope "Fart-ass" (*fartz Esel*), and commissioned woodcuts by Cranach where peasants were depicted as defecating in the papal crown, and one in which the papal church was being expelled from the anus of an enormous she-devil. A handful of unbecoming nicknames are mentioned in Edwards, "Luther's Polemical Controversies," 202–3.

20. Luther, "Of God's Word," 4.

21. *CH* 121B, 145C, 212A; *EH* 536A; *DN* 593B, 636B–644A.

22. Luther, *Works*, 1:235. Also, Rorem, "Martin Luther's Christocentric Critique of Pseudo-Dionysian Spirituality."

that we may learn Jesus Christ and him crucified (1 Cor 2:2). He is the way, the life, and the truth; he is the ladder (Gen 28:12) by which we come to the Father, as he says: "No one comes to the Father, but by me" (John 14:6).[23]

For Luther, the historical trumped the speculative and philosophical leanings yielded to explicit teaching about the redemption brought about by Christ. Thus, he considered Denys "most pernicious [because] he Platonises more than the Christianises."[24] Whether evidence of Platonic influence is a sufficient basis by which to determine Denys's orthodoxy is questionable, but as far as Luther was concerned, there was more *theologia gloriae* than *theologia crucis* in Denys. Both men had a deep appreciation for the hiddeness of God, but Luther used his cross-shaped theology as a sieve to separate out persons like Denys who did not share his broader theological objectives.[25]

## John Calvin

Calvin, too, expressed a palpable aversion to anything Dionysian, and was more pointed than Luther concerning Denys's angelology. His earliest criticism of Denys's *Celestial Hierarchy* is found in the *Institutes*, where he attempts to discount the work by contrasting it with Paul's mystical ascent into the third heaven, described in 2 Cor 12:4:

> None can deny that Dionysus (whoever he may have been) has many shrewd and subtle disquisitions in his *Celestial Hierarchy*, but on looking at them more closely, everyone must see that they are merely idle talk. . . . When you read the work of Dionysus, you would think that the man had come down from heaven, and was relating, not what he had learned, but what he had actually seen. Paul, however, though he was carried to the third heaven, so far from delivering anything of the kind, positively declares,

---

23. Luther, *Works*, 36:109.

24. Luther, *Works*, "Babylonian Captivity," 6.562.

25. A compelling treatment of this facet of Luther's theology is found in Forde, *On Being a Theologian of the Cross*. Forde summarizes Luther's theology: "God refuses to be seen in any other way, both for our protection and to put down the theologian of glory in us. . . . The cross therefore is actually intended to destroy the sight of the theologian of glory. In the cross God actively hides himself. God simply refuses to be known in any other ways" (79).

that it was not lawful for man to speak the secrets which he had seen.[26]

It is to Calvin's credit that he familiarized himself with the *Celestial Hierarchy*, and knowing what we know of his ministry, one can surmise that his spirited reaction to it was based upon pastoral concern. Like Luther, Calvin seems to fear that Denys was not only an unreliable theologian, but a threat to the Reformation itself, which may explain why he frequently defaults to *ad hominem* attacks when speaking of Denys.

For instance, in his commentary on 2 Cor 12:4, Calvin again seizes the opportunity to use Paul's ascent to reiterate his critique of Denys:

> From this, too, we may gather a most useful admonition as to setting bounds to knowledge. We are naturally prone to curiosity. Hence, neglecting altogether, or tasting but slightly, and carelessly, doctrine that tends to edification, we are hurried on to frivolous questions. Then there follow upon this—boldness and rashness, so that we do not hesitate to decide on matters unknown, and concealed. From these two sources has sprung up a great part of scholastic theology, and everything, which that trifler Dionysius has been so daring as to contrive in reference to the Heavenly Hierarchies. It becomes us so much the more to keep within bounds, so as not to seek to know anything but what the Lord has seen it good to reveal to his church. Let this be the limit of our knowledge.[27]

Though Calvin's theology maintains boundaries and parameters every bit as distinct and tidy as "that trifler" pseudo-Denys's angelic and ecclesiastical orders, the exploratory tone of the *Celestial Hierarchy* compels him to judge it as "frivolous." How the act of speculation leads one down the slippery slope of "boldness and rashness," however, Calvin does not say. Yet one ought to press him on this issue, because holy conjecture is at least assumed of Christians to some degree if God is able to do "abundantly far more than all we can ask or imagine."[28] Biblical imagery, poetry, the use of parallelism, parables, and the apocalyptic genre, are all predicated upon the deeper assumption that listeners and readers of the Bible have the capacity to inspect what is at first blush, concealed.

---

26. Calvin, *Institutes of the Christian Religion* 1:14:4, 92.

27. Calvin, *Commentary on the Epistles of Paul the Apostle to the Corinthians*, 2:370.

28. Eph 3:20b.

Calvin urges us to set "bounds to knowledge," to "keep within bounds," and to let God's revelation (Scripture) "be the limit of our knowledge," but an integrated creation cannot be explained by theology alone. In fact, human knowledge *advances* only via the study of unknowns, and many things now taken for granted: movable type, human flight, the combustion engine, genetic research, even the age of the earth or the non-Mosaic authorship of the Pentateuch, were at one time, purely speculative.

Furthermore, is it any less speculative to insist with Calvin that God is present to us in a supernaturally-inspired Text than to say with Denys that God uses orders of angelic and human intermediaries? At least Denys's point in the *Celestial Hierarchy* that the ineffable Godhead becomes present to us via a telescoping network of emissaries provides an *ontological* answer to the connection between the world and the ascended Christ. Nevertheless, even if Calvin's caution about Denys's angelology is warranted, his proof-text is not. What Paul was "not permitted to utter" in 2 Cor 12:4 has nothing to do with the theological use of imagination, but the peculiars of a private, ecstatic experience—a meta-textual, epiphanic event—corroborated by visual and auditory revelation.

The *ad hominem* emerges again in Calvin's discussion of Ezekiel 13:20–23, a passage that declares Yʜᴡʜ's warnings to those who lead Israel to believe false visions. It is noteworthy that Calvin assumes his readership was conversant with pseudo-Dionysius's writings and theories.

> For we know that false prophets boasted in this artifice, when they either raise, or pretend they raise, men's minds aloft, and curious men desire this only; and hence it happens that the doctrines of the Law and the Gospel are insipid to them, because subtleties alone delight them. And we see at this day how many embrace the follies of Dionysius about the celestial hierarchy, who treat all the prophets, and even Christ himself, as of no value.[29]

Whether Calvin's universals ("only," "alone," "all") are hyperbolic, is difficult to tell. Like Luther, he appears concerned with the eternal destiny of persons who accepted Denys's angelology, as if the *Celestial Hierarchy* was capable of transforming individuals into uncivilized pagans. Calvin was terribly cautious, even when interpreting biblical verses that assume

---

29. Calvin, *Commentaries on the First Twenty Chapters of the Book of the Prophet Ezekiel*, 2:37.

the existence of distinct orders of angels. Commenting on Daniel's inter-action with an angel, he writes,

> The philosophy of Dionysius ought not to be admitted here, who speculates too cunningly, or rather too profanely, when treating the order of angels. But I only state the existence of some differ-ence, because God assigns various duties to certain angels, and he dispenses to each a certain measure of grace and revelation, according to his pleasure. We know there is but one teacher of men and angels, the Son of God, who is his eternal wisdom and truth.[30]

Even while conceding that "some difference" and "various duties" exist among the angels, Calvin consistently treats Denys as a sacrilegious phi-losopher bent upon cunning speculation rather than as a fellow Christian.

One wishes Calvin's criticism of pseudo-Denys's angelology had been more constructive and explicit at points, given that Calvin reveals a greater familiarity than Luther with the broader *Areopagitical Corpus*. His commentaries reveal a man who had genuinely interacted with De-nys's works, albeit with a jaundiced eye. For instance, in his interpretation of Acts 17, where the authentic Dionysius the Areopagite appears, Calvin provides a terse review of the *Celestial Hierarchy*, *Ecclesiastical Hierar-chy*, and the *Divine Names*. His pejorative criticism does little to advance Christian charity and reveals that his distaste for Denys also extended to Denys's readership.

> For those who ascribe to Dionysius the books about *The Celestial* and *Ecclesiastical Hierarchies*, and *The Divine Names*, are indeed extremely, crassly stupid. For the *Celestial Hierarchy* is not only stuffed full with many silly and monkish trivialities, but also abounds with many absurd fabrications, and impious speculations. On the other hand, the books about *The Ecclesias-tical Hierarchy* reveal that they were composed many centuries afterwards, when as the purity of Christianity had now been adulterated by a mass of ceremonies. But although the book of *The Divine Names* contains certain things that must not be absolutely despised, yet it breathes subtlety rather than sound godliness.[31]

Denys's theology never stood a chance with Calvin, who maintained that the theologian ought to "confirm the conscience, by teaching what is

---

30. Calvin, *Commentary on the Book of the Prophet Daniel*, 2:382.

31. Calvin, *The Acts of the Apostles*, 7:127.

true, certain and useful."[32] One can only surmise that Calvin's consistent disapprobation of Denys's "trivialities," "absurd fabrications," and "impious speculations" was partially a reaction to practices in the Church of Rome that he considered superstitious. Perhaps he even considered Denys's writings about the choreography surrounding the Eucharist to be reminiscent of the "mass of ceremonies" in the church he was attempting to reform; though it is clear that for Denys, it is Jesus' divine work in the Eucharist, not the angels, that empowers the believer.[33]

Thus far, Calvin has poisoned the well of Denys's teachings by comparing him with pagan philosophers and the Roman Church; he continues to use this same tactic in the introduction to his commentary on Colossians by also allying Denys with the Judaizers who "contrived a way of access to God through means of angels, and put forth many speculations of that nature, such as are contained in the books of Dionysius on the *Celestial Hierarchy*, drawn from the school of the Platonists."[34]

Remarkably, Calvin took Denys's angelology seriously enough to denounce with regularity, even if his arguments were occasionally fallacious. Yet while Calvin stands opposed to the "school of the Platonists" throughout his polemic against Denys, it is interesting that he and other Reformers supported Augustine's soteriology despite the fact that he had also been greatly influenced by Neoplatonism.[35] One wishes they had extended the same liberality to Denys, because it is patently obvious from *Divine Names* 816C–817A that he eschews the Neoplatonic tradition of other beings intruding upon God's relationship to the world.

> I do not think of the Good as one thing, Being as another, Life and Wisdom as yet another, and I do not claim that there are numerous causes and different Godheads, all differently ranked,

32. Calvin, *Institutes*. 1.14., 93.

33. *EH* 372AB. For Denys, theurgy is not magic, but a "consummation of theology" that affirms the inherent possibility that God is active within the sensible world. *EH* 432B.

34 Calvin, *Commentaries on the Epistles of Paul the Apostle to the Philippians, Colossians, and Thessalonians*, 133.

35. However, in his *Commentary on John* (1:3), Calvin does criticize Augustine at one point as one "who is excessively addicted to the philosophy of Plato," though this passing comment fails to minimize Calvin's overwhelming esteem for Augustine as a theologian. Dennis Tamburello maintains that a mystical strain also runs throughout Calvin's work. He finds the clearest examples in Calvin's discussion of the believer's union with the ascended Christ, a subject that was also expounded by Bernard of Clairvaux in the medieval period. See Tamburello, *Union with Christ*.

superior and inferior, and all producing different effects. No. But I hold that there is one God for all these good processions and that he is the possessor of the divine names of which I speak and that the first name tells of the universal Providence of the one God, while the other names reveal general or specific ways in which he acts providentially.[36]

Contrary to what the Reformers intimate, the Dionysian journey, if we may call it that, is hardly about following a Christless, Neoplatonic philosophy where the solitary soul seeks its higher self; nor is it about contriving "a way of access to God through means of angels." Instead, Denys's vision concerns the progressively-mediated presence of a loving God, which is revealed through the Son, angels, sacraments, church offices, and liturgy.[37]

## Modern Detractors

Luther and Calvin were not Denys's only critics, however. Modern-era figures like Ferdinand Baur, suspicious of Denys's philosophical leanings, also publicized their disapproval. Baur compares Denys's view of the Godhead to an amalgamation of stylized monikers, and felt his attention to the achievement of unity threatened to overshadow the doctrine of the Trinity as defined by the Council of Nicea.[38] Baur's greatest complaint, however, was that Denys lacked a robust affirmation of the incarnation, and von Harnack concurred, declaring that the Areopagite's Christology was scarcely more than "a symbol of the universal cleansing and sanctifying activity" of the *Logos*.[39]

Barth also sides with the Reformers against the speculative tone and arrangement of Denys's angelology (smirking at his "annoying . . . omniscience").[40] However, much to his credit, Barth detected the christological element in the *Celestial Hierarchy* (unlike the Reformers, Baur and von Harnack), writing:

36. The categories listed here by Denys roughly correspond to the role of "being, life and mind" in Neoplatonism.

37. It is the beauty and love of God which calls the soul through all things, however. *DN* 701C.

38. See Baur, *Die Christliche Lehre von Der Dreieinigkeit Und Menschwerdung Gottes in Ihrer Geschichtlichen Entwicklung*, 2:207–51.

39. Harnack, *Lehrbuch Der Dogmengeschichte*, 2:170.

40. Barth, *CD* III.3. 388.

> There can be no question of any ranking of the realities indicat-
> ed by them [the angels] because the power which they represent,
> reveal and express is in each instance the power of the one God,
> and because Christ is the Head of them all, and they would not
> be powers apart from the power of this Head. . . . Their differ-
> ence is to be understood from the sequence and differentiation
> of the divine Word and act coming down from the heavenly
> sphere to the earthly.[41]

It is possible that any ambiguity in Denys's Christology is simply
related to his belief that God was beyond naming and being, which also
helps to explain his heavy emphasis on angels as necessary mediators of
divine presence. His reluctance to pursue in detail the theme of incarnation does, however, suggest that he may have leaned in the direction of
Monophysitism, which may account for statements such as, "out of love
for humanity Christ emerged from the hiddenness of his divinity to take
on human shape, to be utterly incarnate among us while yet remaining
unmixed."[42] His tendency to dissolve the humanity of Christ in the ocean
of his divinity may constitute more of an inclination than a dogmatic
ascription, however.

Hans Urs von Balthasar, on the other hand, adamantly defended
Denys as orthodox.[43] "The Monophysitism of the Areopagite," he writes,
"which is often treated as though it were an obvious fact, does not seem
to have been established."[44] He mounts an impressive defense in volume
two of his *Glory of the Lord* in an attempt to whittle back this "unten-
able hypotheses" resulting from "a certain spiritual color blindness" on
the part of most nineteenth-century German scholarship.[45] His central
objection is that Denys's critics are only successful in tearing apart a
straw man due to their unwillingness to see the "radiance of holiness that
streams from this unity of person and work."[46] After reading Calvin and
Luther's unflattering interpretations of him, one gets the sense that the
Reformers also suffered from this same Denys-blindness, though Barth
and Balthasar managed to see more clearly. The following section aims
to counterbalance the presuppositions of Denys's detractors concerning

41. Ibid., 459.

42. *EH*, 444C.

43. See the section on "Denys" in Balthasar, *Glory*, 144–49.

44. Balthasar, "Scholienwerk," 17. Quoted in Pelikan, *Works*, 21.

45. Balthasar, *Glory*, 146.

46. Ibid.

his orthodoxy by exploring the strengths of his Christian theology of hierarchy.

## DENYS'S PRESENTATION OF HIERARCHY

### Angels and Hierarchy

Denys coined the term "hierarchy," which he constructed from *hieros* (sacred) and *arche* (source), to describe the relationship between God and lesser instrumentalities ordained to mediate and participate in sacred realities. His theology is comprised of two principal hierarchies, the celestial and the ecclesiastical. The sacraments are also arranged into something of a hierarchy, but appear to be nestled in the interstice between angels and clergy. Denys's hierarchies complement one another so that God's self-revelation is a downward procession through the celestial hierarchy and the ecclesiastical hierarchy facilitates the worshippers' return to God. Angels are an important part of this system because they are closer than humans to the transcendent God, both in terms of position and nature. About the angels, Denys writes:

> Their thinking processes imitate the divine. They look on the divine likeness with a transcendent eye. . . . That is why they have a preeminent right to the title of angel or messenger, since it is they who first are granted the divine enlightenment and it is they who pass on to us these revelations which are so far beyond us.[47]

It is not merely that angels live closer to God or that they are more like God that makes them significant for Denys, but that they participate *with* the ecclesiastical hierarchy and the sacraments to facilitate a "sacred uplifting to the divine."[48]

Denys's angelology is built around the seven titles St. Paul used for higher-order beings in Eph 1:12 and Col 1:16, to which he adds archangels and angels. This construction of nine angelic orders is further divided into a triad of triads, each with capacities and tasks peculiar to their rank.

---

47. *CH* 180A-B.
48. *EH* 501D.

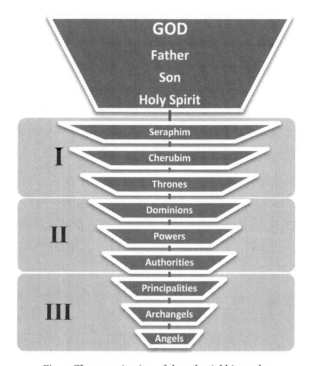

Fig. 2. The organization of the celestial hierarchy

Apart from St. Paul, pseudo-Denys was not the only Christian theologian to arrange the angels in hierarchical fashion; one finds similar delineations of nine angels in earlier works by Cyril of Jerusalem (ca. 315–86);[49] Gregory of Nazianzus (ca. 330–90);[50] Ambrose (ca. 338–97);[51] and Chrysostom (ca. 347–407);[52] though they ranked the orders differently from Denys.[53] Rorem speculates that rather than expressing Denys's Trinitarianism, the three angelic triads reflect the Neoplatonic fascination with the way a mean between two extremes creates a third category.[54]

49. Cyril, "Catechesis Lectures" 23.6.

50. Gregory of Nazianzus, *Discourse* 28.31.

51. Ambrose, *Apologia Prophet David,* 5.

52. Chrysostom, *De Incomprehensibili Dei Natura,* III.48.724.

53. Augustine was reluctant to speculate about the ranking of angels: "Let those who are able answer these questions, if they can prove their answers to be true," he mulls, "but as for me, I confess my ignorance." *Enchiridion,* ch. 58.

54. Rorem, *Pseudo-Dionysius,* 20, 160. A fascination with the mean is hinted

Whether or not this model bears a hidden message about the Trinity misses the point, however; Denys's angelology is primarily concerned with disclosing God's revelation to creation and facilitating creation's return to the Godhead. In fact, when coupled with the *Ecclesiastical Hierarchy*, it forms an egalitarian theory that presumes *all* beings, as they fulfill their role, have the capacity to apprehend and participate in the Godhead, albeit by different degrees.

While his detractors associated Denys and his angelology with Neoplatonism, I would argue that, given his Syrian *milieu*, it is equally likely that his angelology was influenced by works circulating throughout the region during his time. For instance, the *Transitus Mariae*—a Syriac document deemed apocryphal in the late fifth century by the Gelasian Decree—tells of the apostles being miraculously transported to Mary's side from the various cities where they had been preaching just moments before her assumption. Immediately following this miracle, the narrator continues:

> Our Lord Jesus Christ came with a band of the seraphim before
> Him holding trumpets and singing, and a row of angels bearing
> horns and blowing, and choirs of cherubs came holding lamps
> of glory, and crowds of guardian angels came.[55]

The hagiography features Christ and four orders of his angelic retinue whom the apostles behold while the Virgin is assumed into heaven. These clusters of significant figures—Christ, seraphim, cherubim, and angels emerging from heaven, Mary in-between heaven and earth, the apostles upon the earth—resembles Denys's paired hierarchies who participate in the outpouring and ascribing of glory across different strata.[56]

Next, *The Book of the Cave of Treasures*, written in Syriac before the fourth century, arranges eight angelic orders from least to greatest:

> God created the . . . hosts which are invisible (that is to say the
> Angels, Archangels, Thrones, Lords, Principalities, Powers,

---

at in Ovid's *Metamorphoses* II.138, where Phaeton is told to fly "keep the mid way, the middle way is best," but it is more formally rooted in Pythagorean mathematical theory and harmonics, and Aristotle's golden mean. Plato also argued for such a mean in human government: "The mode of election which has been described is in a mean between monarchy and democracy, and such a mean the state ought always to observe." *Laws* 757A.

55. Lewis, *Apocrypha Syriaca*, 14.

56. See *DN* 681D–684A, where Denys claims to have witnessed the Dormition of the Virgin with Hierotheus.

Cherubim and Seraphim) and all the companies and ranks of spiritual beings. . . . All these were created on the first day.[57]

While it is evident why this list of angels is noteworthy to Denys's angelology, it is surpassed by another celestial hierarchy described in the *Apostolic Constitutions*. The work is a pseudo-apostolic collection of writings, likely compiled/edited by a figure in western Syria during the late fourth century.[58] From a liturgical prayer in the eighth book, one finds the same beings listed as in the *Celestial Hierarchy*:

> You [God] do the innumerable hosts of angels, archangels, thrones, dominions, principalities, authorities, and powers, Your everlasting armies, adore. The cherubim and the six winged seraphim, with two covering their feet, with two their heads, and with two flying, say, together with thousand thousands of archangels, and ten thousand times ten thousand of angels, incessantly, and with constant and loud voices, and let all the people say it with them: Holy, holy, holy, Lord of hosts, heaven and earth are full of His glory: be blessed forever. Amen.[59]

This hierarchy of nine angels appears more official and developed than its peers and its use in liturgical settings provides a viable, Christian back-story to the development of Denys's angelology. If Denys drew inspiration from such legends, lists, and liturgies circulating around Syria during his day, his codification, which explores the angels' relationship to one another and the church, expanded upon an already rich tradition.[60]

## Angelic Movement in the Hierarchy

It should now be obvious that Denys's list of angels was not especially original, nor was his hierarchical arrangement, which differed only slightly from earlier models. What is significant, however, is the way he envisioned the angelic hierarchy as a dynamic, indefatigable, harmonious

57. Budge, *The Book of the Cave of Treasures*, 43–44.

58. The compilation is known to us only through extant Syriac versions, though the original third-century works were written in Greek. Bradshaw, *The Search for the Origins of Christian Worship*, 84–85.

59. Donaldson, "Apostolic Constitutions."

60. Also, the *Testament of Adam*, a fourth-century Syriac text, contains a hierarchy identical to the list in the *Celestial Hierarchy*, except that it transposes cherubim and seraphim.

unit and interpreted it in light of ecclesiology. There is no need to survey the entire hierarchy with Denys, but one ought to note that the function of each angelic triad, and each order within it, corresponded to a sacred triad of activity: purification, illumination, and perfection.[61] Altruistically, each order assists the order below it to conform to the divine image.

One way to picture his scheme is to imagine each triad of the hierarchy as part of an integrated, concentric structure (like a gyroscope), held in orbit about the Creator in a trajectory peculiar to their order of being, or as Denys puts it, their "capacity."[62] Thus, because the first triad enjoys the tightest course about the immeasurable spectacle of God's presence, the more its members are drawn toward and saturated with his goodness and light, which they reflect to those orders that comprise the outlying spheres, and so on, out to the church. This centripetal-*cum*-centrifugal movement is also found in Aquinas's theology; like pseudo-Denys, he felt that every object was meant to be understood as united to its source, the equidistance of eccentric movement symbolizing perfect motion because "its terminus is united to its beginning."[63]

Ladder imagery was another accepted model among mystical theologians, so pseudo-Denys's hierarchical angelology can also be understood as a series of symbolic rungs that represent steps closer to or farther from the Creator.[64] Since the angels do not leave their ranks, their "movement" upon this ladder, as they participate in the outreaching love of God, is primarily affective and intellectual. Given his penchant for triads, it is not surprising that Denys's own reflection upon the kinetic activity of angels also included three, metaphorical types of movement:

> The divine intelligences are said to move as follows. First they move in a circle while they are at one with those illuminations which, without beginning and without end, emerge from the Good and the Beautiful. Then they move in a straight line when, out of Providence, they come to offer unerring guidance to all those below them. Finally they move in a spiral, for even

61. Gregory of Nyssa held a similar view in his early writing; see *De Virginitate*, ch. 11.

62. *CH* 208D.

63. Aertsen, "Aquinas's Philosophy in Its Historical Setting," 31. Also, pseudo-Denys taught that God himself has a yearning to extend his love, which travels in a circle, "ever in the same direction, always preceding, always remaining, always being restored to itself." *DN* 712D–713A; cf. *DN* 596C; 701C.

64. Perhaps the most well-known example is *The Ladder of Divine Ascent* by John Climacus.

while they are providing for those beneath them they continue
to remain what they are and they turn unceasingly around the
Beautiful and the Good from which all identity comes.[65]

What may have appeared to Calvin and Luther to be gross speculation at this point can be easily interpreted, if given a chance: Denys's
vibrant arrangement of angelic movement renders the angels as omni-
directional beings because they are (albeit ontologically distinct), exten-
sions of God's plenitudinous love, to which they are eternally united.[66]

Each model of angelic activity raises difficulties for communication
between this world and the place where God abides, however. Spatially, it
appears the farther one travels from God as the subject and source of all
that cannot be articulated, the more dependent one is upon the limitations of words and *vice versa*. This is certainly assumed in the *Mystical
Theology*. While pseudo-Denys recognized that angels occasionally reveal things via human language in the Scriptures, he felt the seraphim
that move about the top rung are less equipped to communicate with
persons than are the archangels or angels who occupy the lower rungs.
Nevertheless, the orbit/ladder imagery illustrates the idea that words
become trivial the closer one soars to the unmediated presence of God,
before whom, every mouth is stilled. He writes:

> The more we take flight upward, the more our words are con-
> fined to the ideas we are capable of forming; so that now as we
> plunge into that darkness which is beyond intellect, we shall
> find ourselves not simply running short of words but actually
> speechless and unknowing.[67]

Figuratively speaking, to ascend this invisible ladder is to be swept
up into a hierarchical conversation where language proves unnecessary.
Denys uses the stratification of angels, whom he calls "heralds of the divine silence," to illustrate why it is necessary for angels to "move" into
our world: so that they might disclose what lies beyond the reaches of
terrestrial language.[68]

65. *DN* 704D–705A.

66. Perhaps the nearest approximation for this simultaneity of motion lies with
multi-dimensional algebraic manifolds, which are used in theoretical physics to unify
quantum mechanics and general relativity.

67. *MT* 1033B.

68. *DN* 696B. Denys argued that it would be highly irregular to see God apart
from angelic intervention since, according to Scripture, "no one has ever seen God."

Furthermore, the *Celestial Hierarchy's* precise chain of command is significant for modern Christian theology not because it classifies all beings and activities on a Cartesian coordinate system, but because it affixes a participative dimension to the action of God-becoming-immanent.[69] Though Noll misunderstands Denys's hierarchy as a vehicle of salvation rather than revelation and presence, his instincts are correct that angels and humans share a common objective that has its end in God:

> Dionysius teaches that to seek knowledge of the celestial hierarchy is not simply a matter of idle curiosity. The hierarchy itself is a kind of vehicle of salvation by which the believer is purified, illuminated, and perfected. Participation in a hierarchical cosmos, church, and society is to provide fulfilment for every saint, just as each angel from top to bottom rank, enjoys the vision of God.[70]

Hierarchical activity is inconsistent with domination. Whatever is above is obligated and designed by God to enlighten that which is below. Denys's hierarchies presuppose continuous layers of movement by which humans and angels lift and are lifted up to a greater experience of, and likeness to, the Divine.[71] Though bearing similarities to Neoplatonic structures, the emphasis here is rather different from the individuality associated with Plotinian contemplation or Iamblican theurgy, because all angelic and ecclesiastical movement is meant to be consecratory and arises out of the beneficence and initiative of God.

By clothing in angelic terminology those moments in life when one senses a sort of alternative reality or ordering, pseudo-Denys intimates that the essence of being human involves living in the presence of a subtle form of perpetual communication that is elegant, structured, transcendent, and ancient—a hierarchical, supernatural order of being

---

He writes, "Of course God has appeared to certain pious men in ways which were in keeping with his divinity. He has come in certain sacred visions fashioned to suit the beholders. . . . Yet it was the heavenly powers which initiated our venerable ancestors to these divine visions." *CH* 180C.

69. Though he disagrees with his conclusions, Barth refers to pseudo-Denys's *Celestial Hierarchy* as "epoch-making." Barth, *CD* III/1, 370.

70 Noll, "Thinking about Angels," 6.

71. He begins the treatise in *CH* 120B with a quote from Jas 1:17: "Every good endowment and every perfect gift is from above, coming down from the Father of lights." Denys completes the thought by adding that this light "spreads itself generously toward us" (procession), and "stirs us by lifting us up" (remaining) before it "returns us back to the oneness and deifying simplicity of the Father who gathers us in" (returning).

that, contra Luther and Calvin's interpretations, beckons one to rediscover the *beauty* of the superessential God, thus throwing earth's disarray back upon itself.

> The goal of a hierarchy, then, is to enable beings to be as like as possible to God and to be at one with him. A hierarchy has God as its leader of all understanding and action. It is forever looking at the comeliness of God. A hierarchy bears in itself the mark of God. Hierarchy causes its members to be images of God in all respects, to be clear and spotless mirrors reflecting the glow of primordial light and indeed of God himself.[72]

Angelic movement within Denys's hierarchy functions to accentuate and reflect God's splendorous presence wherever it may be found; it also acts as a model for the church to replicate.[73] Reminiscent of the way artists use durable materials to stabilize fragile creations—like the role of lead in a stained glass window—the Trinity assembled angels into a nonagonal, supermundane configuration in order to speak into and unite with itself the church of every age.[74] Thus, while Denys animates the celestial hierarchy as a form of divine communication, the question of how the celestial hierarchy relates to Christ's heavenly and eucharistic presence is the subject of the following two sections.

## Christ's Role in the Hierarchy

Denys shifted the paradigm from the Hebrew Scriptures' individualized and episodic angelology by portraying angels in relation to Christian worship, thus transposing angelology from its anecdotal roots into the realms of proposition and experience. He justified this transformation by aligning angels with Christ's message, ministry, and sacramental immanence. Amid forty-six references to "Jesus" and twenty-three to "Christ" in his writings, Denys pressed his thesis forward by emphasizing symbolic and liturgical connections between Jesus Christ, angels, and the church:

> Our most divine altar is Jesus, who is the divine consecration of the heavenly intelligences in whom we, being at once

72. *CH* 165A.

73. *DN* 593D; 596B-C.

74. According to *CH* 260B, an innumerable number of angels also fill the cosmos and oversee the welfare of every nation as an example of God's ongoing activity *within* the creation.

consecrated and in mystery wholly consumed, have according
to the [Scripture] saying "our access."[75]

I speak of the sacraments in greater detail in the following section,
which focuses upon angels in relation to the ecclesiastical hierarchy; for
now the point is to establish, against his detractors, that Christology was
not incidental to Denys's angelology but was *its central framework*. His
hierarchical theology, which begins "and ends in Jesus," sets angelology
within a purely providential and sanctifying sphere of activity.[76] "We must
work together and with the angels to do the things of God," he urges, "and
we must do so in accordance with the providence of Jesus."[77] Thus, the
majority of his assumptions about angelic and ecclesiastical activities rest
upon the conviction that both spheres are connected to and directed by
the Son of God.

The key to summarizing Denys's rather discursive angelology, ecclesiology, and sacramentology, therefore, is to subsume their respective
activities under the greater truth that Christ is "the source and perfection of every hierarchy."[78] This point, that hierarchies only have meaning
inasmuch as they are bound up in Christ, was overlooked by Denys's critics who not only read Denys selectively, but emphasized Scripture as *the*
means of Christ's self-revelation.[79] If taken too far, such a view restricts
mediation to a literary medium and limits the degree to which the rest of
the creation may define its identity and activity as a participation in, and
testimony about, Christ. Contrary to the Reformers' accusations, Denys's
angelic mediation was not meant to sidestep Scripture or to circumvent
Christ, but to make his glory known. This is why the *Celestial Hierarchy*
bears Denys's confession that he trusts only Christ—"my Christ"—to
guide his discourse, since Christ is the very "inspiration of what has been
made known about the [celestial] hierarchy."[80] After all, it is Denys's high
Christology, not its absence, that demands that angels become necessary,

75. *EH* 484D.

76. *EH* 505B.

77. *DN* 953A.

78. *EH* 373B.

79. Calvin says Scripture "conveys Christ to us," and Luther depicts the Bible as the
"swaddling clothes and the manger in which Christ lies." See Calvin, *Institutes*, I.9.3;
Luther, *Table Talk*, 6.16.

80. *CH* 145C.

albeit secondary, vehicles through which the Savior remains present to the church.[81]

His lofty Christology, however, did not dissuade Denys from aligning Christ, the timeless one who entered temporality, as something of an angelic being "because of his generous work for our salvation he himself entered the order of revealers and is called the 'angel of great counsel.' Indeed, when he announced what he knew of the Father, was it not as an angel?"[82]

Denys is no doubt playing with the semantic range of the word "angel" here to illustrate Christ's function as a sacrificial messenger of God on behalf of the church. He is not promoting a Docetic, angel Christology, but his image of Christ as a type of angel is striking given our convention of rendering Christ only in terms of deity and humanity. Denys also describes the ineffable, angel-like Son descending into the flesh during his earthly ministry, which again, helps defend his Christology from Docetism.

> Jesus himself, the transcendent Cause of those beings which live beyond the world, came to take on human form without in any way changing his own essential nature . . . and he obediently submitted to the wishes of God the Father as arranged by the angels. It was the angels who announced to Joseph the Father's arrangements regarding the withdrawal into Egypt and return to Judea.[83]

This articulation of Jesus' birth and ministry in terms of angelic ministration shows that while committed to the cosmic Christ as the head of all hierarchies, Denys was neither ignorant of Jesus' humanness nor the details surrounding his birth; like the angels, Christ himself had descended from the Father and entered into the terrestrial sphere.

81. Still, pseudo-Denys believed that the *lowest* ranks of angels function largely as celestial intermediaries between the hierarch and God, a view that, incidentally, distinguishes him from his most notable commentator Eriugena, who went so far as to argue that "humans become peers with the highest angels." Duclow, "Isaiah Meets the Seraph: Breaking Ranks in Dionysius and Eriugena?" 241.

82. *CH* 181D.

83. *CH* 181C. Denys was possibly referring to the ancient idea that the law was delivered to humanity by angels, but Scripture provides no explicit statement supporting this proposal with respect to Jesus, even allowing for angelic intervention in Jesus' temptation in the wilderness and Gethsemane. References to their role in the giving of the law can be found in the Greek version of Deut 33:2 and Ps 68:17. We also see evidence of this tradition reflected in Acts 7:53, Heb 2:2, and 3:19.

Elsewhere, after formulating a *précis* concerning how Gabriel foretold and announced the incarnation to Zechariah, Mary, and Joseph, Denys offers that "Jesus' love for humanity was first revealed to the angels and that the gift of this knowledge was granted by the angels to us."[84] This spilling-over of divine ardor, which Christ first disclosed to his celestial audience before making it known to humanity, highlights the oneness of purpose Denys perceived between Christ and his angels; more importantly, it affirms that the procession of divine love is shared by the entire chain of being, not just between Christ and humanity. In fact, angelophanies in Scripture were often meant to reinforce the presence of divine love, which the church first experienced, according to the Scriptures, in the form of angelic intervention.[85] Just as Christ descended from the Father to put on human flesh, so the angelic hierarchy descends in order to recapitulate his love and immanence in the absence of his physical presence.

Denys's view that the Father mediated his directives to Jesus or that Christ mediates his love to the church by way of angels is not unlike God's use of angelic mediation in the lives of Jesus, his family, and early followers. What but love explains the angels' role in the Annunciation, the holy family's flight to Egypt and back, Jesus' temptation, resurrection, ascension, and the protection and preservation of jailed apostles? Each of these events revealed the divine presence to humanity via the angels without relinquishing omnipresence or glory in the process. Although the veneration of angels in Syria around Denys's day was so robust that Philoxenus of Mabbugh (d. 523 CE) condemned it and destroyed its icons, Denys is careful to emphasize the love of God and Christ as the purpose of angelic mediation.[86] The angels' indispensability was predicated upon their being divinely ordained and illuminated by Christ, and they remained so subordinate to the Son that they could never outshine his glory.[87]

So rather than conceiving of Christ's mediation as a solitary effort, our author implies that the ascended, cosmic Christ is not only the *creator* and end of the angelic hierarchy, but was a *beneficiary* of angelic intercession while he was in the world and mediates his love to humanity

---

84. *CH* 181B.

85. Acts 5:18–19; 7:53; 8:26; 10:3–6, 22; 12:15; 27:23, 24.

86. Peña, *The Christian Art of Byzantine Syria*, 145, 149.

87. *CH* 165A.

through the same.[88] Christ's bodily ascension means one's access to his physical presence is restricted in a sense, thus because of his present transcendence, one way Christ enters back into the world is under the auspices of his angelic equipage. The *Celestial Hierarchy* offers a meaningful insight into a forgotten Christology that, even if only symbolically, unifies creation through a series of benign, angelic processions. "Every divine enlightenment," writes Denys, "proceeds, out of its goodness, toward those provided for, it not only remains simple in itself but also unifies those it enlightens."[89] Reflexively, through this angelic obedience and activity heaven and earth are again united: Christ is made immanent to his church and the church is drawn to her Savior. The next section explores further the idea of Christ's presence as it mediated beyond the angels into perceptible hierarchies of clergy and sacraments.

## The Role of Clergy and Sacraments in the Hierarchy

Denys's angelology is as horizontal as it is vertical. It establishes a connection to the transcendent Christ while providing a pattern for the ecclesiastical hierarchy, who translate this transcendence into the language of immanence. Like its angelic counterparts, the ecclesiastical hierarchy is entirely dependent upon Jesus, the supreme hierarch: "Jesus enlightens our blessed superiors," writes Denys, "Jesus who is transcendent mind, utterly divine mind, who is the source and the being underlying all hierarchy . . . who is the ultimate divine power."[90] While Denys emphasizes the transcendence of the ascended Christ here, it is the experiential and christological dimension within the sacrament that allows Denys to circumvent difficulties associated with accentuating divine immanence in a post-ascension world. The clergy function as a perpendicular extension of celestial grace, human envoys who mediate Christ's presence through the distributed medium of physical sacraments. Thus, the clergy and sacraments provide a fuller understanding of the conjunction Denys sustains between heaven and earth.[91]

88. Cf. fn. 83 above.

89. *CH* 120A.

90. *EH* 372AB.

91. The absence of Christ's physical body is significant; the earliest polemic against the resurrection and ascension was that the disciples had stolen it (Matt 27:64; 28:12–3), and the Spirit is given in anticipation and in response to Christ's physical absence (John 14:16–8, 26; 16:7–14; Acts 1:1–2, 8; 13:2).

In the *Ecclesiastical Hierarchy*, Denys describes an ideal church that is in its own way inhabited by corporeal angels, apprehensible sub-mediators of Jesus' irreplaceable mediation. He endeavors to cast hierarchs (bishops) in this angelomorphic mold, "Hence, I see nothing wrong in the fact that the Word of God calls even our hierarch an 'angel,'" because he is "raised up to imitate, so far as a man may, the angelic power to bring revelation."[92] Touched with an indelibly angelic character as God's terrestrial messengers, hierarchs were moved by the Spirit to contemplate heavenly things and to distribute means of grace in the form of sacraments. While the primary human mediator for their congregations, like the angels, they were not self-sufficient figures. In fact, that the four treatises (the *Celestial Hierarchy*, *Ecclesiastical Hierarchy*, *Divine Names*, and *Mystical Theology*) were all addressed to Timothy, a bishop, suggests that hierarchs required vocational training, and that Denys was providing them with a manual.[93] Nonetheless, bishops were a divinely-appointed conduit between two additional channels of divine mediation, one spiritual (angels), the other physical (sacraments), which Denys refers to as "the reverend symbols by which Christ is signalled and partaken."[94] These two live wires, once connected to the hierarch, complete the mediatorial circuit between heaven and earth.

Mystically speaking, the angels transmit their illumination to the ever-contemplative hierarch (bishop), so that it might be projected outward to the orders of the ecclesiastical hierarchy and reflected throughout the church.[95] Like a human seraph, the hierarch "sacredly hands down his unique knowledge of the hierarchy to the subordinates," and so becomes a revealer of mysteries to lower-ranking clergy, who in turn, uplift the church.[96] Resembling the Old Testament high priest, the bishop was considered by Denys as the human point of reference within the believing community, and as the lower clergy followed their bishop and immediate

92. *CH* 293A.

93. It is possible that the *Ecclesiastical Hierarchy* was written as a polemic, meant to chastise influential Monophysite monks who questioned the legitimacy of bishops during this time. See Arthur, *Pseudo-Dionysius as Polemicist*, 101–40.

94. *EH* 437C.

95. "The being and proportion and order of the Church's hierarchy are in him [the bishop] divinely perfected and deified, and are then imparted to those below him according to their merit, whereas the sacred deification occurs in him directly from God." *EH* 373A.

96. *EH* 429B. Denys, like Ignatius of Antioch and Cyprian of Carthage before him, saw the bishop's role as central to the unity of the church.

superiors they became a means of grace to their inferiors, so that through "this inspired, hierarchical harmony each one is able to have as great as possible a share in him who is truly beautiful, wise and good."[97]

Denys expressed the earthly, ecclesiastical hierarchy in terms of two triads, ranging from bishops to catechumens; it is my view that the sacraments ought to be considered as part of this model, not simply because they allow the ecclesiastical hierarchy to become a triad of triads (though this is not irrelevant), but because of their function within Denys's theology, which I shall explain shortly.

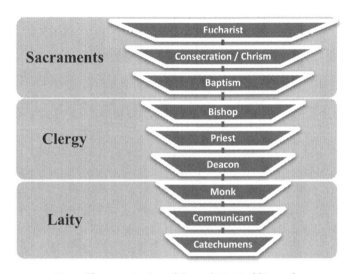

Fig. 3. The organization of the ecclesiastical hierarchy

In such an ecclesiastical schema, clergy are gradually uplifted through a process of *theosis* and remain subordinate to the transcendent presence of God within the sacraments they administer. They were charged with the responsibility of using and interpreting an array of veiled symbols for the purpose of guiding believers into angel-like unity with Christ, bearing a heavy, but distributed responsibility.[98] However, some subtle theological reasoning was also expected of the congregants. For instance, Denys wrote in *Ecclesiastical Hierarchy* 484B that by sym-

97. Ibid.

98. "This [celestial] arrangement is copied by our own [ecclesiastic] hierarchy which tries to imitate angelic beauty as far as possible, to be shaped by it, as in images, and to be uplifted to the transcendent source of all order and of all hierarchy." *CH* 241C.

bolic, liturgical actions such as pouring *myron*-ointment into the shape of a cross, the bishop "shows to those able to contemplate it that Jesus in a most glorious and divine descent willingly died on the cross for the sake of our divine birth, that he generously snatches from the old swallowing pit of ruinous death anyone who . . . has been baptized 'into his death' and renews them in an inspired and eternal existence."

Just as the hierarch is responsible for publicly disclosing christological symbols to the initiated in the context of worship, the initiated are intended to see beyond what might otherwise appear as mere choreography or perfunctory liturgy.

The sacraments, like the angels, are "perceptible symbols" that act to uplift, unify, and "divinize" the church.[99] It remains difficult to grasp how sacraments produce such effects unless one understands the Eucharist, which Denys calls the "sacrament of sacraments," as having an actual, rather than a metaphorical, relationship with Christ himself.[100] Thus, Meyendorff's opinion that Denys reduced the Eucharist "to a moral appeal" should not be admitted here.[101] In speaking about the Eucharist, Denys spoke in terms of genuine unification with the word made flesh:

> For because of his goodness and his love for humanity the
> simple, hidden oneness of Jesus, the most divine Word, has
> taken the route of incarnation for us and, without undergoing
> any change, has become a reality that is composite and visible.
> He has beneficently accomplished for us a unifying communion
> with himself. He has united our humility with his own supreme
> divinity.[102]

The celestial and ecclesiastical communities exist in order that Christ and the church might be brought together in this wonderful exchange, so that when partaking of the sacrament, all believers might "come to look up to the blessed and divine ray of Jesus himself."[103] This experience, which the Reformers distort by making too much of the hierarchies themselves, is merely facilitated by clergy and angels, but is

99. *EH* 376A.

100. *EH* 424C.

101. Meyendorff, *Byzantine Theology*, 202.

102. *EH* 444B. Also, in *EH* 121D he writes, "the reception of the most divine Eucharist is a symbol of participation in Jesus, and so it goes for all the gifts transcendently received by the beings of heaven, gifts which are granted to us in a symbolic mode." Simply because something is symbolic does not mean that it is *only* symbolic, however.

103. *EH* 372B.

ultimately accomplished by Christ's presence as communicated through the visible Eucharist.

Denys's epic narrative also features the choreography of liturgical worship: the procession into the sanctuary, the lifting of bread and cup, the wafting of incense, are reminiscent of his explanation of multidirectional angelic movement discussed earlier. The liturgy is the progression of sacred action emulating the omni-directional love of God-in-Christ. Within this theology of holy movement, the Eucharist represents the intermingling of the celestial and ecclesiastical worlds: the visible beauty of the sacrament, the symbolic beauty of movement, and the underlying moral beauty of Christ's presence within the elements. This mystery also ripples out into the congregation after being disclosed and elevated by the bishop, who

> lifts into view the things praised through the sacredly clothed symbols the bread which had been covered and undivided is now uncovered and divided into many parts. Similarly, he shares the one cup with all, symbolically multiplying and distributing the One in symbolic fashion. With all these things he completes the most holy sacred act.[104]

The ecclesiastical hierarchy mirrors the activity of the celestial hierarchy by communicating the oneness and transcendence of God through a dynamic distribution of Christ's glorious and immanent presence; what angels disclose *in situ*, the clergy disclose in sacrament.

Subordinate to their celestial counterparts, the clergy help to express the beauty and mystery that is Christ's love for, and proximity to, his church. The bishop and his subordinates move as one unit with the sacraments; deacons serve to purify, priests provide illumination, and bishops make up the perfecting order just as "the holy sacraments bring about purification, illumination and perfection."[105] This harmony of purpose brings about the transformation and beautification of the church so that it might fulfill its calling to

> imitate and contemplate the heavenly hierarchies . . . because he [God] wanted us to be made godlike . . . so that he might lift us in spirit up through the perceptible to the conceptual, from

---

104. *EH* 444A.
105. *EH* 536D.

sacred shapes and symbols to the simple peaks of the hierarchies of heaven.[106]

The horizontal axis of Denys's theology uses the perceptible world of clergy and sacraments to foster a contemplative, angelic community, even though it is principally indebted to the immanence of Christ in the Eucharist. This pattern of thought contradicts Calvin and Luther's presentation of Denys as a trivial, rather pagan, figure who failed to ground his angelology within Christian worship.

Nonetheless, what Denys posits is a continuum of mediation that highlights the symbolic and ontological dimensions of a Savior who is seated above angels who adore him and is contemplated by clergy who, starting with the angel-like hierarch, uplift and distribute his eucharistic presence to the church. Nurtured by the love and service of its leaders, whether divine, angelic, or human, the Christian's spiritual journey is also inextricably linked to the sacramental body of Christ and the church. What makes the church an institution of truly cosmic proportions is its unbroken connection with the beautifying presence of the Godhead, which when expressed through angelic and ecclesiastical hierarchies, teaches believers that love is meant to lead all beings outside of themselves for the good of the other.

One must keep in mind that hierarchical imagery was also rife within the liturgical practices of the Syrian Christians prior to and contemporaneous with Denys's time. For instance, the congregation was typically obligated to stand about a centrally located platform while the Holy Scriptures were read from an ambo;[107] whereas the bishop, as Christ's representative, would typically sit enthroned in what can best be described as Christianity's version of Moses' seat.[108] After the readings were complete, the laity and the clergy would walk as a group toward the altar (and *bema*) to prepare for the Eucharist; once there, they faced eastward in a sign of eschatological solidarity, awaiting the return of Jesus along with their bishop who had moved from his seat in order to preside at the Supper.[109] Early Syriac Christians relied upon a clear sense of liturgical space and designed their worship to flow in relation to ecclesiasti-

106. *EH* 121D. This is reminiscent of Plotinus' emphasis upon beauty.

107. Milburn, *Early Christian Art and Architecture*, 123–31.

108. Kieckhefer, *Theology in Stone*, 40.

109. See Addleshaw, *The Ecclesiology of the Churches of the Dead Cities of Northern Syria*; Larson-Miller, "A Return to the Liturgical Architecture of Northern Syria."

cal architecture. This suggests that pseudo-Denys's custom of portraying liturgical and doctrinal matters in an anagogical (and hierarchical) light was likely a reflection of what was already occurring within his culture's profoundly embedded form of spirituality.

Denys spoke to a culture that was relatively receptive to the idea of angelic, human, and sacramental intercalation.[110] He has not always translated well into movements, like the Reformation, which have a propensity to emphasize the objective presence of Christ within Scripture. Yet the human dimension described in Denys's ecclesiastical axis is not incompatible with the biblical narrative; I am thinking here of figures like Abraham, Melchizedek, Moses, the Aaronic priesthood, judges, kings, high priests, prophets, Mary and Joseph, apostles, bishops, pastors, and deacons. The essence of what Denys maintains is that the church, too, requires individuals who are similar in function to these individuals, many of whom received messages from angels, spoke for God, and found themselves inducted into a narrative that reached far beyond the margins of the sacred page.[111]

In conclusion, after reviewing the opinions of Denys's detractors, who suggested that he had adopted too much of Neoplatonism to be taken seriously as a biblical theologian, I argued that his theology was thoroughly Christian in its aim to connect the Godhead, angels, sacraments, clergy, and laity into one, loving community. His emphasis upon Christ as the source and final purpose of hierarchies, in addition to the downward trajectory of grace as prior to human response, is entirely compatible with orthodox Christianity. Moreover, the hierarchies also exhibit a larger pattern of pastoral concern that should not be devalued; rather than being preoccupied with angels or authority, they are meant to amplify the presence of Christ to a church that longs to be near their Lord in light of his ascended, physical absence.[112] Nonetheless, given the persistence of the accusations

110. However, I recognize that Denys may have been trying to persuade certain Monophysite clergy who were less receptive to hierarchies because of their suspicion that bishops were not rooted firmly in God's order. For an overview of issues and primary figures involved in this power struggle, see Arthur, *Pseudo-Dionysius as Polemicist*, 101–40.

111. For instance, see Gen 14:18–20; 18:23–32; Exod 7:1; Lev 16; 2 Sam 7:5–17; etc.

112. In, *Ep.* 9 (1113B), Denys draws upon Luke 12:37 to imagine what the eternal state will be like; "It is Jesus himself who gladdens them and leads them to table, who serves them, who grants them everlasting rest, who bestows and pours out on them the fullness in beauty."

made against him since the Reformation, it is now necessary to turn to the philosophical underpinnings of Denys's angelology—starting with Plato, Plotinus, and Proclus—before establishing the degrees of separation between it and Neoplatonic cosmological models.

## DENYS'S NEOPLATONIC INSPIRATION

Plato's *Timaeus* explored the tension of a two-tiered creation in terms of the relationship between the static eternal world and the dynamic physical world. Since nothing exists without a cause, he reasoned that a coherent cosmogony required a demiurge as the creative agent, proposing that by manipulating the four classical elements of earth, air, fire, and water, the demiurge had reorganized the pre-existent chaos into a mathematically-precise order based upon paradigmatic Forms.[113] Thus, humans "became" children of a demiurge who was thought to have left a tincture of something "divine" and "immortal" within them.[114] This spark, in turn, rendered persons as rational souls capable of appreciating higher insights about reality, which mainly deal with the eternal truths of beauty, goodness, and justice. After Plato's death in 348 BCE, a revised version of his theory, known as middle-Platonism, acted as an ideological bookmark until Plotinus's (ca. 204–270) work led to the noteworthy paradigm that ultimately informed pseudo-Denys.[115]

Most of what is known about Plotinus, who was either a Greek born in Lycopolis, Egypt, or from a Hellenized family of Egyptian or Roman descent, comes from a biography written by his pupil, Porphyry.[116] At the age of twenty-seven he moved to Alexandria, where he studied for eleven years under the philosopher Ammonius Saccas, who also trained Origen, and whose eclectic theory it was that Plato and Aristotle were in agreement. Ammonius and Plotinus's relationship has been compared to that of Plato and Socrates, and directly influenced Plotinus's development

113. According to *Tim.* 29d2, Plato himself did not consider the proposal to be much more than a "likely story" (*eikos muthos*) or a plausible explanation.

114. *Tim.* 41c.

115. The middle Platonists were eclectic in their beliefs, borrowing from other systems like Stoicism; for example, Philo leaned heavily upon Judaism and Plutarch argued for a literal interpretation of the *Timaeus*. Ammonius' academy in Alexandria marks the early transition from Middle Platonism to Neoplatonism.

116. Gerson, *Plotinus*, xiii.

of Neoplatonism.[117] After an attempt to study philosophy in Persia came to naught, Plotinus spent the majority of his later life in Rome where he gained notoriety as a philosopher in his own right. Though slightly overstated in light of Ammonius's influence, Plotinus is often referred to as the father of Neoplatonism, a monistic, metaphysical system inspired by Plato's cosmogony.[118]

In the *Enneads*, Plotinus adapts the *Timaeus* and elaborates upon Plato's "Form of the Good" as found in the *Republic* and the *Parmenides*. He maintains the existence of a first principle that transcends all categories of thought and being, which he referred to as "the One" (*to hen*) or "the Good" (*ta kalon*). Plotinus believed the nature and activity of the One to be so inseparably and causally related that its very *nature* was to bring things into being and to compose them as a reflection of that being. The One was the purely good, self-caused, absolute basis of all reality, from which emanates, by necessity, all dimensions of reality. Thus, as the One upwells like a perpetually-bubbling cauldron it produces the *Nous*, which was a form of universal consciousness that made intelligibility possible. Likewise, from the *Nous* emanates the *Psyche* (including both individual and world-soul), which remains in contact with the *Nous* but stands between it and the intelligible world. Finally, from the *Psyche* radiated the *Physis*, what today we may refer to as "nature."

117. Gatti, "Plotinus: The Platonic Tradition and the Foundation of Neoplatonism," 16.

118. Other candidates are Moderatus of Gades (ca. first century CE) and Numenius (ca. second century CE); see Corrigan, *Reading Plotinus*, 101. Gerson, *Plotinus*, 386. Sorabji, *The Philosophy of the Commentators, 200–600 AD*, 6. O'Meara, *Plotinus*, 113.

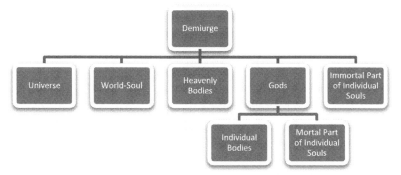

Fig. 4. Fundamental Principles in Plato's *Timaeus*

Fig. 5. Fundamental Principles in Plotinus's *Enneads*

This elegant scheme suggested that the observable order occupies the lowest rung of a cosmic chain of being, yet allowed for the rational (and immaterial) mind to ascend upward in an exploration of these higher derivations—the place where the human soul would inevitably return upon death. Since Plotinus follows Plato by assuming that all things desire the good and long for unity, his description of the intrinsic connectedness of creation fell into two dynamic stages or movements: *procession* from, and *return* to, the origin.[119] Thus, his system is a devotional exploration of both ontic and functional dimensions of metaphysics.

119. *Enn.* I.12–6.

Plotinus summarizes this concept in what was essentially his philosophy of religion:

> The One is all things and no [sic] one of them; the source of all things is not all things; all things are its possession—running back, so to speak, to it—or, more correctly, not yet so, they will be. . . . Seeking nothing, possessing nothing, lacking nothing, the One is perfect and, in our metaphor, has overflowed, and its exuberance has produced the new: this product has turned again to its begetter and been filled and has become its contemplator and so an Intellectual-Principle. That station towards the one [the fact that something exists in presence of the One] establishes Being; that vision directed upon the One establishes the Intellectual-Principle; standing towards the One to the end of vision, it is simultaneously Intellectual-Principle and Being; and, attaining resemblance in virtue of this vision, it repeats the act of the One in pouring forth a vast power.[120]

Plotinus's *Enneads* reinterpreted the Platonic tradition for a new generation and laid the groundwork for Proclus, who followed him. His complex spiritual cosmology strove to relate the One and the many, connected one's incorporeal destiny with a contemplative present, and implied that a return to the generating principle is predicated upon detaching oneself from earthly pursuits and pleasures.[121]

## Proclus

Denys was steeped in the thought of Proclus (412–85), Plotinus's successor and the last of the great Platonic philosophers.[122] A polymath, known for his meticulous commentaries on the works of Plato and Euclid, Proclus was also a poet and scientist, and became the director of the Academy in Athens where he had studied under the direction of Plutarch and Syrianus. With the exception of Christianity, with its description of

120. Plotinus, *The Enneads* (II.1.1), 361.

121. Ibid., I.6.8. "He that has the strength, let him arise and withdraw into himself, foregoing all that is known by the eyes, turning away forever from the material beauty that once made his joy . . . one that is held by material beauty and will not break free shall be precipitated, not in body but in Soul, down to the dark depths loathed of the Intellective-Being, where, blind even in the Lower-World, he shall have commerce only with shadows, there as here."

122. While influenced by Iamblichus and Syrianus, it is clear from Book 1 of *Platonic Theology*, that he considers Plotinus to be the most faithful exegete of Plato.

the creation of a temporal world, Proclus was essentially a religious plu-
ralist. Conversant with both Hellenistic and Egyptian purification rites,
which he assiduously observed along with feast days, he also composed
hymns to Helios, Aphrodite, and several other pagan gods.[123]

Proclus followed Plotinus's cosmogony but subdivided it into
distinct categories, fittingly described as "richer in some ways, but less
suggestive; at once dizzying and cramped."[124] Like Plotinus, the core of
Proclus's elaborate and perplexing metaphysic stresses that each level
of being is similarly connected to the One; but while Plotinus limited
himself to only three separate hypostases (the One, Intelligence, Soul),
Proclus doubles their number by interposing additional manifestations
for each of these principles, producing a six-tiered hierarchy (the One-
*henads*; Intelligence-*intelligences*; Soul-*souls*). In addition, every separate
procession issues three additional sub-hypostases so that there are three
orders of henads, intelligences, and souls. Each sub-hypostasis remains
within and emulates its cause—the henads imitate the One; intelligences
imitate the Intelligence; and souls imitate the Soul—so that each distinct
emanation not only *proceeds* from, but *abides* and *returns* to its immediate
cause. Where Plotinus's One, Intelligence, and Soul form the backbone of
reality, the gaps that exist between each emanation require, in the mind
of Proclus, intermediaries that facilitate their unity.[125] To a greater degree
than Plotinus, Proclus also assumes that a strong mediatorial component
is written into matter; thus he leans heavily in the direction of theurgy as
a means by which one attains union with the gods.[126]

There are similarities between Denys's ideology and Neoplatonism,
most notably in the priority given to the non-sensible world and the way
both order reality as a hierarchy that extends between the physical world
and its Source. More specifically, while a contemplative like Plotinus, Denys shared Proclus's belief that contemplation cannot replace experience
in one's upward ascent toward the sacred. However, despite the shaping
force Neoplatonism had upon Denys's thinking, it is possible to make too

123. He refers to Christians as "strangers to our world," "the ignorant," and "the
godless." Proclus, *A Commentary on the First Book of Euclid's Elements*, xv.

124. Louth, *The Origins of the Christian Mystical Tradition*, 162.

125. In Book 1 of his *Commentary on Parmenides* (618.13–23), Proclus sets out
his celestial hierarchy, where he petitions each order to bestow gifts upon him according to their nature. They are, in descending order: intelligible gods, intellectual gods,
transcendent gods, intercosmic gods, angels, daemons, heroes.

126. Also, cf. Iamblichus, defence of theurgy in *De Mysteriis*, II.11

much of the relationship by not taking Denys at his word.[127] The fact that some elements of his angelology are discoverable in Neoplatonism tells us little unless interpreted in light of Denys's Christianity. For instance, one must not ignore the dissimilarity between Neoplatonism's panentheistic, emanative, non-personal supreme divinity (among divinities) and Denys's monotheistic, personal God who intentionally creates and enters into the universe—notions that contributed to Plotinus, Porphyry, Iamblichus, and Proclus's rejection of Christianity.[128] The chapter now turns to discuss these and other points of dissimilarity between Denys and Neoplatonists like Plotinus and Proclus.

## DENYS'S BREAK WITH NEOPLATONISM

### Plotinus

Given similarities between his hierarchical angelology and the role of hypostases in Neoplatonism, one might assume that Denys emphasized angels because he followed the Neoplatonic portrayal of God as a rather impersonal force, but this is not the case. In fact, it would be challenging to capture Denys's angelology without discussing God's *personal* dimensions, since angelic mediation was meant to point beyond itself to the beauty of divine love. For Denys, even "the mystery of Jesus' love for humanity was first revealed to the angels and . . . the gift of this knowledge was granted by the angels to us."[129] Plotinus, however, took a contemplative approach to a god who did not reciprocate love, and Iamblichus, his disciple, advocated theurgy as a means of reaching the dispassionate and remote One. In contrast, Denys's emotive spirituality was neither an upward climb via pure contemplation, nor was it overtly physical or theurgic—a point intimated by his use of *hierourgia* in relation to the sacraments instead of *theourgia*. Instead, his theology flows from the superseding conviction that a self-mediating God who is rapt with his

---

127. Two recent works that stress such similarities also tend to depict Denys as more of a philosopher than a Christian theologian: E.D. Perl, Perl, *Theophany*; Christian Schäfer, *The Philosophy of Dionysius the Areopagite* (Leiden, Brill, 2006). John Dillon and S.K. Wear are more even-handed in, *Dionysius the Areopagite and the Neoplatonist Tradition* (Aldershot, Ashgate, 2007).

128. Proclus was a devout pagan who opposed Christianity because it believed the world would end; see his treatise, *On the Eternity of the World.*

129. *CH* 181B.

creation graciously makes his presence known by spiritual (angels) and physical (clergy and sacraments) gestures of immanence on the basis of love. As Riordan notes, the difference between Denys and Plotinus is that for Denys, "it is the Absolute One *Itself* that descends, not 'eros' coming out from 'the sphere of the intelligences.'"[130]

Additionally, Dionysian contemplation differed from Neoplatonic versions in that it was a prayerful interaction with sacred symbols and the sacred text, leading one "up to the farthest, highest peak of mystic scripture where the mysteries of God's Word lie simple, absolute, unchangeable in the brilliant darkness of a hidden silence."[131] This contemplation is an imitation of the holy angels, who ponder more directly "the primordial and superessential beauty manifested in three persons because they are judged worthy of communion with Jesus."[132] Yet it is also Jesus who raises the Christian up to imitate angelic contemplation, "As for us, with that yearning for beauty which raises us upward (and which is raised up) to him [Jesus], he pulls together all our many differences. He makes our life, disposition, and activity something one and divine . . . ."[133] Denys's affirmation of a connected universe rendered humans and angels as distinct from the Creator but did not prevent them from sharing together the Christocentric contemplation and experience of divine beauty.[134] In fact, it is a loving God who "is the power moving and lifting all things up to himself, for in the end what is he if not beauty and goodness," asks Denys.[135] Although Plotinus also emphasizes the contemplation of the beautiful, he never aligned his contemplation of the beautiful with the idea of worshiping the One in the way that Denys does. Denys's complex relationship between God, beauty, and aesthetics is already well-documented, however, and needs no further amplification here.[136] Simply put,

130. Riordan, *Divine Light*, 93–94.

131. *MT* 1001A.

132. *CH* 208BC.

133. *CH* 372A.

134. Of course, other luminaries like Ambrose, Augustine, and Origen affirmed the same thing. And as Gregory the Theologian insisted, God's beauty is not merely an ideal because God is both beauty itself *and* beautiful. *Oration* 28.30–31.

135. *Enn.* I.6 is a lengthy discourse dedicated to the subject of beauty; in *MT* 1025B, Denys adopts Plotinus' discussion in I.6.9 of a sculptor who chips away "all that is excessive" from a statue until it becomes "all one glow of beauty."

136. See, Putnam, *Beauty in the Pseudo-Denis*; Balthasar, *Cosmic Liturgy*; Balthasar, *The Glory of the Lord, vol. 2*; Rorem, *Biblical and Liturgical Symbols within the Pseudo-Dionysian Synthesis*, 142; Torevell, *Liturgy and the Beauty of the Unknown*, 25.

Denys understands beauty as God himself and the hierarchies as a providential expression of the divine willingness to draw all things toward that beauty that is itself.[137]

Plotinus understood the One as the object of human aspiration to which the longing soul could return after death gave way to an eternity of reflection. Unlike Denys, his soteriology was based upon contemplation rather than the mediation of a Savior or a Creator.[138] The reason for this is simple; emanationism presumes a progressive deterioration or a want of perfection, and Plotinus saw the mind as an immaterial vehicle that allowed one to escape this imperfect, physical world and attain the divine world, what he called "the fatherland . . . from whence we have come."[139] He was not as pessimistic as the gnostics were concerning the natural world.[140] Nevertheless, he considers the baser elements, which are subject to decay and privation, as "evil itself" (though Proclus would later disagree).[141] Denys, however, sees evil as more evenly distributed throughout the ontological spectrum than Plotinus, and takes a stand against affixing moral value to matter.

> There is no truth in the common assertion that evil is inherent in mater *qua* matter, since matter too has a share in the cosmos, in beauty and form. . . . Surely matter cannot be evil. If it has being in no way at all, then it is neither good nor evil.[142]

My feeling is that Denys's reluctance to relate evil with the physical world is partly related to the idea that the angels' primeval fall had nothing to do with matter, but with volition and hubris.[143] Denys did follow Plotinus on the necessity of matter, whose innate beauty rests in its relation to an ultimate Cause, but he does so only to emphasize tangible and intelligible features of divine grace made manifest in the incarnation, Scripture, clergy, symbology, rites, and sacraments.[144]

137. The hierarchies are "an image of the beauty of God." *CH* 165B.

138. *Enn.* I.6, 8, 22; IV.9, 11, 50.

139. *Enn.* I.6.8.

140. He argues against the gnostic view in *Enn* II.9.

141. *Enn.* I.8.5.8–10, 30; I.8.8.37–44; I.8.13.7–14. For a fuller discussion, see Gerson and O'Brien, "Plotinus on Matter and Evil."

142. *DN* 729A.

143. *DN* 725D–C.

144. *CH*, 121C–136A.

For Plotinus the return to the One was a solitary experience whereby the soul seeks its destiny and unites with its true self, which he expressed in the haunting, final words of the *Enneads* as "the flight of the alone to the Alone."[145] Denys, however, anticipates existential unification with the benevolent God; his angelology and ecclesiology are predicated upon an atmosphere of fellowship with fellow pilgrims, eager for the same. "The soul in ecstasy meets God's ecstatic love for herself. Here is no union with Plotinus's One, immutable and unconscious either of Itself or of the soul," writes Louth.[146] Embraced and welcomed, the church participates in and benefits from the otherwise unapproachable vision of God as channelled through celestial, sacramental, and ecclesiastical intermediaries.[147]

Rather than advocating an individualistic pursuit of contemplative and theurgic practices with the aim of self-perfection, Denys envisions a Christian community that contemplates the historic works of Christ and is, in turn, divinely pursued and sustained.[148] So the angels, like Denys's other means of grace, are part of a holy congregation conceived in divine love, and who, with the church, share in the beauty and blessedness of God.

Pseudo-Dionysius portrays an inexplicable and majestic God who remains distinct from the creation, but who, because of his loving-kindness, traverses the yawning ontological and moral gaps separating divinity and humanity. Like a dance between heaven and earth led by angels, clergy, sacrament, and symbols, Denys's model allows *both* realms to promenade within the same sacred spaces. Uncharacteristic of Neo-platonism, he insists that this motif is not only designed and upheld by a transcendent yet personal God, but that God is compelled by love to express his immanence, which he does by entering *into* the creation itself.[149]

> [God] is, as it were, beguiled by goodness, by love, and by yearn-
> ing and is enticed away from his transcendent dwelling place
> and comes to abide within all things, and he does so by virtue of

145. *Enn.* VI.9.9.11.

146. Louth, *The Origins of the Christian Mystical Tradition from Plato to Denys,* 176. Also, see *EH* 556B.

147. Plotinus refers to the participation between the spiritual and physical realms in *Enn.* VI.5.26.

148. *EH* 484B.

149. One could suggest that the canonical structure of the Bible follows such a pattern, with the procession of life occurring in Genesis and returning to God in Revelation.

his supernatural and ecstatic capacity to remain, nevertheless, within himself.[150]

Likewise, "Jesus himself, the transcendent Cause of those beings which live beyond the world, came to take on human form without in any way changing his own essential nature."[151] In response to this benign initiative, the community of faith has for two thousand years been expressing a similar primal desire to return to the source of all being through loving acts of worship. Unlike Plotinus's theory of mystical ascent, however, this longing presupposes love on both sides of the equation. "For Denys," observes Riordan, "the cosmic liturgy of creatures is an ever-greater exultation into the life and beatitude of the three Persons."[152]

## Proclus

Proclus's triadic and cyclical philosophy of remaining-proceeding-returning (*mone-proodos-epistrophe*) appealed more to Denys than Plotinus's two stage dynamic of procession and return.[153] Denys, however, intends to solve this problem that had preoccupied Neoplatonists for decades by sanctifying the concept. He presents the unity of God as an eternal abiding, the persons of the godhead as a procession, and his angelology, ecclesiology, and sacramentology as gestures of divine immanence beckoning for and facilitating the believer's return to the divine.[154] While less refined than the *Timaeus*, *Enneads*, or *Platonic Theology*, such works provided Denys with a comprehensive philosophical framework upon which he could shape his own epic, Christian theology. While some would interpret Denys's adaptations as more of an ideological conquest than a capitulation—a *force majeure* that undermined Neoplatonic suppositions, others, like Krautheimer, argue that Denys was merely a "superficially Christianized version of Proclus."[155]

150. *DN* 712B.

151. *CH* 181C.

152. Riordan, *Divine Light*, 112.

153. However, his writing appears to emphasize Plotinus' two-stage system: the *DN* focuses upon procession; the *EH*, *Celestial Hierarchy* and *MT*, on return.

154. Though, Rorem clarifies, Denys never went so far as to develop a hierarchy within the Trinity itself. Rorem, *Pseudo-Dionysius*, 52.

155. Krautheimer, *Studies in East Christian, Medieval and Renaissance Art*, 245 n.87.

It may appear that Denys substituted the Christian God for Proclus's One and inserted nine ranks of angelic beings where other hypostases once dwelt.[156] Yet, he had a considerably different philosophical outlook from Neoplatonism and did not understand angels as intermediate divinities, interposed between inter-cosmic gods and good daemons by means of emanation, but as subordinate, aeviternal, creations of God and Christ.[157] Angels in the *Celestial Hierarchy* bear only a superficial resemblance to the Procline diffusions; they participate in God, but do not flow forth from him, nor do humans, in turn, flow forth from angels as in emanationism. As Louth observes, Denys

> rejects any idea that *being* is passed down this scale of being: all beings are created immediately by God. The scale of being and the sense of dependence only has significance in the matter of *illumination*: light and knowledge flow from God down through the scale of being—each being becomes radiant with light and thus passes on light to beings lower down.[158]

The implication in Denys is that as agents of a personal God whom they love, holy angels are not indifferent derivations, but devoted spirits who actively assist and uplift their ecclesiastical counterparts toward the light of Christ for the good of the church.[159]

As proposed earlier, Denys built his hierarchical theology around a christological center, thus his emphasis upon angelic and ecclesiastical hierarchies served to accentuate the immanence of Christ within the Eucharist, the physical/spiritual means of ascent that lies between angels and bishops. Is this not simply Christian theurgy imitating Proclus, however? The Neoplatonic understanding of theurgy as a means of employing statues, animals, plants, and stones to become pure like the gods, differed radically from Denys's concept of sacraments. "The use of material elements in the sacraments . . . is a matter of institution, not of occult fitness," Louth writes; "they are vehicles of grace not because of what they are materially, but because of their use in a certain symbolic

---

156. Iamblichus (ca. 245–325) also included angelic beings to a greater extent than either Plotinus or Proclus and may represent another influence upon this aspect of pseudo-Denys's cosmogony.

157. I used "daemons" (*daimones*) here in the Platonic sense of benevolent, spiritual beings; though Denys treats them as fallen angels in *DN* 724CD.

158. Louth, *Denys the Aeropagite*, 85. (Emphasis mine)

159. *CH* 180B; *DN* 696C.

context."[160] Neoplatonic theurgy was about rendering oneself fit for the gods, a self-justifying ritual that raised the theurgist up into fellowship with divinities.

Theurgy "does not draw down the impassive and pure gods to that which is passive and impure," insists Iamblichus, Proclus's predecessor, "but, on the contrary, it renders us, who have become passive through generation, pure and immutable."[161] Denys, however, related theurgy as something received in accordance with the work of God in salvation rather than the work of the hierarch.[162] He writes, "the reception of the most divine Eucharist is a symbol of participation in Jesus, and so it goes for all the gifts transcendently received by the beings of heaven, gifts which are granted to us in a symbolic mode."[163] The Eucharist, which emphasizes through symbols and words the sacred presence and histori-cal activity of Christ, stresses that the present congregation is receiving a heavenly gift that signifies not only their solidarity with Jesus, but with one another; this, too, is a stark departure from the solitariness associated with the theurgic practices of Neoplatonism.[164]

Finally, Denys's belief in "the sacred incarnation of Jesus for our sakes," which he considered "the most evident idea in theology," would have been an absurdity for Proclus, because it represents an external source of divine illumination.[165] I say this because Proclus maintained that "illumination is our individual light. . . . [S]o by the One in ourselves do we apprehend the One, which by the brightness of its light is the cause of all beings, by which all participate in the One."[166]

Neither contemplative nor experiential routes in Denys's spiritual-ity are predicated upon the assumption that one is inwardly inspired, theurgically self-sufficient or destined to re-merge with the divine sphere

---

160. Louth, *The Origins of the Christian Mystical Tradition from Plato to Denys*, 164.

161. Iamblichus, *De Mysteriis* 1.12.

162. Rorem notes that Denys's use of the term *theourgia* is, unlike Iamblichus and Proclus, not employed as an objective genitive concerning human effort, but as a sub-jective genitive referring to God's own work. In Lubheid, *Pseudo-Dionysius*, 52 n.11.

163. *EH* 121D.

164. "The Neoplatonic theurgist . . . appears as more of a lone figure, concerned only, or primarily, with his own personal unification. The 'congregation,' if any, re-mains very much in the shadows." Wear and Dillon, *Dionysius the Areopagite and the Neoplatonist Tradition*, 115.

165. *DN* 648A.

166. Proclus, *Param.* 7.48.

from whence one came.[167] Even if it is possible that Denys transformed Proclus's hypostases and gods into angels or divine attributes while supplanting the detached One with the economic-*cum*-ontological Trinity, his purpose would have been to demonstrate the superiority of the Christian ideology, revealed by the incarnation, angels, church, and Scriptures, and rooted in love.[168] There is no need to be defensive about an overlap between Christianity and Neoplatonism in Denys, however. The Neoplatonic ingredients within his writings were never so strong that they overpowered the Christian flavor of his thought, which was based upon a revealed, monotheistic faith.

## CONCLUSION

Similarities between the language and concepts used by Denys, Proclus, and Plotinus cannot be denied, but Denys is most coherent when read alongside the Christian tradition, rather than interpreted as a crypto-Neoplatonist aiming to subvert it. What is more likely is that he appropriated Neoplatonic concepts for the same reason that Aquinas would later borrow from Aristotelian metaphysics—it was a helpful framework for systematizing doctrines and resolving tensions within Christian theology.[169] His angels are not lesser-divinities to be worshipped, his discussion of the nature and character of God regards God as personal and as one who externalizes himself out of love for his creation, his version of contemplation was rooted in liturgy, Scripture, and the historical acts of God-in-Christ, plus the motivation behind the apophatic and liturgical pursuit of the divine was driven in response to a loving God. In actual fact, the attributes of Denys's providential God could not be more dissimilar to Neoplatonism's series of indifferent emanations. Quoting Louth, "the One has no concern for the soul that seeks him."[170] One should think that this, coupled with Denys's desire to make the transcendent, ascended

167. "The Fatherland is for us [that] place from which we have come," wrote Plotinus. *Enn.* I.6.8.

168. *DN* 588B; 589A.

169. Balthasar writes, "if Aristotle supplies the exact categories [for Aquinas], Denys supplies not just the great frame for the plan of the *Summa*, with procession and return, and many essential adagios, but also the fundamental structure of the doctrine of God, of the angels, of a sacred cosmos (with structures based both on function and rank), of the ecclesiastical hierarchy." *Glory,* 148.

170. Louth, *The Origins of the Christian Mystical Tradition from Plato to Denys,* 50.

Christ immanent through celestial, ecclesiastical, and sacramental hierarchies, would help to distance him from the unflattering profile sketched
during the Reformation and retraced by subsequent generations.

Just as Old Testament angelology deposed YHWH's rivals from their
lofty perch and accentuated his transcendence in the mind of a developing nation, Denys's hierarchical angelology works in the other direction
to connect the conceptual gap between Christ and Christians-at-worship.
The *Celestial Hierarchy* and *Ecclesiastical Hierarchy* are anagogical statements about the sacred presence and activity of God in the midst of
Christian worship, thirsty for mystery. What one discovers in Denys is
his desire to bring the *other* into the here-and-now by emphasizing the
presence of angels as one means of habituating persons, from bishops
and laity, to heavenly states of mind. The need for such an elaborate intervention implies something about human self-sufficiency, but there is
an element of comfort to be found in Denys's imaginative concept that a
highly ordered array of higher-order beings have been assigned to work
in concert with the creation for the glory of God and the good of the individual.[171] What Denys's model asks for in return, however, is the subordination of individual will to the principles of celestial and ecclesiastical
governance, which remains a challenge as society and the church become
increasingly fragmented.

Characterizing him as sub-Christian, Denys's critics kept their followers from his works, but his angelology is not the threat they said it
was. It describes a possible means by which God uses beings most similar
to himself to disclose his love, as one gear in an existential system that
intends to compensate for humanity's momentary separation from the
personhood of Christ. Still, the Reformer's disparagement of his angelology should not be dismissed entirely. He certainly could have contributed
more concerning the laity's experience of God or their role within the
wider society, but the bigger problem is that his vision does not anticipate
churches that are either not eucharistically oriented or have no formal ecclesiastical hierarchy. Despite the layers of meaning in his texts, so much
depends upon the relationship between clergy and sacrament that one
occasionally struggles to see how angels might function without these
earthly counterparts.

---

171. This is to cut across Schleiermacher's suggestion that the angels belong primarily to an age "when our knowledge of the forces of nature was very limited . . . when
the connection of human beings with nature was not yet ordered, and they themselves
were not yet developed." Schleiermacher, *The Christian Faith*, 159–60.

Denys's ability to dramatize seemingly innocuous doctrines like angelology, and his influence upon the history of theology is incontrovertible.[172] Like early biblical angelology, his work represents a link between theological eloquence and pragmatism; what he adds to Old Testament angelology, however, is an understanding that the angel's message is not always tied to epiphanic events and often entails symbolic and material forms of communication within the worship setting. As my final chapter will argue, Denys's formal hierarchies have been caricatured in the past, but they contribute a necessary corrective to the familiarity, synchronicity, and individualism present in New Age angelology, which eschews corporate worship. Unlike New Ageism, his theology of divine immanence is not without transcendence and has Christ as its head, rather than the autonomy of angels and persons.

Finally, while theologians are as free to depict the angels how they wish as they are to disagree with Denys's version of angelology, one cannot fail to notice that the biblical narrative itself endorses a strong correlation between higher-order beings, hierarchies,[173] worship,[174] divine revelation,[175] significant religious figures,[176] wildly imaginative visions,[177] liturgical symbols,[178] and most importantly, the presence of God.[179] So while the danger exists that Denys's breed of angelology may become an escape for those with a penchant for the esoteric, what it advances is no more fantastic than the Scriptures themselves. Aquinas picked up the relationship between angels and other doctrines where the controversial Denys left off, and the fruit of this theological succession is the topic of the following chapter. In closing, despite his imperfections, Denys's dynamic and original theology is admirable for its portrayal of angels as integral to one's experience of divine love and beauty, an intriguing principle that insistently demands more attention.

---

172. Among them are Aquinas, Bonaventure, Eriugena, Gregory Palamas, Hugh of St. Victor, John Damascene, Julian of Norwich, Maximus Confessor, and more recently, von Bathasar, in his discussions of the cosmic aspect of liturgy in Balthasar, *Cosmic Liturgy*.

173. Eph 1:21; 3:10; Col 1:16; 1 Thess 4:16; Jude 1:9.

174. Pss 103:20; 148:2; 1 Cor 11:10; Rev 4–5; 7:11.

175. Gen 18–19; 28:12; Luke 1:11; 2:10; Matt 28:5.

176. Gen 18; Judg 13; 1 Kgs 19:5–6; Dan 8:16; Luke 1:26; 22:43.

177. Isa 6:1–7; Ezek 28:14–16; Dan 7:9–10.

178. Exod 25:18; 1 Kgs 6:27; Rev 8:3–5.

179. Gen 16:7–11; 18–19; 22:11–12; Rev 8:2.

# Chapter III

# Recovering the Significance of Aquinas's Imaginative Angelology

## INTRODUCTION

PRESSING ONWARD AT THIS POINT, both chronologically and thematically, we shall now explore an uncharted region of Thomas Aquinas's angelology. Assessments of his angelology are too often based upon the *Summa Theologiae*, leading many to characterize his adaptation as overtly philosophical, rather than biblical and exegetical. However, his commentaries on Scripture, most of which are still in Latin, reveal imaginative, Christocentric, and scriptural dimensions of his angelology. While these elements are present in the *Summa Theologiae*, it is in the less formal setting of Aquinas's commentaries that the angel emerges from the text to become compatible with the creation, a hermeneutical device he uses to indicate the cosmos is thick with supernatural presence. As with Old Testament writers and pseudo-Denys, Aquinas was not merely reconstructing old truths about angels, but inventing new patterns of use. His flexible interpretation of higher-order beings transforms the planet into a place that ultimately points to God by bringing him closer to the perceptible world. Picking up where Denys left off, Aquinas pushes the semantic range of the word "angel" as a means of permanently saturating earth with heaven, rather than restricting angels to liturgical roles. His approach provides a template for imagination in modern angelology as well, and in the final chapter, I illustrate how Aquinas's playful contributions correct the disenchanted and dour world of pure environmentalism.

Although a number of books written about Aquinas in the last century cover the historical, ideological, and theological aspects of his life and teaching, few of them mention his angelology. One explanation for this gap is that much of the emphasis within Thomistic scholarship has been placed upon producing reliable Latin copies of his oeuvre. Formed in 1880 in response to Leo XIII's encyclical *Aeterni patris*, the Leonine Commission accepted the monumental task of creating critical versions of Aquinas's works from extant medieval manuscripts. Rather than producing English translations of his writings, this international, and exclusively Dominican, endeavor aims to provide the academy with authoritative editions of the originals. Valuable though this may be, one is still left wanting when it comes to easily-accessible versions of Aquinas's angelology; in fact, while the papal imperative also spurred a renewed interest in Aquinas among Catholic scholars, only J. D. Collins—in his 1947 dissertation *The Thomistic Philosophy of the Angels*—has produced a thorough evaluation of the Angelic Doctor's angelology.[1] Collins work is far from exhaustive, however, because he fails to interact with the commentaries on Scripture.

During the middle of the last century, scholars like Etienne Gilson and Ludwig Ott addressed general philosophical components of Scholastic angelology.[2] However, they skipped the theological use of angels in Aquinas's commentaries in order to focus upon issues like the different metaphysical assumptions in Aquinas's and Bonaventure's angelology.[3] Moreover, post-Vatican II authors have attempted little with the topic of angels in general—the glosses of McBrien and Rahner being among the exceptions.[4] More recently, Steven Chase emphasized the role of angels in mediaeval spirituality (though he does not deal with Aquinas

1. Collins, *The Thomistic Philosophy of the Angels*.

2. Gilson, *The Philosophy of St. Thomas Aquinas*, 160 ff.; Ott, *Fundamentals of Catholic Dogma*, 114–21.

3. Perhaps the most significant disagreement between Aquinas and Bonaventure on this issue had to do with their application of Aristotle's hylomorphism to angelology. Bonaventure felt that since God is the only pure spirit, all other things, including angels, must be regarded as composite beings composed of form and matter. Aquinas argued that since angels are purely intellectual beings, like God, they are purely spiritual.

4. McBrien, *Catholicism*, 255–56. Rahner, "Angels," 4–13.

specifically).[5] A number of essays compiled in *Angels in Medieval Philosophical Inquiry* highlight the ubiquitous function of angels in cosmology, epistemology, ethics, and theology during Aquinas's era.[6]

Like the tiny network of literature that addresses the topic of Aquinas's angelology, only recently has there been an effort to evaluate his biblical commentaries. Several years ago *Aquinas on Scripture*, and its predecessor, *Aquinas on Doctrine*, aimed to introduce readers to his views on *sacra Scriptura* and *sacra doctrina*, respectively.[7] Eleonore Stump has dedicated a chapter to his biblical commentary in *The Cambridge Companion to Aquinas* as well.[8] The problem, again, is that none of these volumes addresses the matter of angels within Aquinas's biblical commentaries.[9] Thus the present chapter is directly influenced by this gap in the literature and seeks to fill the lacuna in a manner that may inspire further research into Aquinas's angelology. By illustrating his approach to angels within his commentaries on Scripture, I also hope to undermine, albeit indirectly, any misgivings about the theological convictions that animated Thomas and his angelology.

## AQUINAS IN HIS HISTORICAL CONTEXT

Numerous theologians had already advanced a variety of theories regarding the doctrine of angelology by the time Aquinas arrived on the scene during the mid-thirteenth century. The rabbinical authors of mystical Hekhalot literature forged a highly allegorical approach to angels by attempting to decipher the deeper significance of the composite beings found in Ezekiel 1 and elsewhere.[10] Earlier theologians like Origen,

5. Chase, *Angelic Spirituality*.

6. Iribarren and Lenz, *Angels in Medieval Philosophical Inquiry*. Of special note is Iribarren's chapter on the controversy between Aquinas and Durandus of St. Pourcain concerning the angel's role in the perfection of the universe. Also, see Nichols, *Discovering Aquinas*, 82–90. While Nichols provides a strong introduction to Aquinas's angelology, the work is essentially a reflection upon the angels of the *Summa Theologiae*.

7. Weinandy, *Aquinas on Scripture*.

8. See Kretzmann and Stump, *The Cambridge Companion to Aquinas*, 252–68.

9. This includes other works such as: Levering, "A Note on Scripture in the *Summa Theologiae*," 652–58; Waldstein, "On Scripture in the Summa Theologiae," 73–94; Valkenberg, *Words of the Living God*.

10. For a good overview of the genre, see Halperin, *Faces of the Chariot*; Elior, "Mysticism, Magic, and Angelology." Jim Davila refers to the essence of Merkavah mysticism and its heavy reliance upon angelic motifs as a form of Jewish shamanism

though also heavily engaged in allegorical interpretations, furthered the doctrine by musing about angelic guardianship, and whether Christ's atonement might extend to even the most depraved angel.[11] While many Greek fathers wrote extensively about angels, it was John Damascene who indirectly popularized the doctrine by collating their views in *De Fide Orthodoxa*.[12] During the early High Middle Ages, Anselm asked critical questions about the ratio of holy angels to redeemed humans (though Augustine introduced the topic in the fourth century), which eventually led to his assertion that fallen humanity has a duty to obey God as the holy angels do, a view he ultimately tied into his Christology, anthropology, and theory of atonement.[13] Finally, it is clear that pseudo-Dionysius's *Celestial Hierarchy* was a standard text in the academic curriculum of Aquinas's day, and was supplemented with commentaries by Eriugena, Hugh of St. Victor, and John the Saracen.[14] The tone of these myriad contributions ranges from the self-evident to the esoteric, but despite their differences, it is our ancestors' mutual confidence in the significance of angels which aligns them with one another. Should one expand this abbreviated history of angelology by including the number of Christian thinkers who have broached the subject since the earliest days of the church, it might appear that everything that could be said about celestial beings had already been written by Aquinas's time.

Nevertheless, it is almost impossible to overstate the widespread fascination with higher order beings during the thirteenth century, a period that David Keck has aptly distinguished as "the flowering of medieval angelology."[15] It is not that earlier angelologies were discarded during this period as much as it is that angels were interpreted and systematized according to new rubrics; the old angelologies, it appears, had lost some of their luster
in light of new philosophical frameworks that had been trickling into Europe. During this time when theology was still unburdened from

---

in Davila, *Descenders to the Chariot.*

11. See, Origen, *Homilies on Numbers* 24:3; *Commentary on Matthew* 13:26; *Homilies on Ezekiel* 1:10; *De Principiis*, 1.6.1–3; 3.6.5.

12. For an overview of the sprawling angelology of both Greek and Latin fathers, see Danielou, *Angels and Their Mission*. See John Damascene, *De Fide*. III.3–4.

13. See Anselm, *De Casu Diaboli* as well as the first several sections of *De Veritate*.

14. See the editorial notes concerning the Paris Dionysian corpus in Appendix 3 of Aquinas, *Divine Government*, 14:184.

15. Keck, *Angels & Angelology in the Middle Ages*, 93.

the divisions created by the Reformation and Counter-Reformation, there was an overwhelming sense that in order for doctrines like angelology to press forward, one needed to adopt and experiment with innovative points of view. Thus, Aquinas's contribution to the doctrine's history was an attempt to reconcile the angelology of his ancestors with the emerging conceptual frontiers of his day.

By way of a systematic discussion of angels in the *Summa Theologiae*, Thomas distinguishes himself from his theological forebears whose ruminations on angels are peppered throughout their respective theologies. The angelology of the *Summa Theologiae* is, by contrast, deliberate, progressive and focused; one can see the great Aquinas took pains to leave no stone unturned as he applied philosophical categories like being and essence to the angels. While this philosophical influence is also evident in the biblical commentaries, there, Aquinas rejoins his theological forebears by periodically weaving angels into his unassuming reflections on the biblical text. His mind may have been with the logicians, yet his heart remained anchored to his Christian ancestors, to whom he frequently appealed as support for his view of angels. However, the allegorical approach to angelology one finds in Aquinas's commentaries is sufficiently innovative to distinguish him from both ancients and moderns.

Recently, a computerized version of his works revealed that before he died at forty-nine years of age, Aquinas had penned over 8,686,577 words, the equivalent of more than 34,700 pages of typed text.[16] Even with his use of up to four amanuenses at a time—it is thought that he would turn to them in sequence, dictating different topics to each—Thomas's output is astonishing both in quantity and quality. This, combined with his dense logic, demonstrates that he possessed a remarkably systematized mind from which he could dictate for hours at a time.[17]

A cursory glance at this works, overflowing with quotations and citations from diverse fields of study, testifies to the quality of education he enjoyed within the Dominican order. It is easy to understand how Aquinas could be construed as a dry academic in light of these feats of

16. If disputed works are included, the number swells to approximately eleven million. Kenny, *Aquinas on Mind*, 11. My calculation of the page equivalencies is based upon: 250 words per page, doubled-spaced, 8.5 x 11 paper.

17. Given his ability to appeal to hundreds of authorities, it is quite possible that Aquinas had a photographic memory; his contemporaries report that he never forgot anything which he had read. See, Carruthers, *The Book of Memory*, 3.

intellectual prowess. However, Chesterton points out how tragically misinformed one would be to hold such a position:

> It would be every bit as false to say that Aquinas drew his pri-
> mary inspiration from Aristotle. The whole lesson of his life,
> especially of his early life, the whole story of his childhood and
> choice of a career, shows that he was supremely and directly
> devotional; and that he passionately loved the Catholic worship
> long before he found he had to fight for it. . . . It seems to be
> strangely forgotten that both these saints [Aquinas and Francis]
> were in actual fact imitating a Master, who was not Aristotle let
> alone Ovid, when they sanctified the senses or the simple things
> of nature.[18]

So too, even someone as unlikely as Luther held Aquinas in esteem
for his deep spirituality, not least for the way he crossed himself under his
cowl when someone praised him, as a way of guarding against the sin of
pride.[19] "[I]t is also worth considering that Luther, until the end of his life,
never ceased referring to Thomas as 'Sanctus Thomas,' 'Beatus Thomas,'
or 'Divina Thomas,'" observes Denis Janz.[20] Despite the fact that many of
the questions he raised were, and continue to be, of philosophical interest, Christ is anterior to all philosophers, Scripture remains central, and
tradition is crucial in all of Aquinas's theological works.

Furthermore, one cannot separate Aquinas from the influence of his
religious order without doing a disservice to his angelology. Dominican
academics like Aquinas's teacher, Albert the Great, whose writings include commentaries on Aristotle and pseudo-Dionysius's *Mystical Theology*, demonstrate that despite their commitment to Scripture, the order
was comfortable with Aristotelian and Neoplatonic concepts.[21] In fact,
Neoplatonism had already made great inroads into Christian theology
by this time, most notably through the writings of Augustine, pseudo-
Dionysius, and others such as Theodoric of Chartres.[22] While Aquinas
affirmed many older Neoplatonic concepts with respect to angels, it is

---

18. Chesterton, *St. Thomas Aquinas*, 14.

19. One of his earliest biographers shares a tale, apocryphal perhaps, that when
the crucified Christ appeared to Aquinas one day, saying "You have written well of me,
Thomas. What do you want as a reward for your labor?," the monk replied, "None but
thyself, O Lord." See Aquinas, *Summa Theologiae*, vol. 24, 53 n.i.

20. Janz, *Luther on Thomas Aquinas*, 7.

21. See Tugwell, *Early Dominicans*, 25.

22. See D'Onofrio and O'Connell, *The History of Theology*, 208–12.

possible to exaggerate his access to and acceptance of new ideas.[23] John Inglis notes, "In the middle of the thirteenth century members of the Dominican order were forbidden to study the arts, including logic, at the universities. The master of the order, Raymond of Penafort, reiterated this rule in the edition of the Dominican constitutions that he completed in 1241."[24] Inglis notes that the study of Aristotle was an exception to the rule, but Penafort's edict suggests that there may have been more tension between the study of theology and philosophy in Aquinas's day (and in Aquinas) than what is typically assumed. For example, Article 28 of the Primitive Constitutions reads:

> They shall not study the books of pagans and philosophers, even for an hour. They shall not learn secular sciences or even the so-called liberal arts, unless the Master of the Order or the general chapter decides to provide otherwise in certain cases. But everyone, both the young and others, shall read only theological books. We further ordain that each province is obliged to provide brethren destined for study with at least three books of theology. Those so assigned shall mainly study and concentrate on Church History, the Sentences, the Sacred Text, and glosses.[25]

Nonetheless, it was the confluence of Scripture, the Fathers, Aristotle, Avicenna and Averroes in his work that helped establish Aquinas as the figurehead for the theological triumph known today as Scholasticism.

In this brief section, I have introduced Aquinas's doctrine of angels as an extension of several philosophical and theological antecedents. Although his methodology was eventually challenged by the Nominalism of Scotus and the fideism of figures like Francisco Sanche, Michel de Montaigne, and Pierre Charron, Thomas was confident that faith and reason were two ways of knowing; thus, he derived his axioms from Scripture, philosophy, and nature.[26] This threefold witness allowed him

---

23. Wayne Hankey argues that pseudo-Denys is central to Aquinas's understanding of Scripture, Augustine, and Aristotle. Whether his claim that Aquinas transforms pseudo-Dionysian thought to accommodate a Latin political understanding of hierarchy, metaphysics, and Trinitarian theology is true or not, is less certain. See Hankey, "Dionysian Hierarchy in St. Thomas Aquinas."

24. Inglis, *Spheres of Philosophical Inquiry and the Historiography of Medieval Philosophy*, 267.

25. Raymond of Penafort, "Dominican Documents: Primitive Constitutions," *Dominican Central Province*. http://opcentral.org/blog/the-primitive-constitutions-of-the-order-of-friars-preachers/.

26. Of course figures like Kierkegaard pushed faith to its extremes, whereas Locke

to create an obscure masterpiece (which I shall discuss in the latter half of this chapter) in the form of an angel that is as comfortable on earth as it is in heaven. Thus, out of this sketch of a nobleman who swam, against his family's wishes, into the vortex of the world's greatest questions and propositions, emerges a saint with an angelomorphic contribution all his own. Unlike earlier theologians whose system was to collect and organize the glosses of their predecessors, Thomas, who often used theology and her handmaiden to construct his own views, stands as a systematician in the truest sense of the word. What is remarkable, however, is not that Aquinas is still regarded as a figure that influenced intellectual history to a considerable degree, but that many of his contributions to that history in the form of biblical theology have yet to be widely appreciated, especially at the point of angelology.

## AQUINAS'S ANGELOLOGY IN THE *SUMMA THEOLOGIAE*

Citations and bibliographies reveal that many theologians evaluated Aquinas's sprawling angelology based upon the germane sections in his *Summa Theologiae*, namely 1.1.50–64; 106–14. However, this selective sample only reflects one facet of his angelology: a refined, systematized version that reveals little about Aquinas's perception of the angel in the biblical narratives. Incorporating his biblical commentaries into the discussion will provide a more complete picture by making available an alternative genre by which to evaluate Thomas's angelology. Even so, for the sake of comparison, it would be equally unhelpful not to provide an outline of his angelology as represented in the *Summa Theologiae*. There, as a subset of his discussion about the superessential activity and glory of God, Aquinas probes topics such as the substance, intellect, will, origin, speech, and guardianship of angels, subjects that he tends to avoid in his commentaries on Scripture.

His conclusions in the *Summa Theologiae* are that angels are purely spiritual beings who, despite being much less free when compared with God, surpass humans in every direction—specifically with regard to ontology, morality, and intellectual potency.[27] As supernatural beings, they

---

prioritized reason to the point of nullifying faith; eventually, the logical positivists finished the work that Locke began.

27. The obvious caveat is that angels can sin, but only some have. *ST* 1.63–64,

do not share in the human cycle of life; they have no bodies of any sort, are not born, do not reproduce, and cannot die.[28] Furthermore, since angels are non-corporeal, their perception of creation is neither sense-dependent nor inductive. Whether this means they understand things conceptually, as if seeing the world in terms of mathematical coordinates, or simply that they possess the ability to perceive everything in terms of its Platonic *form*, is impossible to say.[29] Nevertheless, Aquinas believed their perpetually-active minds do not learn, but are divinely infused with the ability to know things instantaneously and perfectly.[30] This, however, is different from knowing *all* things, which is an attribute peculiar to God.[31] Kenelm Foster summarizes, "[Aquinas's] teaching on angelic knowledge might be described as a series of answers to the question, *What would thinking be like with no sensations to think about?*"[32]

## Angelic Communication

The peculiarities of angelic communication coaxed Aquinas to extend epistemology's reach beyond the earthly realm; how he gained such insights into heavenly minds is admittedly more a function of his own deductive logic than a verity of Scripture. He infers, for example, that angels communicate with one another effortlessly by sharing their thoughts telepathically. This is a reasonable assumption since angels do not rely upon faculties humans need to communicate with one another: vocal cords, tympanic membranes, facial expressions, and temporal lobes.[33] Though speculative in tone, one need not follow those who consider such theories unbiblical, because many of Aquinas's second-order hypotheses are derived from first-order, Scriptural principles. His assumptions remind one that angels are described by biblical writers as relational beings (Ps 148:2; Luke 15:10; Heb 12:22), and as spirits who communicate with one another (Mark 12:25; Luke 20:36; Heb 1:14; Isa 6:3; Zech 3:4). Aquinas notes that in Isa 6:3, seraphim, who are phantasms (*phantasmatum*), call

---

109, 114.

28. *ST* 1.60.1–3.

29. See *ST* 1.58.4.

30. *ST* 1.58.1–3.

31. *ST* 1.57.3.

32. *ST* 1.53.

33. *ST* 1.107.1–5.

out to one another their praises of God.[34] My view is that inter-angelic communication operates in similar fashion to the way one communicates with God via unspoken prayer. Given depictions of heaven as a sanctuary where angels praise the Godhead (Rev 5:11–14), it is important to think of angelic communication in terms of its content rather than its inner workings.

Since the Scriptures also include examples of angels interacting with humans, Aquinas entertains the question of whether they should be associated with physical bodies. These narratives do not explain why celestial beings appear to have organic bodies, which they use to speak, move, see, eat, and even wrestle.[35] Aquinas suggests in *ST* 1.51.2 that on occasion, angels "need an assumed body, not for themselves, but on our account; that by conversing familiarly with men they may give evidence of that intellectual companionship which men expect to have with them in the life to come." Also, he adds that Old Testament angelophanies were "a figurative indication that the Word of God would take a human body; because all the apparitions in the Old Testament were ordained to that one whereby the Son of God appeared in the flesh."[36] Calvin arrived at the same conclusion concerning both the angels' assumption of physical bodies and the interpretation of Old Testament angelophanies as Christophanies.[37] By attempting to resolve the dilemma of why angels appeared to have human bodies, Aquinas seized an opportunity to interject christological insights where the biblical record might have implied a truth without communicating it explicitly. This propensity to extract spiritual observations and solutions from the biblical narrative, without psychologizing it, is a hallmark of his angelology.

Scripture provided the raw ingredients for discussions about angel-to-angel and angel-to-human communication, and Aquinas assimilated them according to his own recipe before serving them. Equally significant is that Calvin, rather than removing his apron "whenever the Lord

---

34. *ST* 1.107.4.

35. Gen 18:8; 19:1–3; 32:24–30.

36. *ST* 1.51.2.

37. Calvin writes: "Moreover, when we read that angels appeared in the visible form of men and clothed in garments, we must remember that this was done to offset human weakness." Calvin, *Calvin*, 169. In *Institutes* 1.13.10, "[T]he Word of God was the supreme angel," he conjectured, "who then began, as it were by anticipation, to perform the office of Mediator."

shuts his sacred mouth," offers his readers similar fare.[38] Thus, it is worth entertaining the possibility that Aquinas's angelology only appears radical when isolated and sensationalized. Barth, for instance, caricatures it: "This work of probably the greatest angelogue of all church history unfortunately has nothing whatever to do with the knowledge of the *veritas catholicae fidei*, or with attention and fidelity to the biblical witness to revelation."[39] Curiously, Barth's critique fails to interpret Thomas within the context of medieval hermeneutics, choosing instead to impose Neo-Orthodox expectations.

In the final chapter, I evaluate Barth's angelology as one that virtually cuts off the finite from the infinite; for now, his accusations are either embarrassingly misinformed or intentionally selective regarding Aquinas's relationship to Scripture. Others have since jumped on Barth's bandwagon by mischaracterizing Aquinas's angelology as "not very biblical."[40] Even if one is unfamiliar with his biblical commentaries, it requires an astonishing degree of inattention to overlook the 25,000 biblical quotations throughout the *Summa Theologiae*.[41] "[T]he bare enumeration of the texts of Scripture cited in the *Summa Theologiae*," notes Daniel Kennedy, "fills eighty small-print columns in the Migne edition."[42] Excluding biblical allusions, in questions dealing specifically with angels in part one of the *Summa Theologiae*, I tallied sixty-six biblical citations in questions 50–64, and ninety-four in questions 106–14, equating to 4.4 and 10.4 citations per question, respectively. One could hardly demand more of a biblical presence.

As explained later in this chapter, what some have interpreted as unrestrained imagination in Aquinas's angelology was actually a key element of medieval exegesis, which emphasized allegorical interpretations. As Richard Bauckham observes, "Hopeful imagining is protected from mere speculation in that it is grounded in the promises of God and resourced by the images of scripture."[43] Bauckham's theory, which he applied to eschatology, is pertinent to Aquinas's angelology because Thomas had been attempting to codify the deeper implications of biblical

---

38. Calvin, *Institutes* 3.21.3.

39. Ibid., 392.

40. Lightner, *Handbook of Evangelical Theology*, 132.

41. Valkenberg, *Words of the Living God*, 211–27, 259.

42. Kennedy, "St. Thomas Aquinas," 670.

43. Bauckham, "Eschatology," 317.

imagery. He was one for whom the allegories, imagery, poetic retellings, nuanced explanations, and narrative gaps that punctuate every book of the Bible were invitations to imaginative creativity. The *essence* of what Aquinas asks one to imagine in the *Summa Theologiae*, however, is not only that angels are spiritual beings with an extraordinary ability to experience the cosmos above the level of physical and emotional sensations, but that they epitomize the goodness and ingenuity inherent in God's communicative and creative acts.[44]

## ANGELS AS EMBLEMS OF A PERFECT UNIVERSE

Aquinas's angel was not the quixotic, nymph-like figure commonly associated with contemporary greeting cards; instead, he maintained that angels were requisite beings who symbolized the perfection of the created order.[45] Reasoning that if the cosmos is understood as a celebration of God's grandeur and a direct expression of the goodness of his will and being, he argued that it would be incomplete should there be no heavenly spirits.[46]

> There must be some incorporeal creatures, for what is principally intended by God in creatures is good, and this consists in assimilation to God Himself. And the perfect assimilation of an effect to a cause is accomplished when the effect imitates the cause according to that whereby the cause produces the effect; as heat makes fire. Now, God produces the creature by His intellect and will. Hence the perfection of the universe requires that there should be intellectual creatures.[47]

44. Yet he notes in *ST* 1.63–64 that this is not true of all angels, because the evil angels, though they would naturally have known their existence depended upon God, engaged in a form of wilful ignorance that stemmed from pride, and ultimately resulted in their fall. Their activities and thoughts are the polar opposite of the good angels.

45. Despite his disapproval of Aquinas's angelology, Barth's hyperbolic assertion— "to deny the angels of God is to deny God himself"—captures the spirit of Thomas' interpretation. Barth, *CD* III/3, 486.

46. Ps 19:1; 50:6; Rom 1:19–20.

47. *ST* 1.1.50.1. It appears the Medieval Age identified heat with fire; perhaps a more scientifically accurate statement would be that wood burns because of its participation with fire.

Here, Aquinas defines angels as immaterial intelligences who derive their existence from the Godhead.[48] It is from the divine being that they receive their intrinsically good, rational and spiritual essence.[49] The concept is not unlike Neoplatonic emanationism in that higher forms are more like the One than the lower; though as I noted in chapter 2, biblical angels cannot be entirely reconciled with those diffusive divinities.

Nevertheless, Aquinas's larger conclusion, which ties the existence of angels to the perfection of the universe, is not without its problems. He appears to be saying that the *quality* of the world is contingent upon the *quantity* of angels within that world. This may not imply an inversely proportional relationship between quality and quantity, but his argument does require that the universe contain no less than one incorporeal creature, which *is* a quantitative metric. Also, what is meant that the universe *requires* angels for its perfection? Certainly Aquinas cannot be guilty of committing the anthropomorphic fallacy that the universe itself has volition. Instead, is he not proposing that God is required to create these beings if the universe is to be complete? Although Aquinas argues elsewhere that God creates out of will rather than necessity, it is not clear how a necessity peculiar to the quality of the cosmos, like the need for ontological plenitude, does not also obligate God to create angels.[50] According to his argument, the non-existence of such beings would, *de facto*, be a blemish upon the cosmos and the principal intention of God.

The answer may lie with Leibniz's argument that if God creates, he must create the best of all possible worlds; this would mean the current number of angels simply fulfils the requisite quota. However, Aquinas's premise is easier to digest if approached ontologically, which is why his idea of cosmic perfection is better understood in terms of "completeness." As Aristotle's *Scala Naturae* had already suggested, there is something intellectually satisfying about a world where no categories are left unfilled. However, the problem is that this ideal appears to interpose the cosmos between God and the human being, since the angel, not the human, is the indispensable component which defines completeness. This transposition risks exalting cosmology and angelology over anthropology by subordinating humans, as the *imago Dei* for whom Christ died, beneath the primary objective of a complete or perfect creation.

48. *ST* 1.50.1–2.

49. *ST* 1.61.1–4.

50. *ST* 1.61.2.

These objections may be too anthropocentric, because one may resolve the difficulty by allowing that Aquinas's conclusion gives priority to the attributes of God rather than the cosmos, angel, or human. Rather than assuming that an indispensable element of creation—in this case, the angel—impinges upon God's freedom by forcing him to create in a certain way, one might consider the matter from the perspective of God's nature. In other words, God freely and willingly fits angels into the cosmos because his character, not the existence of the cosmos, requires him to do so. This accentuates the fact that the only thing that God is *obligated* to make is that which is consistent with his pure character, since "what is principally intended by God in creatures is good." Seen in this light, the criterion for determining how angels contribute to the perfection of the universe is determined by whether their role illuminates God's glory and goodness. Of course, the presence of the angels also accentuates the difference between God and the material world, further avoiding the difficulty of having divinity and corporeality next to one another on the ontological ladder. It is more significant that angels fill a *moral* gap between God and humanity. Even so, it may still be beneficial to retain the idea that Aquinas's "necessary angel" interposes the objective universe between God and humanity, that is, if it produces the fruit of humility or, better yet, resacralizes humanity's perception of creation as a fellow-participant in worship on a cosmic scale.[51]

Nonetheless, directing his study of Scripture and classical philosophy toward the systematization of doctrine in the *Summa Theologiae* allowed Aquinas to establish his reputation as a leading angelogue. He subtly defends his rationale by oscillating between the doctrine's theological and philosophical implications: creatures, celestial or terrestrial, bear a relationship to the rest of creation. This relationship may be interpersonal, ontological, moral, or as the following sections argue, theological. It remains to be seen whether the future of angelology will have room for Aquinas's questions about how angels communicate, whether they are necessary for the perfection of the universe, or how they move through space. It is important, nonetheless, to uphold the value of an angelology that reconciles the supernatural and physical worlds, faith and reason, special and natural revelation. His dialectic approach may have limited appeal to those outside the discipline and his desire to harmonize as much truth as possible opened his angelology to criticism

---

51. Many instances exist of a biblical writer ascribing characteristics of worship to the creation.

from theologians like Barth, who finds it too exploratory. Yet in defense of Thomas, I remind the reader that even Calvin speculated concerning the purpose of embodied angels and offered christological readings of Old Testament angelophanies (as did Barth).[52]

One step toward alleviating the perception of Aquinas's angelology as overly philosophical is to establish the primacy of Scripture in his teaching, not simply by pointing to the 25,000 citations in the *Summa Theologiae*, but by representing his general interpretive model. Branding him as unbiblical perversely misses the point of his work. He was a theology professor dedicated to the formation of aspiring clerics, and Scripture was his *axis mundi*. While he penned a handful of commentaries on Aristotle's work, he never taught a course on Aristotle's philosophy. The same holds true for Aquinas's other private writings; neither the *Summa Contra Gentiles* nor the *Summa Theologiae* were ever taught in his classroom.[53]

Although it was necessary to illustrate the philosophical implications surrounding higher order beings in *Summa Theologiae* 1.1.50–64; 106–14, the remainder of the chapter focuses upon Aquinas's interaction with angels in the biblical texts themselves. There we see a side of him that calls into question the wax nose that he was a dry academic or more parts philosopher than theologian. Admittedly, the *Summa Theologiae* includes little of his warm, living faith and playful commentary, so it is easy to forget the man whose passion for God was so consuming that he left behind his family's two castles and middle-nobility for the Dominican order, dedicated himself to learning, synthesizing, teaching, and writing some of the greatest theological literature ever known, before abandoning it after what some believe was an epiphanic experience in December of 1273, stating "I cannot [continue writing], because all that I have written seems like straw to me."[54] It is to the undocumented angelology of Aquinas the biblical commentator and exegete that we shall now turn.

52. Barth, *CD III/3*, 490. Barth, however, does not demonstrate how his interpretation of Gen 18 as a Christophany is "faithful to the biblical witness to revelation."

53. One exception to this rule, according to L. E. Boyle, is his commentary on the first book of Peter

Lombard's *Liber Sententiarum*, which he taught while in Rome from 1265–66. See Boyle, *The Setting of the Summa Theologiae of Saint Thomas*, 8–15. Also, Sheets, "The Scriptural Dimension of St. Thomas."

54. Tugwell, *Albert and Thomas*, 266.

## HERMENEUTICS AND ANGELOLOGY IN AQUINAS'S BIBLICAL COMMENTARIES

While nearly all Aquinas's philosophical works have been formally translated and published in English, the same is true of roughly *half* of his biblical commentaries.[55] Aside from *Catena Aurea*, which covers all four Gospels, Aquinas penned commentaries on twenty-one books of the Bible: Psalms, Job, Isaiah, Jeremiah, Lamentations, Matthew, John, Romans, 1 and 2 Corinthians, Galatians, Ephesians, Philippians, Colossians, 1 and 2 Thessalonians, 1 and 2 Timothy, Titus, Philemon, and Hebrews; although early records indicate that he also wrote a commentary on Song of Songs, the work remains undiscovered. The chronology for these works is uncertain, though several (Isaiah, Matthew, John) were classroom lectures recorded by a student or assistant. Regardless, Aquinas is among the leading commentators of the medieval age, a fact often unnoticed by his critics. Though in light of the obscurity of his exegetical work, it is quite understandable why some scholars, like Barth, seem from their bibliographies to be familiar with only the *Summa Theologiae* and *Summa Contra Gentiles*.

Aquinas maintained that Scripture was his primary authority, not as a *primus inter pares*, but as the uniquely revealed Word of God.[56] This cardinal belief is still held by countless Christians today, but in Aquinas it has neither credulous nor literalistic overtones. For instance, he was one of the earliest theologians to reflect seriously upon the human author's role in divine revelation; and while emphasizing the literal meaning of Scripture in his *Summa Theologiae*, his preference for the allegorical approach in his commentaries on Scripture has a profound influence on his angelology.[57] He held the Bible to be divinely inspired, but employed a

---

55. See Nicholas Healy's foreword, which explains why the commentaries are so unfamiliar, in Weinandy, *Aquinas on Scripture*. It should be noted that the Leonine Commission of the Vatican and the Dominican Order are currently working to produce a critical text of all Aquinas's writings.

56. *ST* 1.1.8.

57. Aquinas recognized that biblical interpretation needed to maintain two factors: while God was the ultimate author of Scripture, human authors were the instrumental cause (see *ST* 1.1.8–9). Many fathers like Augustine stressed the author as more of an accessory of the Spirit than an individual (*On Christian Doctrine*, 3.27). See also, Jerome (*Epist* 70.7), and Gregory the Great, who writes in the preface his commentary on Job, "But who was the writer, it is very superfluous to enquire; since at any rate the Holy Spirit is confidently believed to have been the Author."

broad hermeneutical method, allowing him to pose multiple meanings for a single passage. To propound only one meaning would be to prune the subtlety, mystery, and paradox from the text. Although this approach moves his angelology in a less philosophical direction from what we have seen in the *Summa Theologiae*, his elucidation requires a modicum of charity on the modern reader's part as it reveals the silhouette of a man who occasionally proffers subjective interpretations, albeit with the best of intentions.

There are factors that explain why Thomas, unlike contemporary theologians who read the same Scriptures, tends to see angels emerging from the most unlikely verses. He enumerates in the *Summa Theologiae*, four senses in which Scripture communicates its message: literally, allegorically, morally, and eschatologically. While not believing all four could be found in every passage, he maintained the literal meaning was always present. "Thus in Holy Writ no confusion results, for all the senses are founded on one—the literal—from which alone can any argument be drawn."[58] Yet his angelology is distinctive because it projects its presence upon various passages via an allegorized creation. Today, literal views of Scripture are often associated with Christian conservatism, while metaphorical/allegorical interpretations are linked with liberalism. For Aquinas no such conflict exists. In the commentaries, he treats the world as an equally physical and supernatural realm, a sphere where ordinary objects become sacred and sacred objects are spoken of in ordinary terms.

This is not to suggest that Aquinas frequently glossed over the literal sense of a verse, but when speaking of angels, he appears to be more involved with the allegorical sense. Was this because of the interpretive flexibility it offered him, or because the ancestral voices of church doctors echoed in his head? "We have drawn the thin lines of history," wrote Jerome, "now let us set our hand to allegory";[59] Augustine said, "We have heard the fact; let us look into the mystery";[60] and Aquinas's master, Gregory: "Thus far let it suffice for us to have gone through the words of the history; let the discussion of the exposition now convert itself to investigate the mysteries of the allegory."[61] Whatever the case, Aquinas

---

58. *ST* 1.10.

59. *Tenues historiae lineas duximus, nunc allegoriae imprimamus manum.* Jerome, "Commentariorum In Amos Prophetam Libri Tres," *PL*, 25, 1063 D. 317.

60. *Factum audivimus, mysterium requiramus.* Augustine, "Evangelium Joannis Tractatus CXXIV," *PL*, 35, 1760.6.

61. *Sed quia superficies historiae sub brevitate discussimus, quid in his de intellectu*

had an arsenal of compelling theological observations to share, regardless of which sense he chose to emphasize; he often indicated when moving beyond the text's literal sense with the qualifier, "*Sed mystice*."

It would be unreasonable to expect his biblical commentaries to resemble technical, exegetical works in the contemporary sense; for although one will find an occasional reference to the original meaning of a word, Aquinas's genius lies in his discursive maneuvering from text to concept and back to text again, highlighting unobvious relationships between passages in the process.[62] While this presents a challenge for codifying an angelology directly from his commentaries, a pattern emerges from his discussion of verses that feature angels and verses that inspired Aquinas to discuss angels. Angels were a product of his devotion and highlight his beliefs—while the same could be said about pseudo-Denys, Aquinas differs in that his observations are dense with biblical citations, as if compensating for the lack of the same in his predecessor.[63]

The commentaries exhibit Thomas's stylistic panache, fully discharged as a means of stretching and sanctifying the reader's imagination.[64] To convey this idea in musical terms: the *Summae* depict Aquinas as the classical impresario whose command of logic, Scripture, fathers, and philosophers resulted in a highly structured, if slightly synthetic, arrangement; the biblical commentaries, however, are expressive and indulgent, as if informed by the idiosyncratic freedom of improvisational jazz. Thus, this chapter proposes that within the amphitheater of Aquinas's biblical commentaries, angels syncopate the physical world by playing under the auspices of birds, holy people, sacred objects, and Scripture. It

---

*mystico lateat perpendamus.* Gregory the Great, "Moralium Libri Sive Expositio In Librum Beati Job. Pars II," *PL* 76, 139.8.

62. Aquinas does, however, demonstrate an appreciation for text criticism in his commentaries, such as the following comment from his work on Ps 33:8: "Now many codices have 'the Angel of the lord encamps.' Jerome has 'the Angel of the lord encircles about those who fear him.'" (*Multi codices habent, immittit angelus Domini. Hieronymus habet, circumdat angelus Domini in gyro timentes eum.*) McDonald and Loughlin, trans., *St. Thomas's Commentary on the Psalms* [cited 23 September 2009]. Online: http://www4.desales.edu/~philtheo/loughlin/ATP/Psalm_33.html.

63. "The Canonical Scriptures alone are the rule of faith," writes Aquinas. See chapter 21 n. 2656 in Weisheipl and Larcher, trans., *Commentary on the Gospel of John* [ctied 8 December 2009] Online: www.diafrica.org/kenny/CDtexts/SSJohn.htm.

64. See Ryan, *Thomas Aquinas as Reader of the Psalms*. Ryan believes that Aquinas's commentaries, most of which originated as lectures, reflect his attempts to develop his students' memories; I would add their imaginations to this as well.

is in this arena that one hears his ancient refrain, written to harmonize the respective realms of spirit and matter.

## Angels and Avian Imagery

The first example of this pattern comes from Thomas's commentary on Ps 16, where the writer petitions God in verse 8 "Protect me under the shadow of thy wings."[65] Aquinas suggests that the psalmist is using "shadow" and "wings" to evoke a twofold metaphor (*duplex metaphora*) about divine protection; an observation he supports by evoking an image from the natural world, "a hen protects her chicks in her wings against a bird of prey, just as God defends the just from the rapacity of the demons in his wings." Yet Aquinas clarifies that the verse should actually be interpreted to mean "under the protection of the angels," a view he validates from Ps 90:11, "For he hath given his angels charge over thee." Thus he intimates that the wings of God represent angels who protect the righteous as a hen does her brood. This rather free treatment of the passage creates a new lens through which to see it, but given his suggestion in the same passage that the chief threat to one's security is the *rapacitas daemonum,* it is reasonable that Aquinas calls to mind the *custodia angelorum.*

He takes a final pass at the verse by offering that "the two wings are the two arms of Christ extended on the cross," since it is written in Deut 32 that "He spread his wings, and hath taken them and carried them on his shoulders."[66] Nowhere in Scripture are Jesus' arms referred to as wings.[67] Aquinas is aware that neither God nor angels have wings.[68] Nevertheless, he brings them together in his explanation, ostensibly because each defends those under their care. More importantly, he is deepening the meaning of the passage by introducing connections between God, the crucified Christ, and the angels by way of a mother hen (an image which Jesus uses of himself in Matt 23:37 and Luke 13:34). Since intelligible objects correspond to heavenly realities, Aquinas uses them to establish an intersection between the physical and spiritual worlds via intrinsic

65. Note that this section follows the Vulgate's enumeration of the Psalms, which differs slightly from translations arising from the Masoretic Text.

66. McDonald and Loughlin, trans., *St. Thomas's Commentary on the Psalms,* http://www4.desales.edu/~philtheo/loughlin/ATP/Psalm_16.html.

67. Though, Origen interprets Christ's arms as wings in the *Catena Aurea* at Matt 23:37.

68. *ST* 1.51.1–3.

analogy.[69] Just as humans represent the *imago Dei*, he sees a similar complementarity between the temporal and eternal—so that a wing or a bird exemplifies angelic and divine activity. Thus, one way God makes possible a caring world is to ordain the angels to protect his creation beneath their, and Christ's, proverbial wings.[70]

In his biblical commentaries, Aquinas treats Scripture as a maze of interconnected paths conjoining heaven and earth. One can map his preferred route to his exegetical destination thus: he embarks by commenting upon each clause in the verse (sometimes to a fault); meanders through several interpretations in light of significant doctrinal landmarks; and finally, cites scriptures and/or authorities who serve as his travelling companions and support his conclusion(s). For instance, note that in Ps 16:8 alone, he clusters the doctrines of providence, atonement, and angelology beneath the metaphorical image of a bird's wings. Hughes Old labels this heavy reliance upon allegorical interpretation as "the bane of medieval preaching."[71] Allegorical approaches may obfuscate the biblical message if they do not point one, as Thomas does, to God and his works.[72] However, his methods were orthodox by medieval standards. So as paradigms change, centuries from now one may find theologians imposing similar anachronistic expectations upon Old's criteria. Nevertheless, by mixing doctrines, imagery, and biblical verses in Ps 16:8, Aquinas affirms two ways God protects the just: he shields souls under the "wings" of Christ's atonement, and defends bodies under the "wings," or guardianship, of angels.

In a second example, from his analysis of Ps 49:9–11, Aquinas takes greater interpretive liberties in applying avian imagery to angels. In the passage, YHWH rejects Israel's ritual sacrifices of bulls and goats because he already owns every animal of the wood and plain and knows all the birds of the air. First, Aquinas observes that three things were offered to

69. This might also include moral lessons, as when he interprets the "wings" described in the psalmist's desire to fly to God with the wings of a dove (55:6) to mean three things: moral virtue, charity, and wisdom.

70. He also notes in his commentary on Ps 18:10, that "*Item volavit super pennas ventorum, idest super scientiam angelorum: Ps. 103: Qui facit angelos suos spiritus etc.*" So God's own "flight" upon the wings of the wind signifies that angelic knowledge is subordinate to God's.

71. Old, *The Reading and Preaching of the Scriptures in the Worship of the Christian Church*, 3:222.

72. For a history of the exegetical tradition, McNally, *The Bible in the Early Middle Ages*, 53–61.

God under the Mosaic covenant: "four-footed animals, birds and fruit," then transitions with the imaginative assertion that, "mystically [speaking], different kinds of people can be designated by these very animals." After comparing segments of humanity to either domesticated or wild beasts, he returns to the verse to declare that the birds are "to be understood as the holy angels, who are a likeness [to them]."[73] This association between the bird and the angel may be based upon the idea that just as animals and humans occupy the terrestrial sphere, birds and angels live closer to the vault of heaven than humans. It could also refer to the notion that the swiftness with which birds move through the air is like the way angels hasten to do the will of God.

Nonetheless, in Aquinas's world, animals metamorphose into people and birds become a type of angel. The Scriptures become a spiritual lesson *ab natura*. While this method does not deny the passage's literal sense, he is clearly not satisfied until every detail has been accounted for and "supernaturalized." Nicholas Healy explains that during Thomas's era, "the visible surface of the text, its 'literal' sense, was regarded as of secondary importance compared with its invisible depths, for it was in the latter that the true meaning of the text lay, through which one might ascend to God."[74] These are not gratuitous associations, however; they allow Aquinas to introduce a doctrinal layer into the passage by positing a correspondence between birds and angels.

Thomas's angelocentric reading of references to wings and birds in passages like the ones in Pss 16 and 49 distinguishes him from pseudo-Denys, who stressed the dissimilarities between the two orders, emphasizing that birdlike qualities associated with angels are merely accommodations to the human mind. "We cannot," insists pseudo-Denys, "as mad people do, profanely visualize these heavenly and godlike intelligences as actually having numerous feet and faces. . . . They do not have the curved beak of the eagle or the wings and feathers of birds."[75] While Aquinas affirms the same point in his discussion of the angelic substance in *Summa Theologiae* 1.1.50–53, he surpasses his predecessor by styling the bird itself as a symbolic angel. These examples illustrate both Aquinas's commitment to a universe thick with angels and his passion to connect heaven with the commonplace, but some might wonder whether

---

73. Ibid., literally "*qui sunt similitude*."

74. Healy, "Introduction," 7.

75. *CH* 137A.

his angelology arises from, or is foisted upon, the text. His imaginative explanations are insightful, however, because rather than glossing over the word "bird" or becoming preoccupied with technical, linguistic matters like the word's etymology, case, or gender, he chooses an interpretive format that accommodates perfectly the metaphorical and symbolic nature of Pss 16 and 49.

Aquinas harmonizes the Old Testament angelology of divine transcendence and pseudo-Denys's angelology of divine immanence by using angels to illustrate the transcendence of the immanent, material world. Additionally, laying an angel-shaped template alongside images of birds and winged animals allows him to uphold the rich history of Christian symbolism with respect to birds. Birds are a symbol of a higher realm and lend themselves to spiritual interpretations. Scripture hosts numerous examples of this type of imagery. For instance, doves are repeatedly used to convey deeper, spiritual truths: the dove bearing an olive branch in the Noah story is a peaceful symbol; throughout the Psalms the writer associates a dove with vulnerability, as in Ps 74:19, "Do not deliver the soul of your dove to the wild animals"; in various places in the Song of Songs, the beauty of the young woman is compared to a dove; the Holy Spirit is said to descend in the likeness of a dove in Mark 1:10; and Jesus uses the dove to symbolize innocence in Matt 10:16. This perfectly scriptural pattern challenges those who qualify Aquinas's angelology as "unbiblical."[76]

His commentaries on Pss 16 and 49 demonstrate how his hermeneutic affected his angelology, helping to explain why those unfamiliar with Scripture's fourfold sense may object to his angelology, though diversity of meaning was *de rigueur* during his era. Because he thought of words as signs of *things* and was convinced that those things (birds/wings, in this case) also retain a deeper significance, he anchored the spiritual to the literal. He writes in *Summa Theologiae* 1.1.10, "So, whereas in every

76. There are a number of similar expressions concerning birds in non-biblical works; Dante referred to angels as "birds" in the *Purgatorio*. See 2.37 and 4.128. Also, Odo, bishop of Tusculum described humans as different species of birds in "Sermon 92." Some, he says, are innocent like the dove; others, like the swallow, enjoy human company; persons like the turtle-dove are suited to solitude; and those who have a spiritual longing are symbolized by high-flying birds. Cirlot, *A Dictionary of Symbols*, 28. More recently, David Brown illustrates this history of animals as characteristic of medieval attitudes; see Brown, *God and Enchantment of Place*, 98–104. Andrew Linzey's *Animal Theology* explores the role of animals in the history of theology through a critical lens; however, he considers much of theology to be anthropocentric, and urges the reader to move beyond the abstract discussion of animals to consider moral issues (e.g., hunting, experimentation, genetic engineering, etc.).

other science things are signified by words, this science [of theology] has the property, that the things signified by the words have themselves also a signification." Aquinas is not limited by the Bible like the modern exegete for whom the allegorical or spiritual approach is the exception. He treats Scripture as a sacred gallery where the theologian-artist draws inspiration from the narrative, then captures its fullest sense by painting a panoramic, multi-perspectival, landscape.

Given his convictions about the multidimensional character of the biblical message, the reality of higher order beings and the power of a sanctified analogy, it is only natural that Aquinas perceives and portrays angels where today's biblical scholars may not. He agrees with Aristotle that the mind conceives things only by way of phantasms, or mental images.[77] Therefore, since it is impossible to produce a mental image of an incorporeal being like an angel, he argues that these are known "by comparison with sensible bodies of which there are phantasms . . . only by way of remotion or by some comparison to corporeal things."[78] While angels exist primarily as a principle of faith derived from Scripture, Thomas's reinterpretation of analogous (avian) imagery allows angels to become visible, in a sense; comparatively, Denys was not so liberal with his angels, limiting such comparisons to Christ and the bishop, and only once for each.[79] Nonetheless, in the creative transposition of the angel and the bird, Aquinas is not merely dabbling with words, but pulling heaven toward the earth via the animal kingdom. Unsurprisingly, his interpretation of Pss 16 and 49 are not the only instances where he posits imaginative connections between earthly creatures and angels. Next, we turn to consider how he compares angels and humans.

## Angels and Human Beings

The previous section highlights Aquinas's angelomorphic interpretation of birds in his biblical commentaries, maintaining that the pattern derives, at its deepest level, from his desire to connect heaven and earth. One may dispute the strength of this conclusion by arguing that Hebrew poetry is a genre that happens to be particularly compatible with symbolic explanations. However, this same pattern also emerges in his

77. *ST* 1.84.7; *De Anima* 3.7.

78. Ibid.

79. *CH* 181D *CH* 293A.

commentaries on the Gospels and New Testament letters. The following examples demonstrate five instances where Aquinas not only extends this subtle mechanism to other pericopes, but ascends the ontological ladder, associating humans with celestial beings.

The first example appears in his reading of Gal 3:19, a passage that discusses the Mosaic law as "being ordained by angels in the hand of a mediator." Playing with the semantic range of the word "angels," Aquinas asserts that the verse refers to "the messengers of God, namely, Moses and Aaron."[80] It is possible that he interprets the passage this way to emphasize the importance of these two human representatives of the law. Yet his unambiguous analysis of the narrative in *Summa Theologiae* 1.2.98.3—entitled "Whether the Old Law was Given through the Angels?"—clearly affirms that the old law was indeed given to Moses though *heavenly* beings. This seeming inconsistency between the two accounts shows Aquinas applying different hermeneutical principles for stylistic purposes: on one hand, he upholds the literal sense of the passage in the *Summa Theologiae*, but on the other, advocates an allegorical interpretation in Galatians by rendering Moses and Aaron as angels. It should be noted, however, that Thomas confirms elsewhere in the commentary that the passage also refers to literal, angelic beings.[81]

As one steps further away from the text and commentary an additional explanation for the angel/human hypostasis appears, which has to do with Moses' role within Aquinas's general interpretation of Galatians. The Epistle itself does not mention Moses. Yet in Aquinas's commentary on the third chapter alone, the patriarch is mentioned five times. Aquinas typically interprets in accordance with his perception of the biblical author's primary themes, a pattern he normally explains in the opening paragraphs of each commentary. For instance, in his prologue to Galatians, he is concerned with the *superiority* of the "new" to that which is "old" (i.e., NT/OT, gospel/law, forgiveness/guilt). So in light of 190 uses of "old" or "oldness" in this commentary, it is conceivable that Thomas is trying to avoid first-order comparisons between aeviternal angels and the "temporal things in the Old Law." It is easier to deputize Moses and Aaron as temporary angels, since, like the old law, they both passed away.

---

80. Larcher, trans., *Commentary on St. Paul's Epistle to the Galatians* [cited 12 October 2009]. Online: www.diafrica.org/kenny/CDtexts/SSGalatians.htm.

81. "Or: by angels, i.e., by the ministry of angels: 'You have received the law by the disposition of angels' (Acts 7:53). And it was given by angels, because it was not fitting that it be given by the Son, Who is greater . . . ."

Yet given the honor shown to Moses in his Galatians commentary, and in light of the following examples where Aquinas depicts other human messengers as angels, it is equally possible that he interprets the term "angel" here out of respect for the mediatorial office held by Moses and Aaron.

The second instance of angelic humanity also appears in his commentary on Galatians. In 4:14, St. Paul expresses gratitude for the assembly's receptiveness to his preaching, treating him like an angel or even Christ himself. Here, Aquinas infers that not only was the apostle received "with the honor accorded to a messenger announcing God's words," but that it is "[f]or this reason preachers are called angels: 'They shall seek the law at the priest's mouth, because he is the angel of the Lord of hosts' (Mal 2:7)."[82] Whether or not he viewed Paul's analogy as an opportunity to remind the reader that angel/preacher comparisons are not without biblical precedent, Aquinas is more faithful to the original language here than he was in either Pss 16 or 49, where he introduced the angel into the passage.

Although he understood the reference to *angelon* in Gal 4:14 to mean "a supernatural being," it is curious that in Mal 2:7, the verse he uses to corroborate his point, he interprets *mal'ak* as "angel" rather than the usual "messenger" preferred by modern translations. Given Thomas's hermeneutic, it is certainly possible that this was an intentional oversight for rhetorical and stylistic purposes. It is impossible to say whether this is Aquinas's imposition upon the text or a misunderstanding following his use of the Vulgate's rendering: *"labia enim sacerdotis custodient scientiam et legem requirent ex ore eius quia angelus Domini exercituum est."* Also peculiar is the Vulgate's use of *angelus* here rather than *nuntius* or *legatus*, terms it typically employs for human messengers; this pattern is repeated in Isa 18:2; 33:3–6.[83] Nevertheless, while St. Paul was treated like an angel, Aquinas implies from Mal 2:7 that one ought to consider all *praedicatores* as such. It is possible that the appearance of *angelus* influenced Aquinas's interpretation, but the primary matter is that, as with Moses and Aaron, he fastens heaven and earth together again by using incorporeal angels to advance a figurative and hallowed portrait of God's servants.[84]

82. Ibid. The word used in Mal 2:7 is *mal'ak*.

83. It is clear from Aquinas's *Commentary on John* that the Vulgate influenced his interpretation of Isaiah as well; he writes: "Or, the angels are, according to Augustine, the preachers of Christ: 'Go, swift angels, to a nation rent and torn to pieces,' as it says in Isa 18:2."

84. To my knowledge, he does not make this claim for the non-ordained believer

Thomas adopts the angel to affirm preaching as a form of exalted speech, which brings heaven to earth in a more profound way than might the image of a protective bird. In fact, Aquinas intimates in *Summa Theologiae* 1.117.2 that the preaching act is occasionally *super*-angelic: "from the preaching [*praedicantibus*] of the apostles the angels learned certain mysteries." Writing along similar lines in his *Treatise on the Formation of Preachers* is Humbert of Romans, the fifth Master of the Dominican order and Aquinas's contemporary. Humbert reasoned that preachers inhabit a noble, angelic, and divine office: preaching is inherently noble due to its apostolic roots, it is angelic because the angels preach (here, he cites Rev 5:2 and Luke 2:10), and finally, since the Son of God was a preacher, it is divine. Humbert concludes neatly, "the apostles are the most outstanding of all the saints, the angels are the most outstanding of all creatures, and in all that exists, nothing is more outstanding than God. So a job which is apostolic, angelic, and divine must indeed be outstanding!"[85]

Like Humbert, Aquinas was a Dominican, an order that emphasizes the ministry of preaching. So it is little wonder that his esteem for preachers leads him to invoke passages like Mal 2:7 as proof of the angelic character of preaching and the preacher. For instance, when discussing the gift of tongues in his commentary on 1 Cor 13:1, Aquinas takes the reader through a series of premises about the properties of corporeal and incorporeal beings in order to substantiate a similar conclusion.[86]

> But it should be noted what is meant by the tongues of angels. For since the tongue is a bodily member and to its use pertains the gift of tongues, which is sometimes called a tongue, as will be clear, neither seems to belong to angels, who do not have members. Therefore, it can be said that by angels are understood men with the office of angels, namely, who announce divine things to other men according to Mal 2:7: "The lips of the priest should guard knowledge, and men should seek instruction from his mouth, for he is the angel of the Lord of hosts."[87]

---

outside of his general eschatological hope in *ST* 1.98.2 and *SCG* 3.57.1–3, which I discuss below.

85. In Tugwell, *Early Dominicans: Selected Writings*, 184–85.

86. And again in his commentary on Ps 8, as well as in Gal 3:19, which I discussed earlier.

87. Larcher, *Commentary by Saint Thomas Aquinas on the First Epistle to the Corinthians*.

Here again, the mechanics of Aquinas's hermeneutical method are exposed: he interprets Scripture with Scripture along allegorical lines in order to vest angels in earthen vessels. It is especially interesting, however, that he takes the hyperbolic phrase concerning "tongues of angels" literally, yet uses the language of angels in both 1 Cor 13:1 and Mal 2:7 to make a metaphorical point.

Thus far, Aquinas has only drawn correlations between angels and male figures, which may sound patriarchal to a twenty-first-century reader, especially since he clearly held that only *viri*, in the strict sense of the word, may hold the "office of angels."[88] To his credit, Thomas did not reserve his angelomorphic interpretations for males alone when making conceptual transitions between the human and the angel. In his commentary on John 20:14–18, he remarks that Mary Magdalene not only enjoyed "the office of an *apostle* . . . [because] it was her task to announce our Lord's resurrection to the disciples," but that "she had the privilege of being a *prophet* because she was worthy enough to see the angels" at Christ's tomb. What makes this more scintillating is his conclusion that "she had the *dignity or rank of an angel* insofar as she looked upon Christ, on whom the angels desire to look."[89] In Thomas's opinion, Mary Magdalene, who beheld Christ and proclaimed the resurrection to his disciples, is comparable to the apostles, prophets, and angels. He applies a similar judgment to the Virgin Mary, whom he regarded as superior to angels.[90] Where Denys suggested similar angelic interpretations of Christ and the bishop, Aquinas's interpretive system is broader in scope and egalitarian enough to "angelize" biblical figures based upon their virtues rather than their genders, reminding one that incorporeal beings are themselves, sexless.

---

88. In *ST* II.2.177.2, he writes, "publicly, addressing oneself to the whole church . . . is not permitted to women. First and chiefly, on account of the condition attaching to the female sex, whereby woman should be subject to man. . . . Secondly, lest men's minds be enticed to lust. . . . Thirdly, because as a rule women are not perfected in wisdom, so as to be fit to be entrusted with public teaching." Also interesting is that in *ST* 3.67.4, he permitted that a woman could baptize in an emergency, adding that while it would be a sin for her to do so in normal circumstances, "there would be no need of rebaptism."

89. Emphasis added in all three quotations pertaining to the Magdalene.

90. He remarks in *ST* 3.30.2, "The Mother of God was above the angels as regards the dignity to which she was chosen by God." In Aquinas's *Catena Aurea*, he records Jerome's observation of Luke 2:26, "And rightly an angel is sent to the virgin, because the virgin state is ever akin to that of angels."

Thomas's proclivity for correlating angels with sacred offices and holy individuals was not without its limits. He qualifies and clarifies this relationship in his commentary on Ps 8 by affirming a clear ontological separation between orders of being, "The nature above humans is two-fold, namely, the divine and the angelic."[91] Aquinas expands on this line of demarcation when discussing John the Baptist in his commentary on John 1:7:

> [The Evangelist] declares "there was a man." This excludes at the very start the perverse opinion of certain heretics who were in error on the condition or nature of John. They believed that John was an angel in nature, basing themselves on the words of the Lord, "I send my messenger [*angelum*] before you, who will prepare your way" (Matt 11:10); and likewise in Mark (1:2). But the Evangelist rejects this, saying, there was a *man* by nature, not an angel. . . . Indeed, although John was not an angel in nature, he was so by his office, because he was sent by God. For the distinctive office of angels is that they are sent by God and are messengers of God. "All are ministering spirits, sent to serve" (Heb 1:14). Hence it is that "angel" means "messenger." And so men who are sent by God to announce something can be called angels. "Haggai the messenger of the Lord" (Hg 1:13).[92]

Likewise, in his commentary on Galatians, Thomas stresses the profound intellectual differences between angels and humans despite their common share in the *imago Dei*, "The image of God is found in the angels by the simple intuition of truth, without any inquiry; but in humans discursively: and therefore in man only in a certain small degree."[93]

What these little-studied passages reveal is that Aquinas's approach is imaginative enough to propose degrees of equivalence between angels and other beings, yet operates within hermeneutical boundaries that forbade him to erase ontological categories in the process.[94] Though the

91. McDonald and Loughlin, trans. *St. Thomas's Commentary on the Psalms,* http://www4.desales.edu/~philtheo/loughlin/ATP/Psalm_8.html.

92. Given the context, I have substituted "perverse" in place of Weisheipl's "incorrect" because I believe it is a better fit for Thomas' use of *perversam*. Weisheipl and Larcher, trans., *Commentary on the Gospel of John* [ctied 8 December 2009]. Online: www.diafrica.org/kenny/CDtexts/SSJohn.htm.

93. Literally: *In angelis invenitur imago Dei per simplicem intuitum veritatis, absque inquisitione; in homo vero per discursum; et ideo in homine aliquantulum.* Larcher, *Galatians.*

94. See Barth's criticism (*CD III.,* 482) of E. Peterson for embracing views similar

same holds true with respect to his correlation between birds and angels, a fascinating relationship emerges in his interpretation of angelology *vis-à-vis* the biblical text.[95] Namely, Aquinas associated heavenly beings with each level of existence: pure spirit (angels), matter and spirit (human clergy), and pure matter (birds) in his biblical commentary.[96] Thus, his angelology accommodates an informal middle-ground of being where angelic forms coexist within the creation, if only in an analogical sense.[97]

Regardless of whether this synthesis was intentional, it suggests a refreshing degree of optimism in Aquinas's interpretation of Scripture and the angels that has rarely been seen since. Even in the face of a robust harmartiology preventing him from embracing an entirely angelic view of life on earth, he maintains an *eschatological* hope for a realized connection between angels and humans. In his commentary on Hebrews, for example, Aquinas reminds his reader that since Jesus spoke in Matt 22:30 of the believer's life in paradise in terms of correspondence with

---

to that of Aquinas. In chapter 12 of the *Celestial Hierarchy*, Denys also affirms that the angel/human comparison is valid for hierarchs and those who are lovers of God "in the highest degree."

95. Alan Torrance's discussion of Battista Mondin is helpful here. He identifies the relationship between angels and birds as an analogy of proper proportionality: angelic flight is to an angel what avian flight is to birds. See Torrance, *Persons in Communion*, 142.

96. The same is also true outside his biblical commentaries, especially as far as the connection between angels and humans are concerned. He writes in *SCG* 3.57.1–3, "Every intelligence naturally desires the vision of the divine substance. But a natural desire cannot be in vain. Any and every created intelligence then can arrive at the vision of the divine substance; and inferiority of nature is no impediment. Hence the Lord promises to man the glory of the angels: They shall be as the angels of God in Heaven (Mat. 22:30); and in the Apocalypse the same measure is said to be of man and angel: the measure of a man, that is, of an angel (Apoc. 21:17). Therefore often in Holy Scripture the angels are described in the form of men, either entirely so, as with the angels who appeared to Abraham (Gen. 18), or partially, as with the living creatures of whom it is said that the hand of a man was under their wings (Eze. 1:8)."

97. S. J. Davis explores another incarnation of this phenomenon in Ibn Kātib Qaysar's commentary on the book of Revelation where Qaysar conflates the apostle John and the angel in Rev 1:1 because of a mistranslation of the Bohairic Coptic text. Qaysar understood it to say, "The revelatory vision of Jesus Christ that God gave to him who taught his servants about what must come to pass quickly and who gave a sign to them and sent it by way of his angel, his servant John," rather than, ". . . having sent them through his angel to his servant John." Despite the mistranslation, Qaysar runs with the idea of the angel-apostle and characterizes the apostles as uniquely gifted, angelic messengers. Davis, "Introducing an Arabic Commentary on the Apocalypse: Ibn Kātib Qaysar on Revelation."

the angelic nature, it is critical to view the nature of humans and angels in terms of this future state, where each is "without sin in relation to happiness," a point at which "they are then equal."[98]

In this section, I examined the angelic motif in Aquinas's biblical commentaries as a way of drawing attention to his novel analysis of Scripture. His approach was not only dissimilar to modern biblical interpretation, but adds much-needed texture to his comparatively formal discussion of angels in the *Summa Theologiae*. He maintained a reasonable balance between the angel as a literal and allegorical being: they truly existed, but could be interjected into various pericopes for theological reasons. This sanctified, imaginative approach is lacking in modern angelologies, which tend to either deny or over-objectify angels. I defended his angelology by establishing him as an orthodox commentator (by the standards of thirteenth-century exegesis) who distinguished himself by treating the Bible as both an object of faith and an invitation to religio-philosophical inquiry.

I also demonstrated a significant pattern within his commentaries where Aquinas's hermeneutical assumptions lead him to draw allegorical connections between angels, birds, and holy people/offices. This cluster of references establishes the complexity of his interpretation of Scripture, permitting me to reveal uncharted aspects of his angelology absent in his other works. Thomas's angels portray the Scriptures and the world as spheres where the most innocuous figure could be transformed if only seen in a divine and supernatural light. This tactic also meant that he could use the angel motif to hypostasize classes of people like pastors and devout followers of Jesus like Mary Magdalene. Although he affirms the literal sense of the text, I suggested that Aquinas's considerable extension of the angelic motif expresses an inherent heavenliness within the animate world. The following section explores the outer limits of this creative motif by exploring the angel's relationship to inorganic objects like the biblical text and the ark of the covenant.

---

98. Fabian Larcher, trans., *Commentary by Saint Thomas Aquinas on the Epistle to the Hebrews* [cited 11 August 2009]. Online: www.aquinas.avemaria.edu/Aquinas-Hebrews.pdf. This optimism is also found outside his commentaries; in *ST* 1.98.2, Aquinas writes, "In paradise man would have been like an angel in his spirituality of mind, yet with an animal life in his body. After the resurrection man will be like an angel, spiritualized in soul and body. Wherefore there is no parallel."

## Angels, Scripture, and Sacred Statuary

What makes Aquinas's angelology a doctrinal masterstroke is that it presents a theological model of reconciliation between seemingly disparate categories: logic and imagination, heaven and earth, the visible and invisible. This current section adds to the list by drawing out relationships between the animated and inert, focusing upon two instances where Aquinas merges the angels with the Scriptures themselves. In the passages considered, it is unclear whether he is alluding to the Old and New Testaments in metaphysical or objective terms. The difference is that if Aquinas is drawing a relationship between angels and the biblical text as a *book*, it indicates a conflation of angels and the world of inanimate objects. Such an interpretation leads one to see the Bible as a tangible representation of what an angel is—a messenger. The advantage of this option is that it presents yet another accessible image for understanding the angel; just as one uses words for God gleaned from an understanding of creatures and the perceptible world (*ST* 1.13.3), one can speak of an angel by a similar mode, *viz.*, wings, birds, saintly persons, or a sacred book. It would also be more in line with his Aristotelian leanings than if he had been speaking of Scripture as an immaterial, eternal idea. While I pursue this line of interpretation, one must allow the possibility of a metaphysical explanation, which would emphasize the ethos lying beyond the sacred page itself—a messenger *qua* message that begins and ends primarily in the mind of God. Seen thus, the link between angels and the Testaments would stress that both higher-order beings and the Scriptures are equally eternal, heavenly, irreducible, ethereal, and indestructible messengers. Regardless, both explanations communicate the subtle unity of being at the level of analogy.

The first example comes from Aquinas's commentary on the 20th chapter of John's Gospel where he considers the significance of the two angels at Christ's tomb. His initial explanation is fairly tame; "First, what [Mary] saw, which was two angels, which goes to show that all orders of angels, both those assisting and those ministering, were in service to Christ: 'Let all God's angels worship him' (Heb 1:6)."[99] This christological emphasis, which I explore in greater detail in the following section, is characteristic of much of the angelology in Aquinas's commentaries. For now, the two angels' deferential service and worship toward Christ is a synecdochic description for the activities of the entire heavenly host.

99. Lit. "*Primo quid vidit.*"

Thomas takes a second, more daring, pass at the narrative, proposing that these two angels also represent the two natures of Christ since one sat at the head of the tomb and the other at the feet, locations signifying divinity and humanity, respectively. However, the interpretation I wish to highlight occurs one paragraph later,

> We see how they [the angels] were positioned, one at the head and one at the feet. We can refer this . . . to the two Testaments. The word "angel" in Greek means "messenger," and both Testaments brought messages about Christ: "And the crowds that went before him and that followed him shouted, 'Hosanna to the Son of David!'" (Matt 21:9). So the angel sitting at the head signifies the Old Testament, and the angel at the feet the New Testament.[100]

Aquinas's association of the Old Testament with the head, rather than the feet, appears strange given the belief that the New had superseded the Old, a point he belabors in his commentary on Galatians. Once one consults the sermons of his teacher, Gregory, it becomes clear that this idea was not his own. "[T]he Old Testament came before Christ," observes Gregory, "and is therefore like the angel sitting at the head. The New Testament came after, and so is like the angel sitting at the feet."[101] So what appears to be an inadvertent transposition of the two books with respect to covenantal supersession is actually a statement about chronology. In Rom 11, a similar argument is used in the form of horticultural imagery (i.e., root, olive trees, branches) to speak of the relationship between Judaism and Christianity. Uncharacteristically, Aquinas neglected to credit Gregory for his observation even though he is clearly standing upon his master's shoulders in this instance. Nonetheless, the angelic presence allows Aquinas to christen it as emblematic of an inanimate object like the Scriptures (which, ironically, do not appear in the text itself).[102] Thus, he justifies the blurring of ontic boundaries between the angel and the Testaments by invoking messengership as the integrating factor, not

---

100. Weisheipl and Larcher, *John*. Note Aquinas's familiarity with Greek here, "*Angelus enim Graece, Latine dicitur nuntius.*"

101. I, "Homily 25 on the Gospels," 76–77. This point is also attributed to Gregory in the *Catena Aurea*, John 20:12.

102. He does the same with mountains in his commentary on Ps 34:8, a passage that speaks of the *mal'ak YHWH* encamping about God's people. "As Psalm 124 says: round about it are his [God's] mountains, namely angels" (*montes in circuitu ejus, scilicet angeli*).

because of anything inherently sacred about messengers themselves, but because they are conjoined by a sacred message "about Christ."

Aquinas's commentary on Hebrews yields an additional illustration where inorganic elements feature heavily in his christological interpretation of angels; albeit with a slight variation. While describing the obsolete regulations of Hebrew worship in 9:5, the biblical writer makes a passing reference to the cherubim who overshadowed the mercy seat.[103] Therefore, in the following example, the angelic figures Thomas has in mind are not literal beings, but gilded statuettes perched atop the ark of the covenant. His succinct explanation is characteristically imaginative and matter-of-fact:

> The two angels are the two testaments looking peacefully at Christ; or all the angels serving Christ in concord and unity of spirit: "Angels came and ministered to him" (Matt 4:11); "Thousands of thousands ministered to him" (Dan 7:10); "All are ministering spirits" (Heb 1:14). They desire to look on Christ and they overshadow the propitiatory, i.e., guard Christ's Church.[104]

Like his interpretation of paired angels at the resurrection tomb, he relegates angelology under Christology once again by metamorphosing the angel into the unchanging vehicle that bears the message of Christ to humanity, the Scriptures.[105] Thus, by a shared abstraction, the Bible itself is also a type of angel. While he compares these inert, golden figurines to equally inorganic Scriptures, Aquinas also animates them by suggesting that they symbolize the greater reality of the complete host of heaven engaged in the worship of Christ. The evolution of modern exegetical methods make it difficult to overlook the allegorical use of the text in some sections of his biblical commentary, but the absence of modern constraints freed Thomas innocently to pursue unique connections within the doctrine of angelology that appear hidden to modern eyes. No matter how tenuous some of his explanations may be, this particular use of the spiritual interpretation demonstrates how it may yield more edifying and christological observations than if he had merely reiterated the passage's

103. Gk. *"huperano de autes cheroubin doxes kataskiazonta to hilastrerion."*

104. Larcher, *Hebrews*.

105. In his commentary on Matthew, Aquinas corrects Theodore of Mopsuestia for denying that Old Testament texts could refer literally to Christ or the church. He writes, "Another [error] was that of Theodore who claimed that nothing brought forward in the Old Testament is literally applicable to Christ but only accommodated to him."

literal sense about the ark itself. Now that we have explored his efforts to bring heavenly things to earth by using angels as a link between birds, saintly humans, ecclesiastical offices, and the Scriptures themselves, we must shift the gaze from the earth to the heavens, as Aquinas draws a relationship between angels and Christ.

## RELATIONSHIPS BETWEEN ANGELOLOGY AND CHRISTOLOGY IN AQUINAS'S COMMENTARIES

Just as with his angelology, Aquinas's fullest treatment of Christology is found in the *Summa Theologiae*.[106] Beginning with the incarnation, he painstakingly recounts the chronology of Jesus' life.[107] His mastery of the doctrine's intricate history and the heresies associated with it is evident. Yet on the surface, Aquinas appears to do little more than affirm the Christology established by earlier theologians like Athanasius. In brief, he understands the incarnation as a necessary, but entirely gracious, taking up of all that is human into the Word made flesh.[108] This *hypostasis* is fundamentally God's response to original sin and humanity's subsequent misuse of the will.[109] As a result, the human race was isolated from the direct experience of the divine presence of God.[110] However, Jesus exercised his sinless will in conformity with God's will by vicariously accepting the sentence which stood against the human race, thus fulfilling his role as a divine-human mediator and opening a new way for the creation to return to the Creator.[111] Aquinas appears to agree with Augustine that Christ's atonement is essential, despite the fact that only a certain number of angels and humans have been elected; an idea he defends as entirely compatible with God's character.[112] Although God desires good for all creatures, Aquinas reasons, "he does not wish every good to them all."[113]

---

106. Also noteworthy is his lengthy discussion in Book 3 of his *Commentary on the Sentences*.

107. Davies, *Everyday God*, 297–319; Schoot, *Christ the "Name" of God*.

108. *ST* 3.2.3–4.

109. *ST* 1.83.1; 1.85.5–6.

110. *ST* 3.46.4.

111. *ST* 3.46.1–12.

112. *ST* 1.23.7; 3.46.2.

113. *ST* 1.23.3.

Because it was central to his theological perspective, this sweeping
incarnational and soteriological narrative serves as a backdrop for our
second stage of inquiry concerning the role of angels in Aquinas's biblical
commentaries. In my first chapter, I argued that it was not coincidental
that in the Old Testament, angels frequently appeared in close proximity
to YHWH and/or the place of worship. The biblical writers harnessed a
powerful motif that allowed them to make indirect, but clear, doctrinal
assertions about the angels and, most importantly, Israel's God. Then in
the chapter on pseudo-Denys we observed a significant shift in the doctrine's interpretation. Denys affirms the angels as subordinates of Christ,
but emphasized the dynamics and limits of their procession from the
Godhead, with a view to their role in accentuating the divine presence
within the Eucharist.

Unlike Denys, Thomas does not limit the application of angelology
to the church; while the configuration of his angelology was influenced
by Denys, the relationship between Christ and the angels is more pronounced in Aquinas's New Testament commentaries than in Denys's
*Celestial Hierarchy*, where one has to do a bit more digging to find similar
associations. There has been a fair amount of scholarly interest in the subject of angelomorphic Christology in recent decades;[114] yet the studies are
often limited to exploring the theme within biblical books like Luke-Acts
and Revelation, or they are concerned with antecedents of angelomorphism in early Jewish Wisdom literature.[115] Little, if anything, has been
advanced with regard to the confluence of angelology and Christology in
Aquinas's biblical commentaries.[116] Since my larger concern differs from
scholars working exclusively on the question of angelomorphism with

114. While there is no set definition of angelomorphism, I find Crispin Fletcher-
Louis' to be the most representative of the field: "wherever there are signs that an individual or community possesses specifically angelic characteristics or status, though for
whom identity cannot be reduced to that of an angel," *Luke-Acts: Angels, Christology
and Soteriology*, 14–15.

115. For example, see Daniélou, *The Origins of Latin Christianity*; Stuckenbruck
and North, eds., *Early Jewish and Christian Monotheism*; Gieschen, *Angelomorphic
Christology*. Gieschen makes a fair case for such a view in the earliest layers of Chris-
tian tradition by appealing to the writings of Jewish antecedents as well as Justin
Martyr, Theophilus, Irenaeus, Tertullian, Clement of Alexandria, Hippolytus, Origen,
Novatian, Lactantius, and Eusebius. He does not mention Aquinas. Nor do others like
Hoffmann, or Fletcher-Louis.

116. That I am aware of, Edgar Foster is the only Western theologian to pen a
sustained, scholarly reflection of this sort, however, not on Aquinas; Foster, *Angelomorphic Christology and the Exegesis of Psalm 8*.

respect to Christology,[117] I consider the following pages as a means of broaching a subject that is worthy of further study.

Thus far, I have argued that Aquinas was an imaginative commentator whose quest for the heart of every passage led him to associate angels with other forms of terrestrial life. His angelology complements the Old Testament angelology of divine transcendence and pseudo-Denys's angelology of divine immanence by affirming the transcendence of the immanent, material world. However, while this is his main objective, in order fully to assess the scope of his angelology one must also determine whether he takes the same interpretive liberties when discussing the angel's relationship to the second person of the Trinity. So the following sections discuss three relationships between Christology and angelology in Aquinas's biblical commentaries: his comparison of angels to Christ; his insistence upon Christ's supremacy to angels; and instances where he relates angels to the Scriptures, which in turn, point to Christ.

## Aquinas's Comparison of Angels to Christ

Unlike earlier examples where he liberally injects angels into the text even when not mentioned by the biblical author, Aquinas is comparatively reserved in his use of analogy when Christ is concerned. In fact, when paralleling Christ and angels, the angel is *always* part of the biblical text upon which Aquinas comments. His comments typically emphasize how angels are related to particular events in Christ's life, like the incarnation or the crucifixion. Also, apart from one exception mentioned later, Aquinas avoids comparing Christ and angels. There are two reasons why this is likely. First, with a little imagination, analogies are easy to formulate when comparing finite beings, and only slightly more problematic when comparing purely spiritual beings like angels with birds, humans or inorganic items. It is tricky, however, to develop a solid analogy between a finite, created being—angel or otherwise—and an infinite, uncreated being like God without appearing irreverent or risking heresy.[118]

The second reason is similar, but related more to the structure of his analogies. As I will explain toward the end of this sub-section, Aquinas

117. One can hardly improve on Gieschen's historical review of the relevant literature, *Angelomorphic Christology*, 7–25.

118. In the previous section, even given his description of Mary Magdalene and clergy as quasi-angelic humans, Aquinas reacted against those who modelled John the Baptizer as a literal, angelomorphic being.

appears to prefer theology that moves from the ontologically lower being to the higher when making such comparisons. For example, when the bird and the saint are typified as angels, they are being transformed into something *more* spiritual and magnificent than what they already are, but in the case of the Son, there is no such comparison that would not compromise the glory of what it means to be God. Thus, if analogous statements are to be made about Christ, they must always work from the angel upward.

The first example comes from his commentary on John 5:1–9a, and features what Nestle-Aland considers an apocryphal detail concerning an angel at the pool of Bethesda.[119] Aquinas follows Augustine's view that "the angel signifies [*intelligitur*] Christ," adding, "Just as the angel descended at certain times into the pool, so Christ descended into the world at a time fixed by the Father." Note that the comparison is at the point of an abstract action: *descent*. This descent implies a particular attribute of Christ's that Thomas wants to highlight. He does not seem remotely interested in the angel's being, or, as in the *Summa Theologiae*, the dissection of how angelic beings might move through space-time. His task is strictly theological; it is the angel's relationship to the healing pool of Bethesda that Thomas finds redolent of Christ's ministry of mercy and compassion to the infirm. As significant as the angel's action was to the story in Aquinas's day, it should, he intimates, remind one of the infinitely greater benevolence involved in the incarnation rather than the healing power of the angel. The angel is outshone by the Son's light, just significant enough to provide a category into which Aquinas can pour, until overflowing, an interpretation that lifts the mind back to Christ. Incidentally, one characteristic of Aquinas's commentaries is that the title "Christ" appears more frequently than the proper name, "Jesus"; perhaps this is coincidental, but it is a lexical consideration that may illustrate an uneasiness on his part concerning the relationship between angels and Jesus as a human being, almost as if he prefers to avoid the ontic problem of comparing the humanity of Jesus with a celestial spirit.[120]

---

119. See the apparatus in Nestle et al., *Novum Testamentum Graece*, 260.

120. He does speak of this relationship briefly in his commentary on Hebrews 1:4–7, "The answer is that Christ had two things according to the human nature in this life, namely, the infirmity of the flesh; and in this way He was lower than the angels: but He also had fullness of grace, so that even in His human nature he was greater than the angels in grace and glory."

Another comparison between Christ and the angels appears in his commentary on 1 Thess 4:16; the verse states that "the Lord himself will descend from heaven with a cry of command, with the archangel's call, and with the sound of the trumpet of God." Aquinas reflects,

> In the resurrection, some things shall be done through the angels, such as the collection of the dust. But the restoration of the bodies and the soul's reunion with the body will be accomplished immediately through Christ. . . . [The Apostle] presents the power of the angels when he says, "with the archangel's call," not that anything is done by his voice, but rather by his ministry. He says, "archangel's" for all angels minister to the Church under one archangel. "This is Michael, the prince of the Church" (Rev 12).[121] Or perhaps, "with the archangel's call," that is, Christ's, who is Prince of the angels.[122]

Apart from observing the hierarchical ministries of the archangel and angels, Aquinas proposes the archangel of 1 Thess 4:16 may be identified as either Michael or Christ. The archangel is an exceptional figure among the angels, notes Aquinas, and just as other things may be described as a type of angel, so the most sublime angel may also point to Christ's pre-eminence.[123] The common vein that Aquinas sees in Christ and the archangel is that both represent primacy. Thomas's interpretation is ambiguous, but he appears to welcome this imprecision; it allows him to infer that the text might be talking about two beings at a time. The biblical author is undoubtedly describing the archangel as a finite spiritual being; nonetheless, Aquinas's reading portrays Michael as subordinate to Christ. This is a noteworthy clarification given the substantial following generated in response to appearances of Michael, which had been reported around Italy as early as the fifth century.[124]

121. It is worth noting that no accepted text has this reading for a verse in the 12th chapter of the Revelation.

122. Larcher, *Commentary on St. Paul's First Letter to the Thessalonians and the Letter to the Philippians* [cited 4 September 2009]. Online: www.diafrica.org/kenny/CDtexts/SS1Thes.htm.

123. It would be too much to suggest that Aquinas is somehow original at this point given the storied history involved in devotion to Michael; it may simply denote Aquinas's familiarity with earlier tradition.

124. The most popular appearance in Italy occurred upon Mt. Garganus during an invasion of the Goths; of course, Michael's renown predates this appearance; D. H. Hannah proposes that Michael was an eminent figure of devotion as early as the Second Temple period, see Hannah, *Michael and Christ*. Theodoret of Cyrus' commentary on

Similar to pseudo-Denys's *Mystical Theology* where the higher one ascends on the ladder of being, the less they can state in positive terms— once Christ is within view, Aquinas jettisons metaphysical distinctions. Instead, he emphasizes the angel's subordination and functional resemblance to the ever-glorious Son. Therefore, according to this pattern, he is not using the angels to bring heaven to earth so much as he is steering earthly gazes to the One who sits in heaven. While birds and humans were elevated via Aquinas's angelomorphic descriptions, this dramatic, *upward* shift in his use of analogy enhances the angel's profile, but limits its glory. The following section explores this endearing feature of his angelology, showing how he magnifies Christ's splendor by casting the major aspect of his ministry such as prefigurement, birth, death, and the second coming, in the lesser light of the angels.

## Christ's Supremacy to the Angels in Aquinas's Commentary on Hebrews

It is likely that the Hebrews commentary arose from a university course Thomas taught around 1265–68 while living in Rome. This was also about the time he began writing the *Prima Pars* of the *Summa Theologiae*, which tends to focus upon metaphysical aspects of angelology discussed earlier.[125] His evaluation of the relationship between Christology and angelology in Hebrews is more devotional than the *Summa Theologiae*, at least in the classical sense, but bears a similar degree of detail. He scours the text, highlighting and exhausting numerous avenues for discussion at every verse, and his conclusions typically focus upon Christ's exalted position with respect to the angels rather than the angels' service to Christ. Interacting with the Hebrews commentary leaves little doubt that Aquinas's lectures on Scripture were designed to focus his students' attention upon the central figure of the text, Jesus Christ.

Just as the author of Hebrews was ardent about demonstrating Christ's superiority to Israel's most revered figures, traditions and institutions, so Aquinas adopts the same strategy in his prologue to the commentary by adding that in the Old Testament "angels are sometimes called gods: 'When the sons of God came to stand before the Lord' (Job 1:6, 11)," and were treated as such "on account of their rich splendor of

---

Col 2:18 suggests a cult of Michael also existed in Asia Minor during the fifth century.

125. Torrell, *Saint Thomas Aquinas*, 1:255.

divine brightness."[126] Although, he insists, "angels are not like unto Christ among the gods, because He is the 'brightness of the Father's glory' (Heb. 1:3)."[127] Throughout the commentary on Hebrews, with nearly two hundred references to angels, Aquinas uses angels to reinforce the holiness of God and supremacy of Christ.

His Christocentrism is rarely apparent when he summons angels out of the ether by way of allegory, but emerges once angels are featured by the biblical text. In the Hebrews commentary, for instance, he resists the temptation to allegorize or embellish the text beyond adulating Christ. Thus in his reflection upon Hebrews 1, Aquinas simply echoes the author by summarizing four ways that Christ is superior to the heavenly host.[128]

> [T]he Apostle devotes this entire first chapter to extolling Christ over the angels by reason of His excellence; hence he lists four things pertaining to Christ's excellence: first, His origin, because He is the Son; secondly, His dominion, because He is the heir; thirdly, His power, because He made the world; fourthly, His honor, because He sits on the right hand of majesty.[129]

Angels relate to Christ in this commentary in a manner similar to their relationship to God in the Old Testament. They are part of a heavenly court that highlights the Son's majesty and transcendence. This celestial dimension of Aquinas's angelology balances his terrestrial emphasis spoken of earlier, because it establishes the angel as a creature of both natural and supernatural proportions. But it is Christ's eternal Sonship that obliges angels and humans alike to worship him.

Although Aquinas did not hesitate to associate angels with lesser creatures elsewhere, he refuses to foist the same spiritual sense upon the text if it would detract from Christ's immeasurable glory.[130] This is

126  Along similar lines, in his commentary on John 21:1–6, he limns, "Except the gods, that is, the angels, whose dwelling is not with flesh (Dan 2:11)."

127.  Larcher, *Hebrews*, 2.

128.  Incidentally, as a way of illustrating his familiarity with text-critical issues, Aquinas's reference to "the Apostle" here refers to his belief that St. Paul was the book's author. While he is familiar that even before Nicaea some doubted Pauline authorship, he writes in the prologue, "Nevertheless, the old doctors, especially Dionysius and certain others, accept the words of this epistle as being Paul's testimony. Jerome, too, acknowledges it as Paul's epistle."

129.  Larcher, *Hebrews*, 17.

130.  Aquinas also argues in the Hebrews commentary that the relationship between humans and angels is eternal, "But men in glory are equal to angels, not greater." And "for men will be raised to the orders of angels." Ibid., 136.

why he rarely invokes the spiritual sense when speaking of Christ in the commentaries, even when interacting with a highly symbolic book like Hebrews. This is likely an intentional decision on his part out of reverence for the Savior. His analogies have a supernaturalizing effect upon terrestrial creatures, but since "the angels are not creators, but creatures," it is impossible and unnecessary to so embroider Christ, the creator of angels.[131]

Thus, although Jesus was in a sense "made lower than the angels" (Heb 2:9) because of his humanity, Aquinas uses angels to defend Christ's deity. "No matter how great a difference you might imagine [between Christ and the angels]," he insists, "there would still remain a greater difference, because they are *infinitely* apart."[132] He is quick to remind readers that Christ's exalted position over the heavenly host does not imply divine indifference to the state of sinful humanity, however. Although humans stand under "a debt of punishment," he counsels, "[t]o satisfy this debt He offered Himself as a victim on the altar of the cross."[133] Aquinas's brings heaven to earth by styling angels as birds and humans, yet ultimately directs earthly eyes heavenward by depicting angels as inferior to Christ crucified and glorified. Unlike examples in the previous section where he emphasizes similarities between Christ and angels, his correlation in the Hebrews commentary emphasizes *divergence*. This approach affirms more than Aquinas's understanding of the inherent logic of the biblical writers, however, it reveals his passionate devotion to Christ expressed through angelology.[134]

## CONCLUSION

The following diagram summarizes all the relationships I have addressed with respect to the angel as an interpretive motif in Aquinas's biblical commentaries:

131. Ibid., ii.

132. Literally, "*distent in infinitum*," ibid., 18. [emphasis added]

133. Ibid., 15.

134. He does not limit to the Hebrews commentary his contrast between angels and the humbling glory of Christ. "Christ is super-eminent not only over all men, but also all angels." Larcher, trans., *Commentary by Saint Thomas Aquinas on the First Epistle to the Corinthians* [cited 2 October 2009]. Online: www.aquinas.avemaria.edu/Aquinas-Corinthians.pdf.

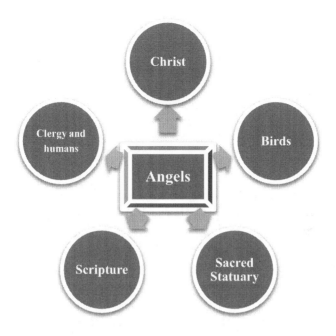

**Fig. 6: The angel's five principal relationships in Aquinas's commentaries**

There are various techniques for hypostatizing the angelic; Milton employed poetry, Michelangelo used a paintbrush, Suger rebuilt an abbey, and Aquinas used the *vox Dei* as his medium. Thomas's descriptions of celestial beings as constituents of the physical world are not dissimilar to the church's attempts to localize the spiritual presence of the ascended Christ; in fact, Scripture, the Eucharist, iconography, incense, sacred architecture, baptism, and even the contemporary use of video projection in the worship service, all presuppose a human need to connect faith with the bodily senses. For this reason, my final chapter suggests Aquinas's angelology serves as an ancient corrective of contemporary, non-theistic, ecological suppositions.

Moving angels from the ineffable to the visible or tactile is Aquinas's way of affirming that God and his heaven are not distant realities. The incarnation is the most profound example of this truth. Each case I have introduced above reveals how an angelic presence might be seen through such things as birds, preachers, Scripture, or sacred statuary. What distinguishes Thomas's discussion of angelology in his biblical commentaries *vis-à-vis* his tone in the *Summa Theologiae* is that he represents physical substances as if they were angels in order to demonstrate the proximity of the divine presence. By this imaginative feat, Aquinas has effectively inserted several different categories into Denys's nine ranks of angelic beings. Just as God can be said to have something in common with the human in terms of communicable attributes, so Aquinas proposes that angels bear similarities to this world: "they [angels] were made in a corporeal place [the uppermost atmosphere] in order to show their relationship to corporeal nature."[135] Yet the angel's incidental similarity to Christ accentuates his point that there is more to life itself than either the present world or the presence of angels.

Although Aquinas held other angelogues like pseudo-Dionysius in high regard, I find his angelology to be more imaginative and reliant upon the biblical text than his mysterious predecessor. Because Aquinas's angelology is more poetic, he pushes Denys's vision beyond purely mediatorial and ontological categories. In his biblical commentaries, Thomas also complements the Neoplatonic inklings of pseudo-Dionysius by infusing more of the supernatural into the natural world that exists *outside* the sanctuary. Yet by no means does he consistently connect the angel with nature, Scripture, or Christ in the *Summa Theologiae*. Sadly, it is the theological-philosophical approach in the *Summa Theologiae* that has been the bane of his legacy in much of Protestant theology.[136] Nonetheless, in defense of Aquinas and his angelology I called attention to the high concentration of biblical citations in those sections of the *Summa Theologiae* that feature questions about angels. Since many of these citations drive and substantiate Aquinas's conclusions in the *Summa Theologiae*, there is nothing intrinsically unbiblical or recondite about his inquiries into how higher-order beings might move or experience the world. This is in light of the fact that Calvin and Barth also flirt with similar avenues of thought, not to mention that such hypotheses were appropriate for *Summae* during his time.[137]

While the weakness of this study is that it cannot cover all that Thomas said about angels in his biblical commentaries or his *Summa Theologiae*, its strengths are significant. In particular, it illustrates that

135. *ST* 1.61.4.

136. However, it is impossible to reduce the *Summa Theologiae* as purely one type of work or another, because the second part of the *Summa Theologiae* is qualitatively different from the first in that it is more original than abstract and rationalistic.

137. See Berman, *Medieval Religion*, 12.

he ventured two rather different approaches to the doctrine, yet many only appear to be aware of one. Because of this lack of familiarity, both Aquinas and his angelology have been falsely rendered as a cautionary tale about the consequences of philosophical approaches to Christian theology. Pursuing the angelology of the commentaries allowed me to demonstrate that Aquinas often used angels as transitional forms and equated them with the present world, which in turn, brought God and heaven closer, if only conceptually.

I introduced the reader to examples from his biblical commentary where he designates angels as birds, preachers, prominent biblical characters of both genders, sacred statuary, both Testaments, and Christ himself. Two themes emerged: first, his creative exegetical approach to angelology represents a strong desire to connect the material world with the spiritual through the use of analogy, which Denys emphasized by focusing instead upon angelic function in relation to liturgy and ontology; secondly, Aquinas's angels functioned to glorify Christ much in the same way that the angelology of the Old Testament often served to magnify God's otherness, whereas Denys's angelology accentuated Christ's eucharistic immanence.[138] Yet however true it may be that the power of a holy analogy allows for new insights into the angelic presence in the world, Aquinas's chief contribution lies in his artful use of celestial beings to direct one's attention to the ultimate concern of God in Christ.[139]

Revealing a semantic transformation of higher-order beings into common elements, the commentaries are not merely a thirteenth-century innovation, however; they mimic the biblical pattern. Just as the biblical writers associated stars and angels, and Jesus compared angels to harvesters and humans to wheat, weeds, sheep and goats, Thomas often speaks in vivid allegories drawn from images in the world around him.[140] Where Denys emphasized the angels in relation to liturgical symbols and their shared participation in the divine, Aquinas broadens the category by suggesting that the world itself participates in angelic forms, which in turn illustrates that the process of sanctifying one's own imagination involves a

138. This is in contrast to the contribution of the angelology in the *Summa Theologiae*, which appears to be more focused upon questions of ontology.

139. This point is abundantly clear in *ST* 1.1.65 where he suggests that Moses deliberately withheld details about the creation of angels in order to prevent the Israelites from engaging in idolatry by focusing upon them instead of God.

140. Job 38:6–7; Judg 5:20; 2 Chr 18:18; Isa 14:12–15; Dan 8:10; Rev 1:20; 9:1; 12:4; 19:17.

willingness to view the Scriptures and the creation, not just the sanctuary, as blessed spaces that overflow with relationships between the mundane and the sacred. Given the precedence set by Jesus and the biblical writers, it is difficult to comprehend the resistance to this sort of preaching and teaching in the church and theology of today; after all, "How can Christianity call itself Catholic," questions Simone Weil, "if the universe itself is left out?"[141] The Angelic Doctor's reading of Scripture opens up such perceptions and makes more connections between the human and the heavenly realm than do many modern versions of angelology. By cultivating this relatively unknown sphere of his theology, I have attempted to broaden the context in which Aquinas and the doctrine itself should be judged in the future.

Finally, as an outstanding intellectual with a mystical streak, Aquinas's two angelologies—one in the *Summa Theologiae,* the other in his commentaries on Scripture—call the world to return to the mystery that surrounds them.[142] Recreating the world imaginatively, Aquinas complements the emphasis upon divine transcendence in Old Testament angelology and pseudo-Denys's angelology of divine immanence, by using angelic imagery to assert the transcendence of the immanent, material world, which points one back to God. However, if Aquinas's angelology is to be assessed on a larger scale, the commentaries will need to be further mined and translated, as will Aquinas's sermons, almost all of which are still available only in Latin. This endeavor will require an interdisciplinary approach, with universities, theologians, historians, liturgists, and linguists working side by side with the church in order fully to reveal this hidden realm within Aquinas's theology. This study is a first attempt to shed some much-needed light upon what I believe may be a promising and edifying subject for years to come.

---

141. Weil, *Waiting for God,* 116.

142. For Aquinas's views on rapturous experiences, see *ST* 2.2.175. For an overview of Aquinas as a mystic, see Weisheipl, "Mystic on Campus," 135–58. Also, Kennedy, "St. Thomas Aquinas," 665; and Norman, "Rediscovery of Mysticism," 449–64. Jones considers Aquinas's commitment to negative theology, which is essentially the description of God's ineffability, to be an example of his mysticism.

# Chapter IV

# Historical Angelology in Dialogue with the Present

## INTRODUCTION

Thus far, my aim has been to unearth layers of intent that have long been buried within ancient approaches to angelology. I proposed that just as one may see more of the universe by looking through the eyepiece of a telescope, so it is possible to read the larger contours of an author's theological objective by gazing into the aperture of their angelology. The chapters have focused upon what I consider to be positive—but misunderstood or misinterpreted—contributions from ancient luminaries, which, to use Dylan Thomas's phrase, have been "bequeathed from pale estates."[1] This is not, of course, to argue for an indiscriminate acceptance of all that has been said about angels in former ages, nor is it to suggest that angelology is the only legitimate lens through which to view themes of immanence, transcendence, and imagination. However, theology must harness the array of perspectives on angels without perpetuating the myth of an historically consistent angelology to which one must capitulate. This said, recent figures and movements have so overstepped the boundaries established by the angelologies represented here that they have compromised the doctrine's usefulness as a theological device for

1. Thomas, "All That I Owe the Fellows of the Grave," 93. "Pale," here, refers to the grave.

accentuating matters of transcendence, immanence, and imagination. Following a concise summary of the book as a whole, it is to these three themes that I shall turn in this chapter.

In the first chapter I suggested that the early biblical authors wrote about angels in order to defend monotheism and the transcendence of God. I maintained that these writers, as the theological elite, compiled, expanded, and transposed oral tradition about angels as a literary means to this devotional end. The metamorphosis of the *mal'ak Yhwh* and the dynamics surrounding conventional angels who were gradually entrusted with titles and proper names, suggests the writers' appreciation for the power of angelic beings grew as they used them to accentuate the being and worship of God. Similarities between biblical accounts of celestial beings and earlier models found in the ancient Near East led me to conclude that while Hebrew authors and redactors leveraged regional mythology to fulfill their theological objectives, Old Testament angelology bears a distinctive message about the otherness of God that neither humanized nor divinized celestial beings. Discussions of divine transcendence in the contemporary period have not always upheld such a balanced angelology. I propose in this chapter that Barth's focus upon God's otherness and his discussion of angelic function at the expense of angelic essence needs to be moderated by the biblical archetype.

My second chapter suggested that unlike Old Testament angelology, pseudo-Denys used a rather formal continuum of angels to express the *immanence* of God within the context of ecclesiastical, sacramental, and liturgical categories. His *Celestial Hierarchy* complements Old Testament angelology, intimating that for God to remain transcendent, yet personal, divine otherness requires degrees of presence. His theory suggests that one way God compensated for Christ's ascended absence was to provide the church with means of divine immanence in the form of angels, clergy, liturgy, sacraments, and symbols. Therefore, angels act as a vital, ontological link between the transcendent, ascended Christ and his church by heightening the outpoured glory of his real, eucharistic presence. Thus, Denys's angelology represents the mitigating transition between divine transcendence and immanence by suspending both in sacramental tension. However, in recent times, the New Age movement has compromised Denys's equilibrium by so isolating and emphasizing the idea of angelic immanence that Creator, Christ, church, Communion, and clergy become incidental paraphernalia. This trend has had the opposite effect to the Barthian mode of angelology, because instead of absorbing angels into God's transcendence, the New Age movement does far greater harm by absorbing God into angelic immanence.

Chapter 3 focused upon the angelology and angel-related themes embedded within Aquinas's biblical commentaries. These forgotten texts highlight his scriptural, Christocentric, and most importantly, imaginative, use of angels. The Bible was a divine resource that allowed him, like the Old Testament authors and pseudo-Denys, to use angelology as a means of leading readers to a particular knowledge of God. Thomas improved upon pseudo-Denys's insights by affiliating angels with the world *beyond* the sanctuary; Aquinas's exegetical techniques pushed the semantic range of the word "angel" so that such beings could be clothed in earthly forms. His analogy of being between the angels and the world helps one to apprehend, by way of relationships and objects present in the creation, what is normally inaccessible: a sense that God and his angels exist alongside our planet, in a heaven that is among us rather than merely above us. Aquinas's transposition of angelology from the supernal to the temporal is especially sustainable because it mirrors, at an imaginative level, the depiction of angels as beings who were progressively infused into Scripture's narrative. Further exposure to his commentaries may renew the study of angelology by pushing for celestial beings to become more of a part of *this* world, in turn, revealing earth as a place where God also resides in holy parallel. Aquinas struck an ideal balance between the Old Testament angelology of transcendence and pseudo-Denys's ecclesiastically-defined angelology of immanence by establishing imaginative points of reference between higher-order beings and creatures of this world. Therefore, this chapter ultimately advances Aquinas's highly imaginative angelology as an obvious solution to the suppression or misuse of spirituality in the ecological movement.

This final chapter concludes by tying together, in a eucharistic knot, all the threads linking angels to transcendence, immanence, and imagination. I draw this relationship between angelology and the sacrament for several reasons, but primarily out of a conviction that if Christ's church is to be "*semper reformanda,*" it must move from the specific to the comprehensive and from the abstract to the evident. In other words, since the act of exploring doctrinal peculiarities is a highly specialized, perspectival, and tendentious activity, doctrines must establish experiential footings wherever possible if they are to appeal to the parishioner and compel worshippers to deeper forms of spirituality. The process of making the insights of academic-level theology *relatable* is the greatest opportunity within doctrinal-like writing today. Therefore, after establishing angelology in relation to attributes of God, the church, and the physical world in the first three chapters, it is equally vital to moor angelology to familiar and tangible practices like the Lord's Supper. My hope is that, under these auspices, angelology might be seen as an approachable and practical topic of discussion once again.

## BARTH'S ANGELOLOGY: TRANSCENDENCE AT THE EXPENSE OF IMMANENCE

As a rule, angelology has not received the same degree of attention in modern and contemporary theology that it enjoyed within Old Testament and post-biblical traditions. Barth's treatment of the subject in his *Church Dogmatics*, however, deserves special mention. His extensive and meticulous angelology, which he regarded as "the most remarkable and difficult of all" doctrines,[2] qualifies his work as an anomaly among Protestant systematicians. Like the Old Testament authors, Barth's reflections are a function of his wider theology. Though he presses for an angelology similar to that of the Old Testament in its emphasis upon the transcendent God, he attenuates the connection between God and the angel at points, resulting in unnecessarily large ontological gaps. First, a very brief synopsis of the underlying principles that led to his conclusions is essential. Barth's theology was forever changed after his former teacher, von Harnack, along with other prominent Christian intellectuals like Schleiermacher and von Rad, were able to rationalize their support of the German war effort in 1914. Barth reasoned that there was something fundamentally wrong about the theological assumptions that allowed them to make such a political misstep. As he and his close associate, Eduard Thurneysen, began to read and discuss the Bible together, both men encountered an entirely different landscape than the one portrayed by their university lecturers.

Published in 1922, Barth's *Romans Commentary* posed a radical dichotomy between God and creation, a theology of crisis that served as a rejoinder to what he perceived as liberalism's romanticism, oversimplifications, and failure to distinguish between God and the world.[3]

---

2. Barth, *Church Dogmatics III.3*, 369.

3. "The power of God," he argued, "can be detected neither in the world of nature nor in the souls of men. It must not be confounded with any high, exalted, force,

Since God was beyond human understanding, a point Barth eventually formalized in the second volume of *Church Dogmatics*, he could not be the domesticated being that liberal Protestantism had attempted to reach by way of a theology from below. Naturally, Barth's stentorian and earnest approach struck quite a different chord compared to the optimistic tune that his liberal forebears and counterparts had been singing. His fear was that the emphasis upon religion and the immanence of God in progressive circles had undermined the importance of Christology, Scripture, and divine transcendence. This led Barth to argue that such a being could only reveal himself, which was the very thing God had done in the person of Christ. Thus God has interjected his "No" to all other alternative means of revelation, because it is in Scripture, the sacred record entrusted to the church, wherein God reveals his "Yes" to Jesus Christ, and through him, a potentially-justifying "Yes" to humanity.

With respect to angelology, Barth's feeling was that the erosion of a scriptural foundation had led liberal theologians to treat higher-order beings as non-beings, for by this time Schleiermacher had already dispensed with angels, Bultmann had demythologized them, and Tillich had begun depersonifying them. Barth, on the other hand, sought to reverse this trend by developing an angelology that augmented the transcendence of God.

> [T]he teacher and master to which we must keep in this matter [of angelology] can only be the Holy Scriptures of the Old and New Testament, that we must not accept any other authority, that we must listen exhaustively to what this guide has to tell us, and that we must respect what it says and what it does not say.[4]

Barth downplayed alternative approaches to angelology in order to give ample recognition to God and Scripture; like Calvin and Luther before him, he treated what he considered to be philosophical and rationalistic approaches to angels with acute suspicion. However, to Barth belongs the unfortunate distinction of being the preeminent Protestant angelogue of the modern era who, by parsing the Scriptures and eschewing the angelologies of persons like pseudo-Dionysius and Aquinas, deprived angels of their splendor even while defending their reality in the light of God's otherness.

---

known or knowable." Barth, *The Epistle to the Romans*, 36.

    4. Barth, *CD III.3*, 372.

One must also appreciate two main characteristics of Barth's angelology in order to understand this shift in emphasis; the first has to do with his desire to reaffirm the biblical description of angels as actual heavenly beings, created by God. He disliked skeptical approaches to angelology, like those lampooned by the late Eric Mascall in his wry adaptation of a classic Christmas carol: "Hark, the herald angels sing: 'Bultmann shot us on the wing!'"[5] In Barth's own words, the task of angelology is to navigate "between the far too interesting mythology of the ancients and the far too uninteresting 'demythologization' of most of the moderns."[6] To be fair, while the present author agrees with Mascall and Barth, Bultmann was reacting in part to what he perceived to be a rigid dogmatism among the pastors of the Confessing church, something that he attempted to alleviate by exposing possibilities that lay behind wooden interpretations.

It is more difficult, however, to endorse the second major feature of Barth's angelology, which happens to be highly correlated with his best-known contribution to the field of theology. His emphasis upon the transcendence of God, which was essentially a reiteration of Kierkegaard's "infinite qualitative distinction" (*unendliche qualitative Unterschied*), led Barth to emphasize the angelic function over against its form.[7] Although my chapter on the Old Testament supports the idea that angels draw attention to the otherness of God, the priority of the transcendent God in Barth's early writings is so overwhelming that it leads to a one-dimensional view of angels. Though he would later balance his doctrine of divine otherness in volume 4 of *Church Dogmatics* and works like *The Humanity of God* by way of Christ's incarnation, his adaptation of angelology remains asymmetrical because he treats the activity of the angels at the expense of their being.[8] Barth's approach captures the basic meaning

---

5. Mascall, *Pi in the High*, 49.

6. Barth, *Church Dogmatics III.3*, 369.

7. He writes, "if I have a system, it is limited to a recognition of what Kierkegaard called the 'infinite qualitative distinction' between time and eternity, and to my regarding this as possessing negative as well as positive significance: 'God is in heaven, and thou art on earth.' The relation between such a God and such a man, and the relation between such a man and such a God, is for me the theme of the Bible and the essence of philosophy." Barth, *The Epistle to the Romans*, 10.

8. Barth argues that the incarnation invites the church to manifest both poles of the *hypostasis* to the world, though he confesses, "I should indeed have been somewhat embarrassed if one had invited me to speak on the humanity of God—say in the year 1920, the year in which I stood up in this hall against my great teacher, Adolf von Harnack." Barth, *The Humanity of God*, 38.

of the words *mal'ak* and *angelos* and understands their function in terms of their messengership. Yet because angels are no less spirits than they are messengers, he has exaggerated the original intent of Old Testament authors and confined the doctrine of angels to a more rigid definition than the Scriptures.

Barth's method falls prey to the same tendency that humans have to classify themselves as occupational beings, (e.g., I am a painter, mechanic, lecturer, etc.), as if it is possible to circumvent ontology by reducing identity to one's primary function in the world. He argues that since angels:

> Do not belong to the establishment and equipment of the lower cosmos ordained for man as described in Genesis 1 and 2, but to the sphere of the heavenly world, of the upper cosmos . . . we can have no knowledge [concerning their nature] even from the word of God or faith.[9]

This assumption strikes me as overly pessimistic, and unnecessarily denies an analogy of being that continues between God, who is spirit, angels as pure spirits, and humans, who are embodied spirits. I am not alone in my alarm; Pannenberg, too, takes umbrage with Barth for intimating that Scripture says nothing about the nature of angels, noting that Barth "refused to examine the nature of angels" and "regarded any study leading to a philosophy of angels as an aberration."[10] Angels, Pannenberg reminds the reader, are clearly called "spirits" in Heb 1:14 and elsewhere.[11] Barth eventually concedes this point as "virtually a definition of the nature of angels."[12] Augustine clarified this matter in the fourth century, "'Angel' is the name of their office, not of their nature. If you seek the name of their nature, it is 'spirit'; if you seek the name of their office, it is 'angel': therefore, from what they are, 'spirit,' from what they do, 'angel.'"[13] As a result of Barth's departure from this classical line of demarcation, his angel is over-identified with its office and function.

---

9. Barth, *Church Dogmatics III.2*, 14.

10. Pannenberg, *Systematic Theology*, 2:103.

11. Ibid.

12. Barth, *Church Dogmatics III.3*, 452. On p. 453, Barth argued that Aquinas's attempts to relate the *angeloi* and *pneumata* went wrong once he tried to associate the *pneumata* with his *substantiae spirituals separatae*.

13. *Angelus enim officii nomen est, non naturae. Quaeris nomen huius naturae, spiritus est; quaeris officium, angelus est: ex eo quod est, spiritus est; ex eo quod agit, angelus est.* Augustine, "Enarrationes in Psalmos 103, 15." 744.

Moreover, there are instances when Barth's version of angelology lacks an appreciation for the similarities between God, angels, and human beings. This marks a rather stark exodus from the interchangeable terminology used by the Old Testament authors, for whom it was possible to utter words like "*enowsh*" and "*YHWH*" in the same breath as "*mal'ak*" without posing a threat to God's transcendence.[14] For example, Barth is exceedingly cryptic in his attempt to shed light upon the epiphanic union found in the figure of the Angel of the Lord; he writes, "The angel of Yahweh in the Old Testament is obviously both identical and not identical with Yahweh Himself. It is quite impossible that the non-identity, too, should not be and remain visible."[15] Barth suggests that since this angel conveyed God's words, it became one with the message. Thus, as a result of this relationship, the Angel of the Lord becomes indistinguishable from God. Nevertheless, Barth appears reluctant to hypostasize this peculiar figure apart from its activity as a messenger for fear that it would undermine the priority of divine unity.

> [W]e are closer to the meaning and text of these Old Testament passages if we accept purely as an angel this one angel of God which is given such prominence, learning from it the supreme relevance of the existence and ministry of angels and their connection with the incomparable and irreplaceable Word and work of God.[16]

One is right to wonder if Barth is uncomfortable with discussions about the *mal'ak YHWH's* ontological relationship to God because he is attempting to preserve the absoluteness of his distinction between the Godhead and the rest of the cosmos of which angels are a part.[17] What makes such a stance awkward is that angels not only embody God's communicable attributes to a greater degree than any other creature, they appear to share certain incommunicable attributes as well, such as

14. Here, I have settled for a relatively conservative point that does not even raise more controversial questions arising from passages like Gen 48:15–16, where a dying Jacob describes God has his "Angel" (*mal'ak*).

15. Barth, *CD I.1*, 299.

16. Ibid., *III.3*, 487.

17. Whether or not he was speaking hyperbolically, Barth rejected the *analogia entis* as the "invention of the anti-Christ," rather than a means of revelation. Barth, *CD I.1*, xiii. He refers to it as "intolerable," "unpardonable," "wicked and damnable," "heathenish," and "incorrigible' in *CD* II.1, 84.

impassibility, and in terms of their ontology, spirituality/immateriality.[18] Simply put, at times Barth's dichotomy nearly humanizes the angels in order to protect God's transcendence, whereas the Old Testament writers achieved the same feat without needing to make such compromises.[19]

Barth interprets biblical angelology as originating in a "sphere where historically verifiable history . . . passes over into historically non-verifiable saga or legend," yet it is unclear why he felt it was valid for Old Testament writers to traverse the permeable veil between history and saga, but scolded theologians like pseudo-Denys and Aquinas for attempting the same thing.[20] The inventive approaches to angelology that were defended in chapters 2 and 3 derive from the Old Testament pattern established in chapter 1, provided it fulfilled a theological purpose with respect to the relationship between God and humanity. Barth depicts the angels as worshipers of God and witnesses to humans—ideas that are certainly prominent in both the biblical text and the history of theology—but his attention to the otherness of God risks making an idol of a human construct because it parenthesizes the trans-ethereal chain of angels that Old Testament writers stretched between heaven and earth. Barth writes that angels are "essentially marginal figures," reasoning that their majesty derives from their subordination to God and his activity.[21]

Lawrence Osborn disagrees: "There is too much emphasis on the divine-human axis within Barth's theology. . . . And, even within this narrow focus, there is too much emphasis on the divine pole. Barth's insistence on divine sovereignty reduces human and angel alike to a state of overawed impotence."[22]

By failing to incorporate celestial beings to the same degree that the Old Testament writers did in their mystical visions and experiences,

---

18. While it may seem as if angels are also simple beings like God, Aquinas argues that it is possible to distinguish the existence (*that* they are) and essence (*what* they are) of angels, whereas God's essence *is* his existence, neither of which he received.

19. Barth's theological vision was strongly oriented upon what God had already achieved in history past, but gives relatively little attention to the future, a fact that holds especially true for his angelology. Though I did not have the space in my chapter on the Old Testament, there are numerous angelophanies in prophetic and apocalyptic books that are entirely focused upon the future. This is even more the case for New Testament angelology.

20. *CD III.*3, 374.

21. Ibid., 371.

22. Osborn, "Entertaining Angels," 284.

Barth adumbrates rather than builds upon the mysteries surrounding angels.

Moreover, Barth's emphasis upon Christ and Scripture as exclusive vehicles of divine self-revelation threatens to undermine apprehensible means of immanence prior to the incarnation and closing of the canon.[23] By closing the door to other forms of disclosure, he seems to suggest that the world in which we live is somehow dissimilar to the world that lives within the pages of Scripture, where angels and nature alike acted as revelatory agents.[24] The Old Testament writers did not marginalize either the natural world or the angels to this degree, because both, like Christ and the biblical text, contributed heavily to the perception that the transcendent God was a being who could be encountered. For instance, God revealed his hiddenness to the unbelieving Jacob, but only after orchestrating an angelic prelude to the encounter at Bethel. Thus God's revelation was not simply in the Word or Scripture, but in true presence and accompaniment within the physical world, so much so that Jacob renamed the plot of land "God's house," as a permanent reminder of this event which occurred in space-time. It is the ascending and descending angels who show this wanderer that heaven and earth are linked, even though Jacob was incapable of anticipating Christ's fulfillment of the ladder trope. The splendor of creation, whether in the form of an angel or an atom, reminds one of the grandeur of its Designer, but as with angelology, too radical a distinction between the two disassociates one's everyday experience from one's ultimate longing.[25]

Given all that has been said about Barth's angelology *vis-à-vis* Old Testament angelology, he still merits praise on several fronts: for his assiduous resolve to reclaim a biblical basis for angelology, for the consistency of his argument, and for reintroducing a largely forgotten subject

23. Barth only concedes that passages like Rom 1:20 reveal that God is *not* perceived through the creation, not that he is present in it. God reveals himself in Christ, instead. Barth, *Epistle to the Romans*, 45–47. Also, Barth's "No!" in Brunner and Barth, *Natural Theology*, 70–128. Brunner complained that Barth always avoided this text, see 61 n.9.

24. For angels as agents of revelation: Gen 22:15–18; Judg 13:3; 1 Kgs 19:5; Deut 33:2. For the role of the natural world: Ps 19:1–3; Rom 1:20.

25. In this historical light, one could wish that Barth had also adopted a more integrative model of revelation which takes into account the entirety of history (after all, the vision of the biblical authors gives an inordinate amount of attention to angels in both Genesis and Revelation), with the angel as a polymorphic and permanently necessary, rather than a marginal, being.

to modern theology. One cannot fault his conclusions given his premises, nor can he be accused of failing to recognize either the angel as an actual being, or the pre-eminence of the Godhead to all that can ever be said about angels. However, Barth's angelology requires an idiosyncratic reading of Scripture and his emphasis upon divine transcendence makes angels too much like humans in order to achieve an effect. Yet, one cannot overlook the fact that God's self-revelation is closely linked to the angels, and that in the taxonomy of being, humans are made lower than these purely intellectual beings.[26] This is why God can say of the angel in Exod 23 "my name is in him" in a way that it cannot be said about mortals.[27] For instance, named angels like "Michael" (Who is like God?) and "Gabriel" (Strength of God) bear a resemblance to God that is more heavenly than earthly, at least one would assume as much from examples like Gabriel's bold proclamation to Zechariah in Luke 1:19, "I am Gabriel, I stand in the presence of God."[28]

The clear distinction between the Creator and his creatures that Barth strives to maintain, threatens to obscure the close relationship between angels and God. The Old Testament writers tie God to the angel in terms of divine participation in the world; in return, the world responds to God in participation with the worship that angels render to God. The radical otherness that Barth imparts between the two worlds merges

26. For instance, in *CD* III/3, 494–95, Barth nearly renders the angels redundant in light of God's unconditioned independence: "Even the frequently heard expression that the ministry of angels consists in mediating between God and earthly creatures is to be used, therefore, only with the greatest caution. God mediates Himself, and does not need a third party for this purpose. He mediates Himself through His own Word . . . His own Holy Spirit." Yet despite this strong opinion concerning angelic mediation, when one turns to p. 497, it appears Barth has failed to heed his own cautionary advice, "It is the angels who impress this stamp [of co-operation with God] as it were on the acts of God. They serve God in this sense. They work with Him in this sense. And in this sense we can and *must speak of a mediating ministry of angels between God and earthly creatures.*" Barth is willing to speak of angels as mediators only in the sense that they are present and active on the periphery of divine activity; their presence distinguishes God's actions from all others.

27. "I am going to send an angel in front of you, to guard you on the way and to bring you to the place that I have prepared. Be attentive to him and listen to his voice; do not rebel against him, for he will not pardon your transgression; for my name is in him" (Exod 23:20–21). In fact, they are called "sons of God" in Job 1:6; 38:7.

28. Anyone conversant with the angelophanies in Scripture will certainly recall how humans instinctively pay deference to the angels on almost every occasion (Zechariah is struck dumb for days resulting from his disbelief of Gabriel's words). At times this deference overflows into worship, which the angels reject.

in the Old Testament at the point of the angel who uniquely represents heaven *and* the creation, the spirituality of God and the limitations of finitude. Barth strove to avoid the radical immanentism that unravels all distinctions between God and the world, yet the fear is that if modern theology pushes too much in the direction of this absolute distinction between Creator and creation, it may lose the interest of an already skeptical twenty-first-century population. Just as Barth was a much-needed corrective of his predecessors, so the modern theologian must be equally cautious that Barth himself did not go too far by stressing the angels' function over their being and their bidirectional theological use as agents of divine transcendence *and* immanence. Thus it may be that Barth is correct that one has to understand angels in their relation to heaven in order to understand them at all.[29] Yet heaven may be conceived not as merely an otherworldly place dominated by a Being of otherworldly proportions, but as something that Christ ultimately joins together in the form of a new creation. Accordingly, inasmuch as angels are a part of that world, they are more than Barth's marginal figures. Instead, they comprise an eschatological hope in the present, which the Old Testament writers leveraged as a means of reconciling the apparent disparity between a transcendent and immanent God.

## THE NEW AGE MOVEMENT: IMMANENCE AT THE EXPENSE OF TRANSCENDENCE

It is perhaps no coincidence that the growth of the New Age movement in recent decades happens to coincide with the decline in church attendance across Europe, and to a lesser extent, America.[30] A number of factors

29. "When we undertake to think and speak about angels we have to remember that they are not leading characters and that we can thus speak of them only incidentally and softly. . . . After all, it makes a great difference whether we treat a theme independently or in connection with something else. And it is the latter which must obtain in relation to the kingdom of God as the kingdom of heaven and therefore to angels as the heavenly messengers of God." *CD III.3*, 371.

30. Virtually no hard data is available concerning the level of membership in the New Age movement, simply because it is such an amorphous group. The only category the UN measures in its statistical database which would come close to New Age is titled "other religions"—too broad to be reliable. The downward trend in church membership, however, is well documented. A survey published in Jan 2010 showed the Church of England had entered a fifth straight year of decline, with a 5 percent drop in attendance since 2001. Gledhill, "Church of England Congregations Fall Again, and

explain the downturn: increasingly busy lifestyles, distrust of religious figures and organizations, boredom with worship services, disagreement with the church's positions on social issues, and an ageing population are among the most likely precipitants. Of course, others have ceased worshipping simply because they grew weary after years of perfunctory attendance. The not-infrequent clergy scandals involving sexual abuse or theft only seem to validate this exodus. It is not always the case that those who took flight lost their need for faith, however; many simply ceased to believe the church could offer a form of spirituality that could not be supplemented elsewhere. Some who began searching for alternatives to Christian worship discovered that groups like the New Age movement— also known as Mind-Body-Spirit—provide a cornucopia of spiritual insights without the hegemony and inconvenience often associated with organized religion.

Yet so problematic are many presuppositions of the Mind-Body-Spirit movement that the Vatican issued a withering condemnation of the group in 2003. Entitled "Jesus Christ the Bearer of the Water of Life: A Christian Reflection on the New Age," the fifty page work portrays the groups as gnostic cults. The paper accuses New Ageism of misleading people to believe that God is a force to be harnessed rather than a being with whom one is meant to have a relationship. It also takes umbrage with the deeply un-Christian hypothesis that there are many Christs rather than one, and the idea that one's *raison d'être* is to reach a higher form of consciousness. The Vatican's assessment is accurate: New Age spirituality is preoccupied with attaining mystical union with the cosmos. This merger has little to do with meeting the transcendent Godhead in the sufficiency of Christ's reconciling love, relying instead upon meditative practices and the performance of rituals designed to summon spiritual guides like angels.[31]

It is difficult to understand the attraction of a recent movement with no official spokesperson or devotional figure, but this appears to be the strength of New Ageism—it is a syncretistic and diffusive form of spirituality that aims to be all things to all persons. Despite being

---

Half Are Pensioners." In America, there was a ½ percent decline across the top twenty-five Christian denominations. Kwon, "Largest Christian Groups Report Membership Decline | Christianpost.com."

31. Pontifical Council for Culture and Pontifical Council for Interreligious Dialogue, "Jesus Christ the Bearer of the Water of Life—A Christian Reflection on the New Age."

heavily invested in Eastern mysticism, one also finds elements of the Judeo-Christian faith in New Age literature, with angels as the most prominent example of this phenomenon. This veneer of the familiar may explain why some believers do not see any harm in frequenting New Age bookstores, especially when hunting for information about angels. In fact, an American study published in 2000 reveals that Christians appear as likely to purchase New Age resources as any other person in society.[32] The researchers concluded, "neither individual, nor community-level religious factors appear to exert any influence on consumption of New Age materials."[33] Yet while dozens of titles about angels flood the bookshelves of alternative bookstores, the angels featured by the New Age movement only retain the most superficial attributes of their Judeo-Christian origins and operate largely at the writer's caprice. For instance, author and hypnotherapist Diana Burney, a leading figure in the movement, writes,

> Since the angelic kingdom respects the Universal Law of Free Will, its members will only come forth or intercede when they are summoned or invited. These angels love you and will assist you unconditionally. The types of angels that come forth are often connected with the individual's level of spiritual evolution. . . . There are many types of angels dedicated to assisting people who seek spiritual growth and well-being. These include angels of healing, transformation, balance, love, mercy, grace, mastery, protection, and vision, to name a few.[34]

Burney's thoughts are representative of the esoteric, individualistic, and heavily immanent angelology of the New Age. Unlike pseudo-Denys's angelology of immanence, the movement imports the transcendent into modern experience without recognizing the jurisdictional restrictions typically associated with celestial hierarchies. Mind-Body-Spirit angelology promises an instantly accessible form of spiritual support, often emphasizing what is better described as a symbiotic cult of humanity and

32. The study was limited to Texas (N = 1,014 with a response rate of approximately 60 percent) and may not be representative of circumstances elsewhere in the world; however, it is significant to note that Texas is one of America's most religiously conservative states, hosting some of the largest churches in the world such as Lakewood church, which boasts a weekly attendance of 43,000 persons. Approximately nine million Texans are distributed among Roman Catholic, Southern Baptist, and United Methodist churches alone, and an estimated fourteen million across all denominations. "State Membership Report: Denominational Groups, 2000."

33. Mears and Ellison, "Who Buys New Age Materials?"

34. Burney, *Spiritual Clearings*, 114.

angels, made possible by the circumvention of ecclesiology. As Burney suggests, the angels interact with persons on an "unconditional" basis provided that individuals choose to summon them. Though Burney differentiates classes of angels as did Denys, she does so according to the powers and attributes they supposedly introduce into people's lives (e.g., healing, transformation, balance, love, etc.), whereas he followed the biblical writers by recognizing angels' titles and their function in relation to the Creator. This difference in emphasis is revealing, because it suggests the New Age movement is interested in ways that *humans* may use the angels, where Christian theology chooses to depict angels as beings used by *God*, which in the *Celestial Hierarchy* was to act as a form of divine immanence.

Unlike Burney, Denys did not suppose the angelic presence was immediately accessible. His cosmology interprets relationships as bound to the stepwise arrangement that emanates from the Triune God—as if a river of access issues forth from the divine throne, cascades through the angelic and ecclesiastical hierarchies, then saturates the sacraments and liturgy, before accumulating within the church. Centuries of theology build up to the idea that human attempts to circumvent this contiguous order would be interpreted as presumptuous and contrary to divine purpose and design. Although New Ageism has invested heavily in the idea of angels as celestial aides, it is far less interested in monotheism, the legitimacy of the church, or the sacraments. The movement expresses an unspoken longing within individuals who remain equally unsatisfied by answers proffered either by positivism or Abrahamic faiths. Neither scientific understanding nor the kingdom of God are the ultimate concern of this utilitarian spirituality, but rather the attainment of a higher form of awareness, often referred to in the literature as "angel consciousness." The angels are important because they are a means to this humanistic end.[35] Where pseudo-Denys called for an angelology that respected the distinctive roles of clergy and liturgy in their relationship to the angelic hierarchy and the Godhead, the prophets of the New Age sound an inclusive call for all persons to dabble with angels as if angels were an ap-

35. A stark contrast to pseudo-Dionysius' almost compulsive theositic desire to meet with God through apophasis and kataphasis, Faivre paints a compelling portrait of the esotericist who "appears to take more interest in the intermediaries revealed to his inner eye through the power of his creative imagination than to extend himself essentially toward the union with the divine. He prefers to sojourn on Jacob's ladder where angels (and doubtless other entities as well) climb up and down, rather than to climb to the top and beyond." Faivre, *Access to Western Esotericism*, 12.

paratus for spiritualevolution. As an ideological reservoir where nearly everything is acceptable and almost nothing is heretical, the Mind-Body-Spirit movement is a welcome exception for those who perceive as patri-archal, bookish, and narrow the conventions of Christianity.

The emphasis of the New Age movement upon angel-human en-counters allows its gurus to shroud in piety their individual experiences without facing the demands of credibility, as if by filtering angelology through their own eccentricities, such occurrences authenticate and uni-versalize the imperatives and methodologies found in their literature. Purporting to reveal the requisite knowledge that would permit new-comers to engage with celestial beings in similar fashion, they intimate that not only is the practice safe and valid, but contra-Denys, invalidate relationships between angels and the church, clergy, or sacraments. Rather than drawing upon such an august marriage of systems and his-torical reflection as Dionysian angelology does, the New Age adaptation celebrates a catalog of pragmatic works with titles like: *How To Hear Your Angels; Healing with the Angels: How the Angels Can Assist You in Every Area of Your Life; Past Life Regression with the Angels; 100 Ways to Attract Angels; The Angel Connection: Utilising Your Angels in the New Energy; The Angels within Us; Emotional Healing with Angels: A Spiritual Guide to Knowing, Healing and Freeing Your True Self by Angels; Angel Prayers and Messages; Romance Angels: How to Work with the Angels to Manifest Great Love.* Often infallible in tone, the rituals prescribed within this literature smack of the highest Dionysian churchmanship, but their accessibility reveals that the authors are equally reluctant to differentiate themselves from their "parishioners."

Pseudo-Dionysius is generally regarded among Mind-Body-Spirit authors in the same way some Americans regard Columbus or Lincoln, as a forgotten but tangentially relevant figure who made a new world pos-sible, but whose vision is almost entirely lost upon the present genera-tion. Similarly, these authors often draw upon Scripture and figures like pseudo-Denys as an appeal to authority, to support their esotericism. For instance, after awkwardly describing Denys as the sixth-century origina-tor of a spiritual "system [of angelology] most commonly followed by Westerners," J. E. Trayer, whose *nom de plume* is Silver RavenWolf, then uses Denys's outline to launch into a discussion about how one gains ac-cess to these nine ranks of angels. In her book, *Angels: Companions in Magick,* now in its eighth printing, RavenWolf writes,

> The Seraphim, those closest to divinity, concentrate on vibra-
> tional manifestations to keep divinity constant and intact . . .
> they make sure nothing rocks the boat, no negative energy gets
> through to divinity. . . . Magickal [sic] people can access the
> Seraphim because we are excellent at praying and raising power.
> . . . To reach the Seraphim, burn a white candle for divinity, and
> a purple candle for the Seraphim.[36]

A prolific and popular author, Ms. RavenWolf's seventeen books disseminate her philosophy far beyond American shores, having been translated into various languages, including Czech, Spanish, Italian, German, Russian, and Hungarian. However skilful she may be at detaching Denys's angelic hierarchy from the church and Christianity, her characterization of seraphim takes profound liberties with Scripture. Passages like Isa 6 highlight the point, where the seraphim shake the temple's foundations with their antiphonal trishagion; then, only at Yнwн's command do they interact with an overwhelmed Isaiah, pronouncing absolution by cauterizing his unclean lips. Neither Scripture nor Denys supports her candle-lighting theory as a means of access. In fact, Ms. RavenWolf makes only one reference to Scripture in the book when she describes how, in the past, angels had been relegated to the "bottom of the Bible cabinet at the whims of religious leaders."[37] It appears she, like other New Age authors, has returned the favor by relegating the Bible to a position beneath the whims of "magickal" angelology.

The angelology featured in the Mind-Body-Spirit movement borrows eclectically from Scripture and Christian theology, but takes pains to avoid the crucifixion and atonement, seeking instead a mystical approach to spirituality that never has to deal directly with radical evil or the angels' relationship to Christ. Given that the New Age movement is generally opposed to sectarianism in all forms, it is unsurprising that its writers are especially wary of traditional religions. "Religions tell people what to do and what to believe," insists Mind-Body-Spirit author Diana Cooper, "Spirituality tells people to listen to their own guidance and follow their hearts."[38] Notwithstanding the fact that Cooper's endorsement of spirituality over against religion sounds itself like a veiled imperative about "what to believe," later in her book, *A Little Light on Angels*, she cannot avoid telling her own followers "what to do": "Simply focus on

36. RavenWolf, *Angels*, 39–40.

37. Ibid., 2.

38. Cooper, *A Little Light on the Spiritual Laws*, 114.

angels!"[39] Cooper, however, is more conservative in her emphasis upon angels than some of her comrades who perpetuate the idea that every individual is entitled to select their own means of access to the spiritual world from a smorgasbord of entities: "there are many levels of guides, entities, energies, and beings in every octave of the universe . . . ," one author insists, "They are all there to pick and choose from in relation to your own attraction/repulsion mechanisms."[40]

This new breed of angelology places such an emphasis upon synchronicity that nearly everything becomes paranormal, and because angels are intimately involved in all aspects of life, every event, however trivial, is laden with spiritual significance. From a Christian perspective, it is unfortunate that this endeavor for greater depth of meaning, rather than evoking a sense of awe and reverence for the Godhead, only serves to communicate that the individual and his or her angels are able successfully to manipulate the world, or worse, that one is entitled to the financial reward that lies within the giving power of an anthropomorphized Universe. "The next time you find a coin on the ground," writes Doreen Virtue,

> know that it was purposely placed in your path. The angels realize that we love to receive gifts, and the gift of a coin helps us feel supported—financially, emotionally, spiritually, and physically. Coins are a reminder of the Universe's infinite abundance of all that is good.[41]

Thus, immanence is not necessarily understood in terms of proximity to or intensity of God's presence, but in the identification of angelic gestures on the behalf of a self-conscious cosmos. Like pseudo-Denys, there is a strong emphasis in New Age culture on the connectedness of the world, but the difference is that while it treats the angels as celestial suzerains, it also fashions them as vassals, eager to satiate one's thirst for serendipity, and ever-willing to hear and answer requests for healing, wisdom, success, or love. Furthermore, not only does this omni-angelology remove the prospect of being judged by a transcendent God, but it brings heaven to earth in such a way that longing is consistently realized and never deferred, provided that one approaches the angels with candles, chants, prayers, and an openness to suggestion that borders on absurdity.

39. Ibid., 119.

40. Griscom, *Ecstasy Is a New Frequency*, 82.

41 Virtue and Virtue, *Signs from Above*, 68.

Since they are thought of as purely benign creatures, always celebrating, helping, listening, and guiding, New Ageism has used angels to synthesize a Procrustean cosmos in which higher order beings inhabit spaces where only God used to reign. Take, for example, George Trevelyan's description of an angel as a guide who "can speak in your thinking with the still small voice. He can use your faculty of intuition to suggest to you a course of action into your Higher Self."[42] Divine condescension, celestial and ecclesiastical hierarchies, means of grace, and transcendence are unnecessary when the imprimaturs of New Age publishers allow authors to bequeath their readers with keys of theurgic access to every higher order being. Thus, heaven has become immediate and accessible—pedestrianized by a new Cultural Revolution, which itself is driven by the insatiable iconoclasm that tramples underfoot everything that undermines its regime. Pseudo-Dionysius's angels preserve the inscrutability of God and complement the Old Testament emphasis upon transcendence by enhancing God's immanence in light of Christ's presence in the Eucharist. By shifting the focus from God to the individual, however, New Age angelology is like a bird with one wing, transforming Denys's elegant theology of divine immanence into a flightless religion of human self-actualization.

At its worst, New Age religion downplays Judeo-Christian concepts of theism and transcendence in order to exalt human transcendence, which explains why persons are exhorted to work in concord with angelic beings, who in turn, become surrogates for the Father, Son, and Holy Spirit. This inclination veers precariously close to the warning against apostasy in Gal 2:18, "Do not let anyone disqualify you, insisting on self-abasement and worship of angels, dwelling on visions, puffed up without cause by a human way of thinking . . . ." In fact, the most egregious examples of heterodoxy in the twenty-first century come not from radical atheists, but from New Age gurus who put heretical theology into the mouths of angels: "Angel consciousness means you know that you are a divine being and that you are guided by a higher wisdom in the universe that operates for your highest good."[43] Similarly, "The main lesson the angels have for us is that *we are love, we are God on earth*, and it is time to love ourselves and open our hearts."[44]

---

42. Trevelyan, *Exploration into God*, 118.

43. Taylor, *Messengers of Love, Light & Grace*, 47.

44. Taylor, *Creating with the Angels*, 54.

So the version of angelology that has likely gained the largest following in recent decades does not follow pseudo-Denys as a means of
enhancing the immanence of God *per se*, but uses angels to mediate the
fantasies of its architects to persons in search of the hope, power, and
mystery that are ultimately found in Christ. Given that humans and angels share a Creator, the longing to interact with these supernatural beings is not any less rational than the desire to interact with lower beings
like dogs and cats, nor are the Scriptures in any way opposed to the idea.
However, what the Mind-Body-Spirit culture insists upon experiencing
now is an event which Jesus envisioned in the context of the life to come,
when persons will be like, and worship with, the angels who gather the
church into one eschatological congregation.[45] While this impulse to develop a religion of immanence is understandable given the absence of
the Son's personal presence, the New Age movement's tendency to over-
-personalize angels as a way of mitigating the gap between the self and
the transmundane dissolves God in the process, rendering angels as little
more than the lackeys of a human longing that Denys fulfils liturgically
and sacramentally. In other words, the quality that recommends the Dionysian angelology over against its newest contender is its reverence for
the hierarchical dynamic between God, angels, and the individual, which
it locates, as the New Testament does, as embodied within the church's
eternal worship of the Godhead rather than the self.

## ENVIRONMENTALISM: CREATION AT THE EXPENSE
## OF SACRED CREATIVITY

Thus far, I have argued that Barth departs from the Old Testament model
of angelology by emphasizing divine transcendence to the point that angels, rather than playing a distinguished role in the context of the divine-
human relationship, become "essentially marginal figures" standing on
the sidelines of redemption history.[46] Next, I proposed that the New Age
movement exaggerates the Dionysian emphasis on divine immanence
by placing too much importance upon the angel-human relationship;
by locating transcendence within the individual instead of with God, it
seeks immanence in the form of an immediate access to angels. Due to
their misplaced emphases, both sets of presuppositions negatively affect

45. Rev 4–5 Matt 13:49–50; 22:30; 24:31; Rev 4–5.

46. *CD III.3*, 371.

angelology's role as a theological tool for enhancing divine transcendence and immanence. Consequently, I have proposed that the church must regain in its angelology a sense of complementarity whereby the angels are *greater* than Barth's overawed and amorphous spectators of God's glory, yet *less* than the quasi-omnisicent, quasi-omnipotent, and quasi-omnipresent beings of the New Age movement.

This brings us to the final segment, which concerns the role of Thomas Aquinas as the figure who emphasized, more than others, the angel as a heavenly being of both literal and anagogical proportions. As with the Old Testament writers and pseudo-Dionysius, Aquinas's angelology is also an effective means of moderating ideologies which inhabit the extremes of an ideological continuum that I define as the space between pure imagination and pure reality. Therefore, I contend that Aquinas's angelology offers new insights into environmentalism, because unlike some popular ecologists, he is less afraid to posit a relationship between the natural and supernatural realms. By an approach that is both imaginative and true to Scripture, he sees angels relating to the planet not only as literal beings who occupy earth's sphere, but as analogical inhabitants of the physical world itself. Consequently, I propose that the proper way to relate to the earth is not as if it is simply a network of natural ecosystems, but a habitat for supernatural activity and an icon of God's profoundly creative activity.

In the last half century, environmentalists, government agencies, scientists, historians, and theologians have all advanced numerous works in response to the overuse of natural resources and the effects of pollution. While only a fraction of this collection is made up of publications addressing the relationship between ecology and theology, these works have heightened awareness within the Christian community concerning the correlation between one's faith and the physical world in which we live.[47] However, for reasons which I will discuss later, there is also an unfortunate trend among secular authors who feel the need to associate ecological progress with a disesteem for the Bible. The converse of this phenomenon is equally apparent among individuals who value Scripture but subordinate environmental considerations beneath their closely-held religious convictions. Examples of superseding concerns for this second group include the perceived futility of environmental action in light of

47. Prominent examples include: Brown, *God and Enchantment of Place: Reclaiming Human Experience*; Bakken, Engel, and Engel, *Ecology, Justice, and Christian Faith*; Moltmann and Kohl, *God in Creation*; Birch and Cobb, *The Liberation of Life*.

Christ's impending return.[48] Further objections to environmentalism may also arise out of economic beliefs about the right of free enterprise to consume the raw materials necessary to feed the growth of consumerism, or might simply reflect attitudes held by one's political party, denomination or peer group. There is little doubt that increased emphasis upon the physical world has highlighted genuine environmental concerns in recent years. For this reason, I believe Aquinas's angelology could potentially add much-needed depth to the discussion by providing a more constructive, less antagonistic approach to the current debate.

Nevertheless, formidable modern voices like historian Lynn White Jr., perhaps the most outspoken critic of theology's relationship to ecology, have a much different starting place from Aquinas. By drawing a correlation between environmental problems and Judeo-Christian theology (which he faults as inherently anthropocentric), White launched the current debate about whether Scripture encourages humanity to abuse the earth's resources. His opinions came to the fore after being published an influential article in *Science* entitled "The Historical Roots of Our Ecological Crisis." In the article, White alleges that "Christianity bears a huge burden of guilt" because it introduced the idea of ecological entitlement that ultimately allowed science and technology "to give mankind powers which, to judge by many of the ecologic effects, are out of control."[49] Yet it is impossible to verify whether White's position is, in fact, correct. As it stands, it is merely an accusation in search of hard evidence. I say this because after checking White's claims against statistical research conducted by the United Nations, I fail to see how, if his claims are true, nations with little or no exposure to Judeo-Christian theology have a *substantially higher* carbon output per capita compared with traditionally "Christian" nations.[50] This fact alone poses a significant barrier for parties seeking to put the Bible in the dock for the collective misdeeds of corporations, governments and persons throughout the centuries.

I do not wish to undermine the positive qualities of White's article, however, because while his perceptions lack any statistical support whatsoever, he leaves room for theologians like Aquinas to make a

48. It is possible that members of the Thessalonian assembly had stopped working because of a similar preoccupation with the Second Coming (2 Thess 3:6–15).

49. White, "The Historical Roots of Our Ecological Crisis," 1206.

50. $CO_2$ emissions per capita (in tones): compare the UK: 9.2 US: 19.7 with UAE 32.85, Qatar 56.24, Kuwait 31.17, Bahrain 28.82. "Environmental Indicators: Greenhouse Gas Emissions."

contribution. For instance, he proposes that since Christian theology is ultimately responsible for destroying the nature-preserving effects once found in pagan animism (another rather dubious assertion), the future of ecology will depend upon religious, rather than scientific and technological, solutions. This point, coupled with the eco-friendly example of St. Francis of Assisi, who tried to establish the idea of the equality of all creatures, led White to conclude that nothing short of a theological uprising will counteract humanity's gratuitous exploitation of nature. While many Christians may disagree with White's premises, there is much to say in favor of his conclusion that theological resolutions must precede an environmental restoration, a concept that reopens a path for Aquinas's angelology as well.

Aquinas speaks most naturally to those areas of the environmental movement where passion for the physical world has become such a priority that it resists becoming anchored to the supernatural in any way. What makes him especially fitted for this work is an interpretive style that frees bodiless intelligences to inhabit places where one might otherwise see nothing beyond a bird, statue, or a person. In other words, Aquinas enhances the physical world by suggesting that the angel and nature are both part of God's creative witness, and are therefore inseparable and interchangeable without being synonymous. So as a figurative device for describing the natural world, his angel becomes a mixed being who reconciles the extremes of spirit and matter by embodying both. Shin Shalom, a modern Israeli poet, captures this sentiment nicely:

> On Tu B'Shvat . . . an angel descends, ledger in hand, and enters
> each bud, each twig, each tree, and all our garden flowers. . . .
> When the ledger will be full, of trees and blossom and shrubs,
> when the desert is turned into a meadow and all our land is a
> watered garden, the Messiah will appear.[51]

Similarly, Aquinas sees within the earth something that originates beyond ecosystems, flora, and fauna: a vision of heaven that eludes those who are focused only upon restoring the world for its own sake. From the viewpoint of aesthetics, Aquinas's ideology could not be more dissimilar to anti-supernatural alternatives that reduce the world to a congregation of biological automatons who are little more than organic computers running their encoded DNA.[52] While Aquinas's opinions may not hold

---

51. Shalom, "Fifteenth of Shevat," 5.

52. Wink observes, however, since both angels and DNA are messengers, one

the same amount of sway with all ecologically minded persons, his voice is worth adding to the current dialogue, if for no other reason than that his integration of angelology and creation is a poetic reading of the world that stretches back thousands of years, and elevates the planet's worth more than pure environmentalism.

As imaginative as it is timeless, Thomas's doctrinal fusion is equally tempered by reverence for the Creator, a sentiment quite contrary to the musings of outspoken environmental activists like the late Edward Abbey, who spent his years pushing for a *geocentric* spirituality. "Why confuse the issue by dragging in a superfluous entity?" Abbey asks rhetorically, "Occam's razor. Beyond atheism, nontheism. I am not an atheist but an earthiest. Be true to the earth."[53] It is unclear what compelled Abbey (and the eco-warriors his books inspired) to prefer the environment to God, but such hostilities often radiate as counter-responses to God's decree, commonly misunderstood, to "subdue" the earth and exercise "dominion" over all forms of life.[54] Andrée Collard, for instance, states that "Genesis presents the view that God created everything and gave it to man to dominate."[55] Similarly, Ian McHarg, asserts that the Bible

---

could interpret the ancient belief that "there was an angel for everything, down to the last blade of grass," as a conceptual prototype of what we now know as DNA. Wink, *Naming the Powers*, 121.

53. Abbey, *Desert Solitaire*, 208.

54. One way for theology to move forward is to encourage the church to embrace the idea of working together with local environmental groups. While they might differ on other issues, both groups could find common ground by committing to reverse the effects of resource domination and exploitation. For Christians, it could be said that just as the angels have dominion over humanity, so it is better to understand our dominion as a duty to care for that which has been entrusted to us, rather than as something to conquer. After all, it would be rather odd if the writer of Genesis went to the trouble of emphasizing that God reflected seven times in creation's goodness (1:4, 10, 12, 18, 21, 25, 31), only to mandate the abuse of the natural world. Furthermore, it is clear from the book of Leviticus alone that one's treatment of the creation is governed by divine laws: one was forbidden to reap to the edges of their field, nor could they gather the gleanings (Lev 19:9); trees must be at least five years old before they are harvested (Lev 19:23); fields are to remain unsown on a regular basis (Lev 25:1–12); and landowners are to tithe from their harvest (Lev 27:30–33). New Testament writers suggest that even though Christ supersedes our concept of "dominion," he is responsible for creating it for his own glory (Col 1:16; 1 Tim 6:16; Rev 1:6). To revisit the connection between angels and the environment again, perhaps the connection is linguistically closer than we have realized, given the class of holy angels known as "the Dominions" get their name from *dominationes*, the Latin translation of *kuriotes* in Col 1:16.

55. Collard, *Rape of the Wild*, 17.

"in its insistence upon dominion and subjugation of nature, encourages the most exploitative and destructive instincts in man . . . ."[56] One the other hand, persons like right-wing author and syndicated columnist Ann Coulter, read Genesis 1:28 as a justification for gratuitous consumption levels, a position that only serves to reinforce anti-supernatural approaches to ecology. Without a hint of irony, Coulter writes,

> The ethic of conservation is the explicit abnegation of man's dominion over the Earth. The lower species are here for our use. God said so: Go forth, be fruitful, multiply, and rape the planet—it's yours. That's our job: drilling, mining and stripping. Sweaters are the anti-Biblical view. Big gas-guzzling cars with phones and CD players and wet bars—that's the Biblical view.[57]

Coulter, a self-identified Christian, may not be alone in her grotesquely irresponsible crusade to interpret the world by the value of its commodities. Stephenie Hendricks's book *Divine Destruction* finds that a number of Fundamentalist Christians also believe environmental protectionism is equally meaningless in light of the immanence of Christ's second coming.[58] It is likely that such views are even more prevalent in evangelicalism than Henricks realizes, given that *Left Behind*, the best-selling Christian fiction series of all time, dramatizes the future earth as a theatre for cataclysmic and draconian events—prerequisites for the return of Christ.

However, with the exception of Aquinas's vision, none of the theories discussed approaches nature as a divine gift or a sacred realm brimming with transcendent truths. Instead, they depict the world as a means to an end, a transient planet that one can worship, pillage, or downplay—thus, either the planet is primary, or the person is primary, or the end times are primary.

By contrast, Aquinas's angelology neither exalts the earth above God as Abbey appears to do (preferring creation to Creator), nor uses God to endorse wanton self-interest as in Coulter. Instead, he is only able to use angels to depict the planet as a multivalent and enduring realm because he presupposes the sacred presence of God within the earth. "God exists in everything," writes Thomas, "as an agent is present to that in which

---

56. McHarg, *Design with Nature*, 26.

57. Coulter, "Oil Good; Democrats Bad."

58. Hendricks, *Divine Destruction*.

its action takes place. . . . So God must exist intimately in everything."[59] This revealing quote begs the question as to whether ambivalence toward creation, as expressed by Coulter and others, may be the result of a theology that affiliates God and angels with the ethereal world alone. Simply put, if heaven is depicted as the distant abode of God and angels, is it any wonder that the earth is in its current state?

Historically, Judeo-Christian theology has striven to affirm a supernatural presence in the world, but without confusing this presence with the world itself. It is difficult, however, to push for a resacralization without erring too much on one side of this presence/absence dichotomy. In fact, because some contemporary Christian ecotheologians like Rosemary Ruether and Sally McFague have been accused of overlooking the distinction between God and nature, it may be wiser to affirm that divine omnipresence means that God, heaven, and angels are present within the earth by remaining alongside it, in a parallel universe that is simultaneously present and absent to our experience, as somewhere utterly real but only accessed through prayer, worship, and the imagination, except when it deliberately reaches into our world in the form of miracles and epiphanic experiences.[60]

Angels, of course, are not literally one with the objects to which Aquinas compares them (birds, sacred statuary, Scriptures, persons, wings, etc.); they simply gilt the pages of God's world, representing the silent glow of omnipresence and glimmers of eschatological potential. His poetic angelology enfolds the earth in mystery. For instance, in his sermon *"Lux Orta,"* preached on the Feast of the birth of the Virgin Mary and inspired by Ps 97:11, which reads: "Light has risen for the just; joy for the upright heart." Aquinas declares, "the angels are called 'light.' Gen 1:3 reads: 'God said: "Let there be light," and light was made'; a gloss says that this is understood as concerning the blessed spirits, that is, the angels." While Aquinas recognizes elsewhere that the Genesis passage is typically interpreted as the creation of visible light, here it is also true of angels by analogy, ostensibly because their goodness, pervasiveness, immateriality, purity, and intellectual brilliance.[61] It is this buoyant quality

59. *ST* 1.8.1.

60. For criticisms of these views, see Hart, *Regarding Karl Barth*, 182–86. Fergusson, *The Cosmos and the Creator*, 8. Hampson, *Theology and Feminism*, 160. For the views themselves, see McFague, *Models of God*; Ruether, *Gaia & God*.

61. For instance, in lecture seven on the fourth chapter of Galatians, he writes: "When I say 'Let there be light' and speak of corporeal light, it pertains to the literal

that safeguards Thomas's incorruptible angel from being confused with the groans of the natural world itself, but at the same time the celestial presence anticipates in the present what the created order will one day be.

What Aquinas provides is a comparatively hopeful alternative to the rather intense and ominous language used in non-theistic interpretations of the planet's future. Care has to be exercised that this model does not detract from the reality of environmental concerns, however. His association between angels and the world will not eliminate resource mismanagement, but since there is no guarantee that technology and legislation will solve the problem either, what Aquinas envisions is immediately attainable: the beholding of nature in a supernatural light. Given White's call for theological solutions, it seems Aquinas's angelology, with its ability to lead the imagination to a spiritual habitat mysteriously contained within the material, would help to inspire "green" action and alleviate unnecessary despair.

Aquinas's contextualized angelology is particularly winsome because it expands upon the language of Scripture.[62] For instance, biblical writers frequently associate angelophanies with aspects of the natural world, purposefully noting details that all but the most assiduous reader may fail to notice. For example, we are told that angels guard access to a tree in the Garden of Eden (Gen 3:24), engage Hagar by a spring of water (Gen 16:7), appear to Moses within a flaming bush (Exod 3:2), detain Balaam by a vineyard (Num 22:24), speak with Abram and Gideon beneath oak trees (Gen 18:1, 8; Judg 6:11), care for Elijah under a broom tree (1 Kgs 19:5–7), and teach Zechariah among the myrtle trees (Zech 1;11); an angel visited Manoah and his wife in a field, commanding her not to eat or drink anything coming from the grapevine (Judg 13:9–14). Similarly, in the New Testament, Jesus portrays angels as harvesters whose labor entails distinguishing between wheat and weeds (Matt 13:39–49), they transform natural pools of water into therapeutic baths (John 5:3–4),

---

sense. If 'Let there be light' is understood as 'let Christ be born in the church,' it pertains to the allegorical sense. If it is understood as 'let us be introduced into glory through Christ,' it pertains to the anagogical sense. If it is understood as 'let us be illumined in our intellects and inflamed in our affections,' it pertains to the moral sense." *Galatians.* Augustine supports the same view in Bk 11, ch 9 of *City of God.*

62. In passages like Ps 104:4, angels are compared to winds and fire and in Rev 1:20 Jesus refers to them as stars. Also in 2 Sam 5:23–24 and 1 Chr 14:14–15, the wind which stirred the tree-tops appears to have been regarded as the presence of YHWH's hosts. So too, the pool of water in John 5:1–4 was imagined to be related to the intervention of an angel, where it is more likely to have been a natural, subterranean force.

their voice is mistaken for thunder (John 12:29; Rev 6:1), they are compared to basic elements like wind and fire (Heb 1:7), and with the stars (Rev 1:20); four angels are given charge of protecting the earth, sea, and forest from wind (Rev 7:1) and one ascends from the rising sun (Rev 7:2). So it appears even from this brief survey that by bringing the angels into the world in a similar fashion, Aquinas is on conceptually sound footing when he writes of the atmosphere as the location for the creation of angels: "They [angels] were made in a corporeal place in order to show their relationship to corporeal nature, and that they are by their power in touch with bodies."[63]

Of course, the relationship between angel and nature is not always positive in Scripture.[64] Ever since the cherubim were placed at the mouth of the Garden of Eden, humankind has been locked in a struggle against weeds and thorns, the collective brows of multitudes still drip with sweat while clawing, with crude tools, the hardscrabble soil beneath their feet. And as one looks to the end of the biblical narrative in hope of respite, they find that before the valleys are lifted up and the mountains made low, the angels of God will move, like chess pieces, from positions of guardianship to opposition: "the angels who are appointed to watch over men will no longer fulfill the office of guardians," writes Thomas.[65] Throughout the book of Revelation the angels exhibit powers of terrifying proportions, which they unleash upon the earth at God's command. No longer do these celestial beings protect Paradise and endure conversations with bewildered humans under shade trees; instead, they introduce malaise-inducing episodes of war, famine, and pestilence. With upper lips stiffened by righteousness, they devastate the trees, grass, lakes, and rivers; and perhaps as an omen of all that is now being said about global warming, they unleash the flames of the sun in order to scorch the flesh of the blasphemous. However metaphorical, the extreme language concerning the angels of the Apocalypse is a reminder that the natural world is, and will always be, connected but subordinate to the celestial.

Fortunately, this is only part of the story, because after the angels raze the earth, the natural world is instantly restored in Rev 21 with the

---

63. *ST* 1.61.4.

64. Commenting on Gen 3:1, Aquinas interprets the serpent's temptations in the Garden as the result of possession by a fallen angel, "the serpent spoke to man, even as the ass on which Balaam sat spoke to him, except that the former was the work of a devil, whereas the latter was the work of an angel."

65. *ST* III suppl. 73.3.

heavenly Jerusalem descending and the beatific vision perfecting the planet. No longer will humankind be alienated from the flora and fauna—here, lambs and lions, children and vipers, live in peace—enjoying Jesus' assurance of living "like the angels." This said, there still needs to be an ecological revision of angelology in the book of Revelation, a rare opportunity missed by Aquinas who does not go far enough in addressing this tale of war and peace, despite his heavy emphasis upon angelology and natural theology elsewhere. Aquinas, however, has broken ground in order to make such a discussion possible, and so the next step for theology is to peer deeply into the creation itself, to find and highlight more identifying marks between it and spiritual beings.

For instance, the angel who is described in Rev 10:1 as wrapped in a cloud, with a face like the sun and a rainbow for a halo could not be more of an embodiment of creation's glory. This resplendent being signifies the natural world as a composite of the spiritual, yet a detailed search of the *Corpus Thomisticum* reveals no traces that Aquinas considered the figure as such. Perhaps these are anachronistic expectations. What Aquinas does comment upon is that the world, in the context of its eschatological future, is not ultimately subject to angels, regardless of how glorious they may appear. Regency belongs to the Godhead. He presses, however, for an appreciation of the angels' supervisory governance until that time:

> But Daniel (chap. 10) says that an angel was the prince of the Greeks and of the Persians, and in Dt. (32:8) it says: "He appointed the bounds of people according to the number of the children of Israel." But it should be noted that they are not subject to them as to a lord, but as to a vicegerent: for all visible creation is administered by angels.[66]

Aquinas understood that it is far better to exegete the earth than to consume it, and his willingness to risk a creative application of angelology makes him a fitting voice for future discussions about the environment as it relates to heavenly beings and the world to come. Perhaps if Aquinas was alive today, he might suggest that while some persons are like the angels of Revelation—destroying the world in an effort to capitulate to the demands of gratuitous consumption—humans can also aspire to be like the angels, who, in their positive relationship to nature, superintend the creation with the same joy and wonder they expressed upon the original

---

66. Aquinas, *Hebrews*, 2:5.

unveiling of the planet.[67] Aquinas may not have been the first to propose an imaginative connection between angelology and the natural world, but in this generation's preoccupation with saving the world, it is possible that we might have overlooked the connection without him.

While it may be improbable that his view would gain a large following from ecologists today, Aquinas's theory opens up homiletical vistas for interpreting the world as a place that is associated with something greater than itself, a point absent in many exhortations to care for the planet. Aquinas's analogies envision the earth as a simultaneously spiritual and organic object. Teilhard's *Mass of the World* captures a similar idea:

> When all the things around me, while preserving their own individual contours, their own special savors, nevertheless appear to me as animated by a single secret spirit and therefore as diffused and intermingled within a single element, infinitely close, infinitely remote; and when, locked within the jealous intimacy of a divine sanctuary, I yet feel myself to be wandering at large in the empyrean of all created beings: then I shall know that I am approaching that central point where the heart of the world is caught in the descending radiance of the heart of God.[68]

There is something unsettlingly diabolical about humans wanting to be alone in the world without God or angels, because it indicates a loss of wonder, the repression of childlikeness. As almost every clergyperson, artist, educator, writer, and filmmaker knows, it is nearly impossible to engage a person's mind without also appealing to their imagination. So it is one thing to speak about emissions that are tainting the thin atmosphere above our heads, and quite another to conceive of the same space as Aquinas did: as a habitat for angelic sentries, who, like birds in flight, wing their way throughout the sky on our behalf.[69] After all, if a similar vision of assembled angels was used in 1 Cor 11:10 to support female head-covering and Heb 12:22 to evoke a sense of wonder and reverence

---

67. Job 38:4–7: "Where were you when I laid the foundation of the earth? Tell me, if you have knowledge. Who set its measurements, since you know? Or, who stretched out its measuring line? On what was its bases sunk? Or, who laid its cornerstone? While the morning stars sang together, and all the angels [lit. 'sons of God'] shouted for joy."

68. King and Chardin, *Teilhard's Mass*, 158.

69. Cf. *ST* 1.61.4.

within the micro-universe of Christian assembly, how much more might it apply to the world that God created?

Aquinas reminds the church that God is no less concerned with the spiritual composition of the world than he is with the physical. One does not have to choose between the two realms as if it was a zero-sum proposition, contrary to what the Abbeys and Coulters of the world might have us believe. Instead, one sphere flows out of the other; the root that bears the fruit of environmental care is deeply buried in an ethic that is spiritual and imaginative. To Aquinas, the very perfection of the universe depends upon the existence of angelic beings, without which, the earth would be rather like a disconnected bubble floating on a sea of nothingness than a playground for heavenly activity. Hence, "[e]verything that happens among creatures," Aquinas maintains in his *Commentary on Ephesians*, "occurs with the assistance of the angels."[70] Analogically, the angels, like Christ, incarnate the physical world, clothing themselves with temporary flesh, eating Abram's bread, separating wheat from tares in Jesus' parables. They represent the completeness of creation, as the Creed reminds us: God is the maker of *horaton te panton kai aoraton*. What may seem like a creedal dichotomy is not meant to suggest that the visible and invisible are separate realms, but that what is for God a unified creative act, is only partly perceptible in the present life.

If the church is orienting people to look to the future and the New Age movement is telling them to look inward, the absence of a spiritual presence in ecology has taught persons to look outward to the world. Yet because it is often unwilling to accommodate the idea that the hand of God is at work within the creation, I have suggested that non-theistic environmentalism is a myopic solution to what is essentially a spiritual matter. Equally troubling are those in the Christian community who interpret the moribund ecosystem as a foregone conclusion of either Christ's return or a divine mandate to reap without sowing. Introducing Aquinas's model to the ecological dialogue would serve to make us aware of more connections between this and the heavenly realm. It would also help to challenge the orientation that suggests that faith is a spiritual, personal, and interior issue that has little to do with our activities within the natural world. So rather than seeing the creation as an object entirely distinct from humanity, Aquinas's angelology, through the medium of imagination, brings one *into* the creation with the angel as a member of

70. Aquinas, *Ephesians*, 48.

the same narrative. Thus angelology, creatively conceived and applied, can be a tool that encourages a love for nature while also preventing us from displacing God with a disenchanted environment.

## THE EUCHARIST AS THE FULFILLMENT OF ANGELOLOGY

Unlike angels and the departed in Christ who dwell in the immediate presence of the Godhead, the believer must wait until their mortal lives are over before gaining admission into the blessed state. The one who wishes to alleviate a sense of alienation from God must therefore find a way to appropriate God's future promise into their present life. I have offered a number of ideas in this work that orient angelology as an anticipation of the special presence of God. However, because not everyone is willing and able to take purely conceptual leaps into categories like transcendence and immanence, or capable of mustering the imagination required to "see" the angel within nature, my theories lack the sort of experiential dimension that may appeal to a broader Christian demographic. I shall attempt to remedy this weakness in this final section by proposing an association between angelology and the arch-sacrament of Christ's church, the Eucharist.

Like an angelophany, the Eucharist serves as a means of mediating the intensity of divine presence to the physical world. Although neither angel-visions nor partaking of the Lord's Supper are equivalent to being in God's presence, they each provide a source of encouragement to those who cannot defer their longing indefinitely. The Eucharist and angel are both means of transport, bringing into the present, glimpses of the future which God has promised to the Christian and the creation. However, since the Eucharist is repeatable and operates within the predictable structures of liturgy, it enjoys a distinct advantage over angelophanies, either as real events or theological devices.

In Scripture, incorporeal angels appear to clothe their nothingness with visible forms so that they may interact with humans outside the world of dreams and heavenly voices; in fact, biblical hospitality to strangers is predicated upon the idea that any unknown man or woman one encounters may actually be an angel in disguise.[71] So too, the Eucharist could be considered Christ's present disguise. Yet it is a not a

---

71. Heb 13:2. Cf. Gen 18:2, 16; Ezek 9:2; Dan 10; etc.

hypostatic union between angels and humans, or deity and humanity, but between *deity* and *creation*. Christ himself seems to endorse this view by describing his body and blood in terms of bread and wine, broken and poured out to be ingested by those who hunger for eternal life:

> Very truly, I tell you, unless you eat the flesh of the Son of Man and drink his blood, you have no life in you. Those who eat my flesh and drink my blood have eternal life, and I will raise them up on the last day; for my flesh is true food and my blood is true drink. Those who eat my flesh and drink my blood abide in me, and I in them.[72]

The passage reveals what the resurrection reinforces; eternal life is best interpreted as more than a promise of unending felicity in a disembodied future state, it is a present possession which ensures the redemption of the material and immaterial constituents of a human being, the physical body as well as the soul. This reconciliation of the material and immaterial is a fitting description of the eucharistic mystery, Aquinas's angel as a composite being, and eternal life as something that one receives while still living upon the earth. Each is an admixture of the noumenal and phenomenal, the physical and spiritual, the present and future life.[73]

The connection between the angel and the Eucharist is most pronounced in traditions that recognize the sacrament as the liturgy's central feature. Every week millions of Christians embroider the celebration with angelic themes by singing or saying the *Te Deum*, *Gloria*, and the *Sanctus*, praying suffrages and collects, and even petitioning for the prayers and protection of angels. As John Paul II observed, the eucharistic prayers, which honor angels are not insignificant:

> This is an aspect of the Eucharist which merits greater attention: in celebrating the sacrifice of the Lamb, we are united to the heavenly liturgy. . . . [T]he Eucharist is truly a glimpse of heaven appearing on earth.[74]

The act of prayer reminds the church of the angelic presence during a worship service, evoking a sense of cosmic solidarity to the proceedings; at these moments the church acknowledges that she is truly one congregation, visible and invisible. Another particularly interesting example of

72. John 6:53–56. The image of Jesus as one who provides the bread/food that gives eternal life is a major theme of this chapter.

73. Composite in the sense that his angel overlaps with the physical world.

74. Paul II, "Ecclesia de Eucharistia," I.19.

this intentional camaraderie comes from the *Book of Common Prayer*, which includes the following petition for the consecration of a church, with the Bishop laying a hand upon the Table:

> Lord God, hear us. Sanctify this Table dedicated to you. Let it be to us a sign of the heavenly Altar where your saints and angels praise you for ever. Accept here the continual recalling of the sacrifice of your Son. Grant that all who eat and drink at this holy Table may be fed and refreshed by his flesh and blood, be forgiven for their sins, united with one another, and strengthened for your service. Blessed be your Name, Father, Son, and Holy Spirit; now and for endless ages. Amen.[75]

By recollecting angel and altar imagery used throughout the Scriptures, the prayer of dedication envisions the Eucharist as the *axis mundi* where humans imitate the devotion of celestial beings.[76]

In its biblical and liturgical environment, angelic imagery serves to heighten the sense of the Eucharist's importance, a point similar to the one I have made throughout this work about the angel as a theological motif for the transcendence of God. Thus, since biblical references (many of which have sacrificial overtones), predate such liturgical interpretations, it will not do to view the relationship between angels and the Eucharist as purely artificial. On the other hand, the correlation is not indefectible; the Lord's Supper links tangible elements with an immediate access to the supernatural in a way that incorporeal angels may still long to look into. It is impossible to overestimate the epistemological assurance many derive from contact with the Eucharist as a *physical* version of the transcendence, immanence, and creative activity of God. Nevertheless, both angels and sacraments are an imaginative pledge from God to humanity, reminders that one is never ultimately far from the presence of God who is *other*.

In my first chapter I described, among other things, how the Old Testament depicts angels in relation to sacred places: they flank the ark's mercy seat, guard doorways and sanctuaries, and appear at makeshift altars where sacrificial blood was shed. The second chapter illustrated how pseudo-Denys positioned angels in a hierarchy that is contiguous with the Eucharist, establishing christological union between heaven

75. The Episcopal Church, *The Book of Common Prayer*, 574.

76. For instance: Judg 6:19–21; 13:19–20; 1 Chr 21:18; Luke 1:11; Rev 8:3–5; 9:13; 14:18.

and earth within the confines of the church sanctuary. My final chapter focused primarily upon Aquinas's imaginative use of angels as a way of resacralizing the natural world, but one also discovers in his works a relationship between angels and the Eucharist that draws us back into the sanctuary. For instance, when discussing 1 Cor 11:23–24, Thomas writes that Christ commands us to *take* the eucharistic bread, "As if not from any human power or merit is it proper for you to use this sacrament, but from an eminent gift of God: 'Thou didst give thy people the food of angels' (Wis 16:20)."[77] Here, Christ provides the bread with its heavenly character, and so the sacrament becomes a form of angelic food whose metaphysical properties derive not from anything that resides in the celebrant or laity, but are supernaturally supplied by God.[78]

Aquinas could have strengthened this particular image of the Eucharist as angelic food had he addressed supporting biblical accounts. Clearly, Ps 78:25 is the *locus classicus* for the statement that mortals ate "the bread of angels," which refers to the manna that Yhwh sent from heaven to fortify Moses and the people of Israel. Numbers 11:8 recounts how they formed the substance into cakes and ate it as they travelled through the wilderness for forty years. This manna, also called "bread" in Exod 16:31, characterizes God's persistent grace toward his people, providing them with "the bread of angels" to sustain them. It is also worth keeping in mind that, apart from Jesus, only two individuals are said to have fasted for forty days, Moses and Elijah. We are not told details about Moses' fast, *per se*, but Dale Allison raises the point that Jewish tradition puts angels on Sinai with Moses, and a Samaritan text, *Memar Marqah* 4:6, describes Moses eating the bread of angels.[79]

Similarly, in 1 Kgs 19:5–7, an angel feeds Elijah bread and water twice under a broom tree, which sustains the prophet for his forty-day journey to Horeb. Finally, in the Gospels, we are told that after his fast and the devil's attempt to get him to turn stones into bread, angels came

---

77. Aquinas, I Corinthians, 120.

78. In his discussion of Ps 51, where the repentant David predicts a time when God will again "delight in right sacrifices, in burnt-offerings and whole burnt-offerings; then bulls will be offered on your altar." Aquinas offers that burnt-offerings represent "lesser saints," whole burnt-offerings the "greater saints," and that upon their death, it is the angels who offer them back to God—a form of reverse-Eucharist—by "lay[ing] the saints upon thy altar, that is, into heavenly glory."

79. See Allison, 202 n.28.

to minister to Jesus.[80] In light of the miraculous feedings during Moses' and Elijah's era, it is plausible that the angels ministered to Jesus in a similar way by providing him with food to break his fast.[81] Therefore, one could expand Aquinas's original idea by saying that not only is the Eucharist God's provision for the church as it hungers for his presence, but that it ought to make us mindful of how God may still use his angels to provide for our physical and spiritual needs today.

Stronger still is the connection Aquinas drew between the angels and the Eucharist in the *Summa Theologiae*. At one point, he identifies the angels as celestial concelebrants and thurifers who amplify the prayers of the priest and congregation during the eucharistic liturgy:

> The priest does not pray that the sacramental species may be borne up to heaven; nor that Christ's true body may be borne thither, for it does not cease to be there; but he offers this prayer for Christ's mystical body, which is signified in this sacrament, that the angel standing by at the Divine mysteries may present to God the prayers of both priest and people, according to Apocalypse 8:4: "And the smoke of the incense of the prayers of the saints ascended up before God from the hand of the angel."[82]

Here, Aquinas's celebratory and mystical tone underscores a belief in the church as a hierarchical body with strong ties to the Eucharist as a metaphysical event, language that is less likely heard in circles where the emphasis upon Scripture, preaching, conversion, and sanctification has virtually supplanted the role of sacraments, angels, and church offices.[83] Whether this suggests that by turning their back upon the angel's relationship to worship—either in the form of liturgy or the Eucharist—the church is in danger of producing Christians who are out of touch with heaven itself, is uncertain. Yet one cannot help thinking that by moving closer to the biblical imagery, which plays a commanding role in Aquinas's angelology, the church may discover and explore new elements of its birthright—that one's communion with God is superintended by the angelic.

80. Only found in Matt 4:11; Mark 1:13.

81. This is all the more likely since Jesus is often portrayed as a new Moses or Elijah. For other angel/bread references, see Judg 6:20–21; 1 Kgs 13:18.

82. *ST*, III/83.4. 9.

83. Some elements within the Charismatic movement, however, maintain a high regard for their own elected bishops. Nevertheless, Communion is typically celebrated infrequently and there is a high priority upon spiritual gifts.

In our present circumstances, angels can only accentuate what the Eucharist is *in situ*: the presence of the transcendent Christ in the material world. However, the biblical writers, Denys, and Aquinas are not alone in their depiction of angels in relation to the sacrament. For instance, in *Vested Angels: Eucharistic Allusions in Early Netherlandish Paintings*, the late historian Maurice McNamee, SJ, reveals how painters of this school often portrayed angels as celestial clergy. By examining over one hundred pieces of artwork, McNamee catalogs the number of ways in which these artists used sacerdotally-apparelled angels to make eucharistic references to nearly every episode of Christ's life.[84] Surprisingly, he discovered only one case in which an angel wore a chasuble, the appropriate garment for a celebrant; in every other instance they are depicted in vestments appropriate for subministers, such as albs, amices, or copes. The reason for this, McNamee determines, is because Christ is already present in the "chasuble of his flesh."[85] So both theological literature and art represent the angels as occupants of a peripheral, yet vital, position in an eternal liturgy; in neither instance do angels overshadow Christ, but nor does his presence make theirs unimportant.

I have suggested that one way for the church to preserve the angel's appeal is to draw a relationship between angelology and the sacrament, because it establishes an affiliation between existential longing and the christological event at the center of worship. This connection is not only evident in liturgy, art, and Aquinas's theology, but can be found in Scripture as well. The reason for maintaining this point is that the experiential dimension is often more memorable than words themselves; so when one sings hymns, recites stages of the liturgy, or takes Communion, it is hoped that they will also experience a taste of angelic spirituality. I am reminded of Chrysostom's words concerning the Eucharist, "At such a time angels stand by the Priest; and the whole sanctuary, and the space round about the altar, is filled with the powers of heaven, in honor of Him who lies thereon."[86] By attempting to relate and demonstrate the doctrine

---

84. Notable examples of non-Netherlandish works on the same theme, include: Claudio Coello's *Adoration of the Holy Eucharist*, *The Victory of the Eucharistic Truth Over Heresy* by Rubens, Bartolome Esteban Murillo's *The Infant Jesus Distributing Bread to Pilgrims*, and the enormous brass Ciborium which rests on the shoulders of four angels, designed by Giovanni Ricci and housed in the Sistine Chapel, Basillica Di Santa Maria Maggiore.

85 McNamee, *Vested Angels*, 204.

86. Chrysostom, *St. Chrysostom On the Priesthood*, 146.

in this way, my wish is that angels might again be perceived as nothing less than what they were for the earliest Christians: tokens of divine grace and figures that are synonymous with the guardianship and leadership of Christ's church.[87]

## CONCLUSION

In the course of this book I demonstrated that angelology once enjoyed a considerable role in Judeo-Christian theology as a means of supplementing the larger narrative of God's relationship with the world. I proposed that this apparatus—which was so central for biblical authors, pseudo-Denys, and Aquinas—is poised for rebirth despite having been oversimplified, demythologized, and intellectualized.[88] Since the Reformation, theology has attempted to navigate the existential gorge between heaven and earth without much reliance upon angelology, preferring instead to emphasize the centrality of Christ in God's reconciliation of the world to himself. As this work reveals, however, our ancestors were not oblivious to the primacy of the Godhead when they inlaid their theologies with angelomorphic ornamentation, but mischaracterizations of their ideological constructs obscured their true contributions. Therefore, in view of numerous biblical precedents, I proposed that their angelologies are relevant to our day and worthy of further exploration because they are metonyms for theocentric and christological themes.

Consequently, I sought to depict ancient angelologies in a sympathetic light and in a manner that is as sensitive to their historical milieu as it is to the needs of the modern church. In this final chapter, I have argued against recent theologians like Barth and movements like New Ageism and secular environmentalism that I feel have either minimized or exaggerated the role of angels with respect to the Godhead. The discussion culminated in the exploration of a relationship between the Eucharist and angelology, which I proposed contributes a much-needed experiential dimension to the doctrine. While my primary focus was upon angels as a means of enhancing dimensions of transcendence, immanence, and imagination, this book also aspires to be a summons toward ecumenical harmonization of the doctrine where ancient Hebrew (OT Scriptures),

87. Acts 5:18–20; 8:26–29; 10:3–8; 12:6–11; 27:23–25; Rev 1:13, 20.

88. These three qualities parallel my discussion about reaffirmation, revision, and rediscovery in the introduction.

Orthodox (pseudo-Dionysius), and Catholic (Aquinas) angelologies—combined with a eucharistic spirit—balance and complement more austere Protestant interpretations. Since each of these views comprises an integral part of the church's rich theological heritage, I am reluctant to exalt one above another for fear of oversimplifying a doctrine that is only as iridescent as it is comprehensive.

One can only hope that the convoluted development of angelology and its many-sided expressions in theology, art, and literature will continue to challenge the constraining assumptions of literalism and fideism, but without trivializing the subject. Systematics has tended to produce and preserve conventional templates of angels over the years when it ought to be drawing inspiration from the angelologies described in this work, not to mention the polymorphic exuberance expressed in nature, incarnation, and worship. Rather than perceiving angelology as we do the mercurial clouds that wisp and mingle with the wind, or in its mystical relation to the Bread and Cup, it has been captured like a photograph within mats and frames, static and cut to fit sectarian peculiarities or stuffed and preserved like taxidermy, hung vacant-eyed, between doctrinal kinspersons. This lack of freedom and scope, I believe, has moved the laughter of God but contributed to the marginalization of angelology by muting its splendor and smothering its capacity to speak beyond itself.

Given that there are more things in heaven and earth than are dreamt of in our theology, it will always be possible for the theological community to explore new ways to communicate angelology. It could be argued that other formats, such as art, are equally poised to further this doctrine. In fact, Renaissance-era paintings have informed people's concept of angels as haloed, winged, robed, resplendent beings more effectively than the written word has communicated the angel's more subtle distinctions. Art may also spur us on to rethink some of these earlier images, as in Paul Klee's twenty-nine depictions of angels as less-than-perfect beings or Anselm Kiefer's sculpture "Book with Wings" and painting "The Order of the Angels"—an interpretation of Denys's *Celestial Hierarchy*. Thus, clay, colored charcoal, canvas, pigment, and gold leaf, may provoke discussion in ways that reach beyond the theologian's grasp. Similarly, Wallace Stevens demonstrates that poetry can be a useful medium for applying the language of angelology to everyday life. In his poem, "Angels Surrounded Paysans", Stevens uses angelomorphic imagery to illustrate the relationship between the spiritual and physical realms. Inspired by a Pierre Tal-Coat still life painting, Stevens interprets the artwork by personifying it as an angel who invites onlookers to set their gaze beyond mere images. The rather lonely angel seeks to mediate his presence and knowledge to the imperceptive and jaded individual for whom life has lost its wonder. Representing the coexistence of the natural and supernatural realms, the angel reminds the reader that the fecundity and luxuriousness of the physical world is discovered when one is not looking merely at its physicality. His mission is to call into question the true meaning of the physical world, which can be known in fact, but is, unlike the spiritual world, utterly transitory and subject to the march of time. So he gently reminds the disenchanted onlooker that the created order is not something one ought to observe dispassionately because its meaning is dependent upon ideas that spring from the invisible realm of imagination. Thus the angel encourages the reader to reframe the world as an enchanted place that can be seen through both the eye and mind.

As a purely theological endeavor, what dreams may come as far as angelology is concerned remains to be seen, but the greatest challenges ahead depend upon whether the doctrine can continue its creative evolution without undermining the angel's existence or relationship to God in the process.[89] The prominence of angels in the history of sacred literature reflects the values and experiences of biblical authors and theologians, with angels as a means of accentuating God's transcendence and immanence, his relationship to ecclesiology, his creative work within the world, and his eucharistic self-provision. Yet what is at issue is not simply that our ancestor's angelologies may provide new insights into their theological rationale—though that would be sufficient reason for revisiting their ideas—but whether ideas drawn from their wells and poured out in the Eucharist will help to irrigate the angelologies that have yet to be sown from our pulpits, palettes, and publications. By documenting the variety of ways in which angels have been used as a profound, yet understated, presence throughout the history of Judeo-Christian reflection, I have hoped to pique, in a small way, a resurgence of interest in angels as a theological device that brings glory to the Godhead and reveals a glimpse of Paradise in our midst.

89. This is a fault I find with several modern angelologies like those of Walter Wink, Michel Serres, and to a lesser extent, Geddes MacGregor, who convert the angel into a symbol for human institutions, communication, or even as extraterrestrials, respectively. They do not necessarily inspire the sort of intentional verticality found in the Old Testament, pseudo-Denys, or Aquinas. (See Wink, *Naming the Powers;* Serres, *Angels;* MacGregor, *Angels.*)

# Bibliography

Abbey, Edward. *Desert Solitaire*. Tucson, AZ: University of Arizona Press, 1988.

Addleshaw, G.W.O. *The Ecclesiology of the Churches of the Dead Cities of Northern Syria*. London: Ecclesiological Society, 1973.

Aertsen, Jan. "Aquinas's Philosophy in Its Historical Setting." In *The Cambridge Companion to Aquinas*, edited by Norman Kretzmann and Eleonore Stump, 12–37. Cambridge: Cambridge University Press, 1993.

Albright, William F. "What Were the Cherubim?" *The Biblical Archaeologist* 1 (1938) 1–3.

Allison, Dale. "Behind the Temptations of Jesus." In *Authenticating the Activities of Jesus*, edited by Bruce Chilton and Craig A. Evans, 195–214. Leiden: Brill, 1999.

Alter, Robert. *The Art of Biblical Narrative*. New York: Basic, 1981.

Anonymous. "Dionysius the Pseudo-Areopagite." In *The Oxford Dictionary of the Christian Church*, edited by F. L. Cross and E. A. Livingstone, 315–36. London: Oxford University Press, 2005.

Aquinas, Thomas. *Commentary by Saint Thomas Aquinas on the Epistle to the Hebrews*. Translated by Fabian Larcher. Online: www.aquinas.avemaria.edu/Aquinas-Hebrews.pdf.

———. *Commentary by Saint Thomas Aquinas on the First Epistle to the Corinthians*. Translated by Fabian Larcher. Online: www.aquinas.avemaria.edu/Aquinas-Corinthians.pdf.

———. *Commentary on St. Paul's Epistle to the Galatians*. Translated by Fabian Larcher. Online: www.diafrica.org/kenny/CDtexts/SSGalatians.htm.

———. *Commentary on St. Paul's First Letter to the Thessalonians and the Letter to the Philippians*. Translated by Fabian Larcher. Online: www.diafrica.org/kenny/CDtexts/SS1Thes.htm.

———. *In Librum Beati Dionysii De Divinis Nominibus Expositio*. Edited by Ceslas Pera. Turin: Marietti, 1950.

———. *St. Thomas's Commentary on the Psalms*. Translated by Hugh McDonald and Stephen Loughlin. 2009. Online: http://www4.desales.edu/~philtheo/loughlin/ATP/Psalm_33.html.

———. *Summa Theologiae*. Edited by Edward D. O'Connor. Vol. 24. Cambridge: Cambridge University Press, 1990.

———. *Summa Theologiae: Divine Government: Ia2ae. 103–9*. Edited by T. C. O'Brien. Vol. 14. Cambridge: Cambridge University Press, 2006.

————. *Summa Theologica*. Edited by Kenelm Foster O.P. Vol. 9 (Ia. 50–64). Cambridge: Cambridge University Press, 2006.

Arthur, Rosemary A. *Pseudo-Dionysius as Polemicist*. Farnham, UK: Ashgate, 2008.

Augustine. "Enarrationes in Psalmos 103, 15." *Documenta Catholica Omnia*. Online: http://www.documentacatholicaomnia.eu/04z/z_0354-0430__Augustinus__Enarrationes_in_Psalmos__LT.doc.html.

Bakken, Peter W., et al. *Ecology, Justice, and Christian Faith: A Critical Guide to the Literature*. Westport, CT: Greenwood, 1995.

Balthasar, Hans Urs von. *The Glory of the Lord*. Vol. 2: *Studies in Theological Style: Clerical Styles*. Translated by Andrew Louth et al. Edinburgh: T. & T. Clark, 1985.

Barackman, Floyd H. *Practical Christian Theology*. Grand Rapids: Kregel, 2001.

Barth, Karl. *Church Dogmatics I.1*. Edited by Geoffrey W. Bromiley and Thomas F. Torrance. Reprint. London: T. & T. Clark, 2004.

————. *Church Dogmatics III.1. The Doctrine of Creation*. Edited by Geoffrey W. Bromiley and Thomas F. Torrance. Translated by J. W. Edwards et al. Reprint. London: T. & T. Clark, 2004.

————. *Church Dogmatics III.2*. Edited by Geoffrey W. Bromiley and Thomas F. Torrance. London: T. & T. Clark, 1960.

————. *Church Dogmatics III.3*. Edited by Geoffrey W. Bromiley and Thomas F. Torrance. Reprint. London: T. & T. Clark, 2004.

————. *The Epistle to the Romans*. Translated by Edwyn Clement Hoskyns. London: Oxford University Press, 1968.

————. *The Humanity of God*. Translated by John Newton Thomas. Louisville, KY: Westminster John Knox, 1960.

Bauckham, Richard. "Eschatology." In *The Oxford Handbook of Systematic Theology*, edited by John B. Webster, et al., 306–22. Oxford: Oxford University Press, 2007.

Baur, Ferdinand Christian. *Christliche Lehre von Der Dreieinigkeit Und Menschwerdung Gottes*. Vol. 2. Tübingen: Oslander, 1843.

Berkhof, Louis. *Systematic Theology*. Grand Rapids: Eerdmans, 1996.

Berman, Constance H. *Medieval Religion*. New York: Routledge, 2005.

Berry, D. H., and Malcolm Heath. "Oratory and Declamation." In *Handbook of Classical Rhetoric in the Hellenistic Period: 330 B.C.–A.D. 400*, edited by Stanley E. Porter, 393–420. Leiden: Brill, 1997.

Birch, Charles, and John B. Cobb. *The Liberation of Life: From the Cell to the Community*. Cambridge: Cambridge University Press, 1981.

Boa, Kenneth, and Robert M. Bowman. *Sense and Nonsense about Angels and Demons*. Grand Rapids: Zondervan, 2007.

Bordwell, David, ed. *Catechism of the Catholic Church*. London: Bloomsbury, 2002.

Borg, Marcus. *Jesus in Contemporary Scholarship*. New York: Continuum, 1994.

Boyle, Leonard. *The Setting of the Summa Theologiae of Saint Thomas*. Toronto: Pontifical Institute of Mediaeval Studies, 1982.

Bradshaw, Paul F. *The Search for the Origins of Christian Worship*. Oxford: Oxford University Press, 2002.

Brown, David. *God and Enchantment of Place: Reclaiming Human Experience*. Oxford: Oxford University Press, 2004.

Brueggemann, Walter. *Genesis*. Interpretation. Louisville: Westminster John Knox, 1982.

Brunner, Emil, and Karl Barth. *Natural Theology*. Translated by Peter Fraenkel. London: Centenary, 1946.

Bucur, Bogdan Gabriel. *Angelomorphic Pneumatology: Clement of Alexandria and Other Early Christian Witnesses*. Leiden: Brill, 2009.

Budge, E. A., trans. *The Book of the Cave of Treasures*. London: Religious Tract Society, 1927.

Bultmann, Rudolf. *The New Testament and Mythology*. Edited by Schubert Ogden. Philadelphia: Fortress, 1984.

Burney, Diana. *Spiritual Clearings: Sacred Practices to Release Negative Energy and Harmonize Your Life*. Berkeley, CA: North Atlantic, 2009.

Cabasilas, Nicolaus, and P. A. McNulty. *A Commentary on the Divine Liturgy*. Translated by J. M. Hussey. Crestwood, NY: St. Vladimir's Seminary, 1998.

Calvin, John. *The Acts of the Apostles 14–28*. Translated by John W. Fraser. Grand Rapids: Eerdmans, 1995.

———. *A Commentary on Genesis*. London: Banner of Truth Trust, 1965.

———. *Commentary on the Book of the Prophet Daniel*. Translated by Thomas Meyers. Vol. 2. Grand Rapids: Eerdmans, 1948.

———. *Commentary on the Epistles of Paul the Apostle to the Corinthians*. Vol. 2. Translated by John Pringle. Grand Rapids: Eerdmans, 1948.

———. *Commentaries on the Epistles of Paul the Apostle to the Philippians, Colossians, and Thessalonians*. Translated by John Pringle. Grand Rapids: Eerdmans, 1948.

———. *Commentaries on the First Twenty Chapters of the Book of the Prophet Ezekiel*. Vol. 2. Translated by Thomas Meyers. Grand Rapids: Eerdmans, 1948.

———. *Institutes of the Christian Religion*. Translated by Henry Beveridge. Rev. ed. Peabody, MA: Hendrickson, 2008.

Carruthers, Mary. *The Book of Memory: A Study of Memory in Medieval Culture*. Cambridge: Cambridge University Press, 2008.

Cassuto, Umberto. *The Documentary Hypothesis and the Composition of the Pentateuch*. Jerusalem: Shalem, 2006.

Chafer, Lewis Sperry, and John F. Walvoord. *Major Bible Themes*. Grand Rapids: Zondervan, 1974.

Chase, Steven. *Angelic Spirituality: Medieval Perspectives on the Ways of Angels*. New York: Paulist, 2002.

Chesterton, G. K. *St. Thomas Aquinas*. Fairford, UK: Echo Library, 2007.

Childs, Brevard S. *Isaiah*. Louisville: Westminster John Knox, 2001.

Chrysostom, John. *Six Books on the Priesthood*. Translated by G. Neville. London: SPCK, 1964.

Cirlot, Juan Eduardo. *A Dictionary of Symbols*. Translated by Jack Sage. Mineola, NY: Dover, 2002.

Collard, Andrée. *Rape of the Wild*. Bloomington, IN: Indiana University Press, 1989.

Collins, James. *The Thomistic Philosophy of the Angels*. Washington, DC: Catholic University of America Press, 1947.

Cooper, Diana. *A Little Light on the Spiritual Laws*. Forres, UK: Findhorn, 2007.

Corré, Alan D. *Understanding the Talmud*. New York: Ktav, 1975.

Corrigan, Kevin. *Reading Plotinus*. West Lafaette, IN: Purdue University Press, 2005.

Coudert, Allison. "Angels." In *The Encyclopedia of Religion*, Vol. 1, edited by Mircea Eliade and Charles J. Adams, 282–86. New York: Macmillan, 1987.

Coulter, Ann. "Oil Good; Democrats Bad." *Townhall.com*, October 12, 2008. Online: http://townhall.com/columnists/AnnCoulter/2000/10/12/oil_good;_democrats_bad.

Cox, Harvey. *Fire from Heaven: The Rise of Pentecostal Spirituality and the Reshaping of Religion in the Twenty-First Century*. Cambridge, MA: DeCapo, 2001.

Curtius, Ernst Robert. *European Literature and the Latin Middle Ages*. Princeton: Princeton University Press, 1990.

Danielou, Jean. *Angels and Their Mission: According to the Fathers of the Church*. Allen, TX: More, 1987.

———. *The Origins of Latin Christianity*. Vol. 3. London: Darton, Longman & Todd, 1977.

Davidson, Maxwell. *Angels at Qumran: A Comparative Study of 1 Enoch 1-36, 72-108 and Sectarian Writings from Qumran*. Sheffield, UK: JSOT, 1992.

Davies, J. G. *Everyday God*. London: SCM, 1973.

Davila, James. *Descenders to the Chariot*. Leiden: Brill, 2001.

———. "The Name of God at Moriah: An Unpublished Fragment from 4QGenExoda." *Journal of Biblical Literature* 110 (1991) 577–82.

Davis, Stephen. "Introducing an Arabic Commentary on the Apocalypse: Ibn Kātib Qaysar on Revelation." *Harvard Theological Review* 101 (2008) 77–96.

Duclow, Donald. "Isaiah Meets the Seraph: Breaking Ranks in Dionysius and Eriugena?" In *Eriugena: East and West*, edited by B. McGinn and W. Otten, 233–52. Notre Dame, IN: University of Notre Dame Press, 1994.

Demisch, Heinz. *Die Sphinx: Geschichte Ihrer Darstellung von Den Anfängen Bis Zur Gegenwart*. Stuttgart: Urachhaus, 1977.

Dever, William G. *Did God Have a Wife?* Grand Rapids: Eerdmans, 2005.

Donaldson, James, trans. "Apostolic Constitutions." *New Advent*. Online: http://www.newadvent.org/fathers/07158.htm.

D'Onofrio, Giulio, and Matthew O'Connell. *The History of Theology: Middle Ages*. Collegeville: MN: Liturgical, 2008.

Driver, S. R. *The Book of Exodus*. Cambridge: Cambridge University Press, 1911.

Dunn, James D. G. *Christology in the Making: A New Testament Inquiry into the Origins of the Doctrine of the Incarnation*. 2nd ed. Grand Rapids: Eerdmans, 1996.

Durant, Will. *The Story of Civilization: Caesar and Christ*. Vol. 3. New York: Simon and Schuster, 1944.

Dyrness, William. *Themes in Old Testament Theology*. Downers Grove, IL: IVP, 1979.

Ebeling, Jennie R. "Cherubim." In *Eerdmans Dictionary of the Bible*, edited by David Noel Freedman et al., 233. Grand Rapids: Eerdmans, 2000.

Edwards, Mark U. "Luther's Polemical Controversies." In *The Cambridge Companion to Martin Luther*, edited by Donald McKim, 192–208. Cambridge: Cambridge University Press, 2003.

Elior, Rachel. "Mysticism, Magic, and Angelology—The Perception of Angels in Hekhalot Literature." *Jewish Studies Quarterly* 1 (1993) 3–53.

"Environmental Indicators: Greenhouse Gas Emissions." *United Nations Statistics Division*. Online: http://unstats.un.org/unsd/environment/air_co2_emissions.htm.

Erickson, Millard. *Christian Theology*. Grand Rapids: Baker Academic, 1983.

Eskola, Timo. *Messiah and the Throne: Jewish Merkabah Mysticism and Early Exaltation Discourse*. Tübingen: Mohr Siebeck, 2001.

Fabry, Heinz-Josef. "Nechosheth." In *Theological Dictionary of the Old Testament*, edited by G. Johannes Botterweck and Helmer Ringgren, Vol. 9, 378–80. Grand Rapids: Eerdmans, 1998.

Faivre, Antoine. *Access to Western Esotericism*. Albany, NY: SUNY, 1994.

Fergusson, David. *The Cosmos and the Creator*. London: SPCK, 1998.

Finkelstein, Israel, and Neil Asher Silberman. *The Bible, Unearthed: Archaeology's New Vision of Ancient Israel*. New York: Free, 2001.

Firth, C. H., and Robert S. Rait, eds. *Acts and Ordinances of the Interregnum, 1642–1660*. London: H.M. Stationery Office, 1911.

Fletcher-Louis, Crispin H. T. *Luke-Acts: Angels, Christology and Soteriology*. Tübingen: Mohr Siebeck, 1997.

Forde, Gerhard. *On Being a Theologian of the Cross*. Grand Rapids: Eerdmans, 1997.

*Forms of Prayer for Jewish Worship*. Vol. 2. London: Reform Synagogues of Great Britain, 1977.

Fortescue, Adrian. *The Orthodox Eastern Church*. Whitefish, MT: Kessinger, 2004.

Fossum, Jarl Egil. *The Name of God and the Angel of the Lord*. Tübingen: Mohr Siebeck, 1985.

Foster, Edgar G. *Angelomorphic Christology and the Exegesis of Psalm 8:5 in Tertullian's Adversus Praxean*. Lanham, MD: University Press of America, 2006.

France, R. T. *Jesus and the Old Testament*. Vancouver, BC: Regent College, 2000.

Freedman, David Noel. "Who Is Like Thee among the Gods?" In *Ancient Israelite Religion*, edited by Patrick D. Miller. Philadelphia: Fortress, 1987.

Frennesson, Björn. *In a Common Rejoicing: Liturgical Communion with Angels in Qumran*. Uppsala: University of Uppsala Press, 1999.

Funderburk, G. "Angel." In *The Zondervan Pictorial Encyclopedia of the Bible*, Vol. 1, edited by Marrill Chapin Tenney, 160–66. Grand Rapids: Zondervan, 1975.

Gatti, M. L. "Plotinus: The Platonic Tradition and the Foundation of Neoplatonism." In *The Cambridge Companion to Plotinus*, edited by Lloyd P. Gerson, 10–37. Cambridge: Cambridge University Press, 1996.

George, A. R. "Four Temple Rituals from Babylon." In *Wisdom, Gods and Literature: Studies in Assyriology in Honour of W. G. Lambert*, edited by A. R. George and I. L. Finkel. Winona Lake, IN: Eisenbrauns, 2000.

Gerson, Lloyd P. *Plotinus*. The Arguments of the Philosophers. London: Routledge, 1994.

Gieschen, Charles A. *Angelomorphic Christology*. Leiden: Brill, 1998.

Gilson, Etienne. *The Philosophy of St. Thomas Aquinas*. New York: Random House, 1956.

Giovino, Mariana. *The Assyrian Sacred Tree*. Fribourg: Academic Press Fribourg, 2007.

Gledhill, Ruth. "Church of England Congregations Fall Again, and Half Are Pensioners." *The Sunday Times*, January 23, 2010. Online: http://www.timesonline.co.uk/tol/comment/faith/article6999268.ece.

Gnuse, Robert Karl. *No Other Gods: Emergent Monotheism in Israel*. Sheffield, UK: Sheffield Academic Press, 1997.

Goodenough, E. R. *The Archaeological Evidence from the Diaspora*. New York: Pantheon, 1953.

Goulder, M.D. *The Psalms of Asaph and the Pentateuch*. London: Continuum, 1996.

Green, Alberto Ravinell Whitney. *The Storm-God in the Ancient Near East*. Winona Lake, IN: Eisenbrauns, 2003.

Pope Gregory I. "Homily 25 on the Gospels." In *Reading the Gospels with Gregory the Great*, translated by Santha Bhattacharji, 71–90. Petersham, MA: St. Bede's, 2001.

Grenz, Stanley J. *Theology for the Community of God*. Grand Rapids: Eerdmans, 2000.

Griscom, Chris. *Ecstasy Is a New Frequency: Teachings of the Light Institute*. New York: Simon & Schuster, 1987.

Grudem, Wayne. *Systematic Theology*. Grand Rapids: Zondervan, 1994.

Gunkel, Hermann. *Genesis*. Translated by Mark E. Biddle. Macon, GA: Mercer University Press, 1997.

Halperin, David. *Faces of the Chariot: Early Jewish Responses to Ezekiel's Vision*. Tübingen: Mohr Siebeck, 1988.

Hamilton, Victor P. *The Book of Genesis: Chapters 1–17*. Grand Rapids: Eerdmans, 1990.

Hampson, Margaret Daphne. *Theology and Feminism*. Oxford: Wiley-Blackwell, 1990.

Handy, Lowell K. *Among the Host of Heaven: The Syro-Palestinian Pantheon*. Winona Lake, IN: Eisenbrauns, 1994.

———. "The Appearance of Pantheon in Judah." In *The Triumph of Elohim: From Yahwisms to Judaisms*, edited by Diana Vikander Edelman, 27–44. Grand Rapids: Eerdmans, 1995.

Hankey, W. J. "Dionysian Hierarchy in St. Thomas Aquinas: Tradition and Transformation." In *Denys l'Aréopagite et sa postérité en Orient et en Occident, Actes du Colloque International Paris, 21–24 Septembre 1994*, edited by Ysabel de Andia, 405–38. Collection des Études Augustiniennes, Série Antiquité 151. Paris: Institut d'Études Augustiniennes, 1997.

Hannah, Darrell D. *Michael and Christ*. Tübingen: Mohr Siebeck, 1999.

Hanson, Paul D. *The People Called: The Growth of Community in the Bible*. San Francisco: Harper& Row, 1986.

Harrington, Wilfrid J., and Daniel J. Harrington. *Revelation*. Sacra Pagina 16. Collegeville: MN: Liturgical, 1993.

Hart, Trevor A. *Regarding Karl Barth: Toward a Reading of His Theology*. Downers Grove, IL: IVP, 2000.

Hathaway, Ronald F. *Hierarchy and the Definition of Order in the Letters of Pseudo-Dionysius. A Study in the Form and Meaning of the Pseudo-Dionysian Writings*. The Hague: Nijhoff, 1969.

Hayman, Peter. "Monotheism—a Misused Word in Jewish Studies?" *Journal of Jewish Studies* 42 (1991) 1–15.

Healy, Nicholas. "Introduction." In *Aquinas on Scripture: An Introduction to His Biblical Commentaries*, edited by Thomas Weinandy, et al. London: T. & T. Clark, 2005.

Hendricks, Stephenie. *Divine Destruction*. Hoboken, NJ: Melville House, 2005.

Hengstenberg, Ernst Wilhelm. *Christology of the Old Testament*. Vol. 1. Translated by Theodore Meyer. Edinburgh: T. & T. Clark, 1858.

Heschel, Abraham Joshua. *Heavenly Torah as Reflected through the Generations*. Edited by Gordon Tucker. New York: Continuum, 2006.

Hobbes, Thomas. *Leviathan*. Chicago: Wilder, 2007.

Hodge, Charles. *Systematic Theology*. Vol. 1. Grand Rapids: Eerdmans, 1940.

Hoffmann, Matthias. *The Destroyer and the Lamb: The Relationship Between Angelomorphic and Lamb Christology in the Book of Revelation*. Tübingen: Mohr Siebeck, 2005.

Homer. *The Odyssey*. Translated by Edward McCrorie. Baltimore: Johns Hopkins University Press, 2004.

Hornung, Erik. *Akhenaten and the Religion of Light*. Ithaca, NY: Cornell University Press, 2001.

Hurtado, Larry W. *One God, One Lord: Early Christian Devotion and Ancient Jewish Monotheism*. 2nd ed. London: Continuum, 1998.

Inglis, John. *Spheres of Philosophical Inquiry and the Historiography of Medieval Philosophy*. Leiden: Brill, 1998.

Iribarren, Isabel, and Martin Lenz, eds. *Angels in Medieval Philosophical Inquiry: Their Function and Significance*. Aldershot, UK: Ashgate, 2008.

Janz, Denis. *Luther on Thomas Aquinas*. Stuttgart: Franz Steiner Verlag Wiesbaden GmbH, 1989.

Jędrej, M. Charles, and Rosalind Shaw. *Dreaming, Religion, and Society in Africa*. Leiden: Brill, 1992.

Johnston, Sarah Iles. *Religions of the Ancient World*. Cambridge, MA: Harvard University Press, 2004.

Jones, David Albert. *Angels: A History*. Oxford: Oxford University Press, 2010.

Kadushin, Max. *Worship and Ethics: A Study in Rabbinic Judaism*. Binghampton, NY: Global Academic, 2001.

Kapelrud, A. S. "The Gates of Hell and the Guardian Angels of Paradise." *Journal of the American Oriental Society* 70 (1950) 151–56.

Kaufmann, Yehezkel, and Moshe Greenberg. *The Religion of Israel*. New York: Schocken, 1972.

Keck, David. *Angels & Angelology in the Middle Ages*. Oxford: Oxford University Press, 1998.

Keller, Werner, and Otto Kaiser. *The Bible As History: Archaeologists Show the Truth of the Old Testament*. Oxford: Lion, 1991.

Kennedy, Daniel. "St. Thomas Aquinas." *The Catholic Encyclopedia*, Vol. 14, 663–76. New York: Appleton, 1913.

Kenny, Anthony. *Aquinas on Mind*. London: Routledge, 1994.

Kieckhefer, Richard. *Theology in Stone*. New York: Oxford University Press, 2004.

King, T.M., and Pierre Teilhard de Chardin. *Teilhard's Mass*. Mahwah: Paulist, 2005.

Kitchen, Kenneth Anderson. *Pharaoh Triumphant, the Life and Times of Ramesses II, King of Egypt*. Warminster, UK: Aris & Phillips, 1982.

Kitto, John, assisted by James Taylor. "Cherubim." In *The Popular Cyclopadia of Biblical Literature*, 192–95. Boston: Gould and Lincoln, 1854.

Knibb, Michael. "The Book of Daniel in Its Context." In *The Book of Daniel: Composition and Reception*, Vol. 1, edited by John Joseph Collins and Peter W. Flint, 16–35. Leiden: Brill, 2001.

Knowles, Melody D. *Centrality Practiced: Jerusalem in the Religious Practice of Yehud and the Diaspora in the Persian Period*. Atlanta: Society of Biblical Literature, 2006.

Kratz, Reinhard. "The Visions of Daniel." In *The Book of Daniel: Composition and Reception*, Vol. 1, edited by John J. Collins and Peter W. Flint, 91–113. Leiden: Brill, 2001.

Krautheimer, Richard. *Studies in East Christian, Medieval and Renaissance Art*. New York: New York University Press, 1969.

Kretzmann, Norman, and Eleonore Stump, eds. *The Cambridge Companion to Aquinas*. Cambridge: Cambridge University Press, 1993.

Kwon, Lillian. "Largest Christian Groups Report Membership Decline | Christianpost. com." *The Christian Post*, February 25, 2009. Online: http://www.christianpost.

com/article/20090225/largest-christian-groups-report-membership-decline/index.html.

Lacocque, André. *The Book of Daniel*. Louisville: John Knox, 1979.

Larson-Miller, Lizette. "A Return to the Liturgical Architecture of Northern Syria." *Studia Liturgica* 24 (1994) 71–83.

Letellier, Robert Ignatius. *Day in Mamre, Night in Sodom: Abraham and Lot in Genesis 18 and 19*. Leiden: Brill, 1995.

Levering, Matthew. "A Note on Scripture in the Summa Theologiae." *New Blackfriars* 90 (2009) 652–58.

Lewis, Agnes. *Apocrypha Syriaca*. London: Clay, 1902.

Lightner, Robert P. *Handbook of Evangelical Theology: A Historical, Biblical, and Contemporary Survey and Review*. Grand Rapids: Kregel, 1995.

Linzey, Andrew. *Animal Theology*. Chicago: University of Illinois, 1995.

Livingston, G. *The Pentateuch in Its Cultural Environment*. Grand Rapids: Baker, 1974.

Louth, Andrew. *Denys the Aeropagite*. New York: Continuum, 2002.

———. *The Origins of the Christian Mystical Tradition from Plato to Denys*. Oxford: Oxford University Press, 1981.

Luhrmann, T. M. "Evil in the Sands of Time: Theology and Identity Politics among the Zoroastrian Parsis." *The Journal of Asian Studies* 61 (2002) 861–89.

Luther, Martin. *Luther's Works*. Vol. 36. Edited by Jaroslav Pelikan and Helmut T. Lehmann. St. Louis: Concordia, 1955.

———. *The Table Talk of Martin Luther*. Translated by Wm. Hazlitt. London: Bohn, 1857.

MacDonald, W. "The Angel of the Lord." In *Current Issues in Biblical and Patristic Interpretation: Studies in Honor of Merrill C. Tenney*, edited by Gerald Hawthorne, 324–35. Grand Rapids: Eerdmans, 1975.

MacGregor, Geddes. *Angels: Ministers of Grace*. New York: Paragon House, 1988.

Mafico, Temba L. J. *Yahweh's Emergence as "Judge" among the Gods: A Study of the Hebrew Root Špt*. Lewiston, NY: Mellen, 2006.

Malysz, Piotr. "Luther and Dionysius: Beyond Mere Negations." In *Re-Thinking Dionysius the Areopagite*, edited by Sarah Coakley and Charles M. Stang, 149–62. Chichester, UK: Wiley-Blackwell, 2009.

Marius, Richard. *Martin Luther: The Christian between God and Death*. Cambridge: Harvard University Press, 1999.

Mascall, Eric Lionel. *Pi in the High*. London: Faith, 1959.

Matt, Daniel Chanan. *The Zohar*. Palo Alto: Stanford University Press, 2006.

Mazar, Amihai. "To What God? Altars and a House Shrine from Tel Rehov Puzzle Archaeologists." *Biblical Archaeology Review* 34 (2008) 40–47.

McBrien, Richard P. *Catholicism*. San Francisco: Harper, 1994.

McFague, Sallie. *Models of God: Theology for an Ecological, Nuclear Age*. Philadelphia: Fortress, 1987.

McGarry, Eugene. "The Ambidextrous Angel (Daniel 12:7 and Deuteronomy 32:40): Inner-Biblical Exegesis and Textual Criticism in Counterpoint." *Journal of Biblical Literature* 124 (2005) 211–28.

McHarg, Ian. *Design with Nature*. Garden City, NY: Natural History, 1969.

McIntosh, Jane. *Ancient Mesopotamia*. Santa Barbara: ABC-CLIO, 2005.

McNally, Robert. *The Bible in the Early Middle Ages*. Westminster, MD: Newman, 1959.

McNamee, Maurice B. *Vested Angels: Eucharistic Allusions in Early Netherlandish Paintings*. Leuven: Peeters, 1998.

Mears, Daniel P., and Christopher G. Ellison. "Who Buys New Age Materials? Exploring Sociodemographic, Religious, Network, and Contextual Correlates of New Age Consumption." *Sociology of Religion* 61.3 (2000) 289–313.

Melanchthon, Philipp. "Treatise on the Power and the Primacy of the Pope." In *The Book of Concord: The Confessions of the Evangelical Lutheran Church*, edited by Robert Kolb and Timothy Wengert, 329–44. Minneapolis: Augsburg Fortress, 2000.

Metzger, M. "Der Thron Als Manifestation Der Herrschermacht in Der Ikonographie Des Vorderen Orients Und Im Alten Testament." In *Charisma Und Institution*, edited by Trutz Rendtorff. 250–96. Tübingen: Gütersloher Verlagshaus G. Mohn, 1985.

Meyendorff, John. *Byzantine Theology*. New York: Fordham University Press, 1987.

Migliore, Daniel L. *Faith Seeking Understanding: An Introduction to Christian Theology*. Grand Rapids: Eerdmans, 2004.

Milburn, Robert. *Early Christian Art and Architecture*. Berkeley: University of California Press, 1991.

Miller, Patrick. "Fire in the Mythology of Canaan and Israel." *Catholic Biblical Quarterly* 27 (1965) 256–61.

Moltmann, Jürgen. *God in Creation*. Translated by Margaret Kohl. San Francisco: Harper, 1985.

Morgenstern, Julian. "The Mythological Background of Psalm 82." *Hebrew Union College Annual* 14 (1939) 311–14.

Mullen, E. Theodore. *The Assembly of the Gods: The Divine Council in Canaanite and Early Hebrew Literature*. Missoula, MT: Scholars, 1980.

Munk, Linda. *The Devil's Mousetrap*. New York: Oxford University Press US, 1997.

Nestle, Eberhard, Erwin Nestle, Barbara Aland, and Kurt Aland, eds. *Novum Testamentum Graece*. 27th ed. Stuttgart: Deutsche Bibelgesellschaft, 1993.

Nichols, Aidan. *Discovering Aquinas*. Grand Rapids: Eerdmans, 2003.

Nicholson, Ernest. *The Pentateuch in the Twentieth Century: The Legacy of Julius Wellhausen*. Oxford: Oxford University Press, 2003.

Noll, Stephen F. "Thinking about Angels." In *The Unseen World*, edited by Anthony N. S. Lane, 1–27. Grand Rapids: Baker, 1997.

Norman, Ralph. "Rediscovery of Mysticism." In *The Blackwell Companion to Modern Theology*, edited by Gareth Jones, 449–65. Oxford: Wiley-Blackwell, 2004.

Oberman, Heiko. *The Dawn of the Reformation: Essays in Late Medieval and Early Reformation Thought*. Edinburgh: T. & T. Clark, 1986.

O'Brien, Denis. "Plotinus on Matter and Evil." In *The Cambridge Companion to Plotinus*, edited by Lloyd Gerson, 171–95. Cambridge: Cambridge University Press, 1996.

Oden, Robert A. *The Bible without Theology*. Urbana, IL: University of Illinois Press, 1987.

Old, Hughes Oliphant. *The Reading and Preaching of the Scriptures in the Worship of the Christian Church*. Vol. 3. Grand Rapids: Eerdmans, 1998.

Olyan, Saul M. *A Thousand Thousands Served Him: Exegesis and the Naming of Angels in Ancient Judaism*. Texte Und Studien Zum Antiken Judentum Series 36. Tübingen: Mohr Siebeck, 1993.

O'Meara, Dominic J. *Plotinus*. Oxford: Oxford University Press, 1995.

Osborn, Lawrence. "Entertaining Angels: Their Place in Contemporary Theology." *Tyndale Bulletin* 45 (1994) 273–96.

Ott, Ludwig. *Fundamentals of Catholic Dogma*. Cork: Mercier, 1955.

Pannenberg, Wolfhart. *Systematic Theology*. Translated by Geoffrey W. Bromiley, Vol. 2. Grand Rapids: Eerdmans, 1994.

Paul II, John. "Ecclesia de Eucharistia," 2003. Online: http://www.vatican.va/edocs/ENG0821/__P3.HTM.

Pauline, Albenda. *Le palais de Sargon d'Assyrie*. Paris: Recherche sur les Civilisations, 1986.

Peña, Ignacio. *The Christian Art of Byzantine Syria*. Reading, UK: Garnet, 1997.

Perl, Eric D. *Theophany: The Neoplatonic Philosophy of Dionysius the Areopagite*. Albany, NY: SUNY Press, 2007.

Phillips, John. *The Reformation of Images: Destruction of Art in England, 1535–1660*. Berkeley: University of California Press, 1973.

Plotinus. *The Enneads*. Edited by John M. Dillon. Translated by Stephen Mackenna. London: Penguin, 1991.

Pontifical Council for Culture, and Pontifical Council for Interreligious Dialogue. "Jesus Christ the Bearer of the Water of Life—A Christian Reflection on the New Age." 2010. Online: http://www.vatican.va/roman_curia/pontifical_councils/interelg/documents/rc_pc_interelg_doc_20030203_new-age_en.html.

Pope, Marvin. *El in the Ugaritic Texts*. Leiden: Brill, 1955.

Pritchard, James. *The Ancient Near East: An Anthology of Texts and Pictures*. Princeton: Princeton University Press, 1958.

Proclus. *A Commentary on the First Book of Euclid's Elements*. Princeton: Princeton University Press, 1992.

Propp, William. *Exodus 1–18: A New Translation with Introduction and Commentary*. New York: Doubleday, 1999.

Propp, William Henry. *Exodus 19–40*. New York: Doubleday, 2006.

Pseudo-Dionysius. *Pseudo-Dionysius: The Complete Works*. The Classics of Western Spirituality. Translated by Colm Luibhéid. New York: Paulist, 1987.

Putnam, Caroline Canfield. *Beauty in the Pseudo-Denis*. Washington, DC: Catholic University of America Press, 1960.

Rahner, Karl. "Angels." *Encyclopedia of Theology*, edited by Karl Rahner, 8–13. New York: Continuum, 1982.

———. *Theological Investigations*. Vol. 19. Translated by Graham Harrison. New York: Seabury, 1975.

Randolph Joiner, Karen. "The Bronze Serpent in the Israelite Cult." *Journal of Biblical Literature* 87 (1968) 245–56.

Rapaport, Samuel. *Tales and Maxims from the Midrash*. New York: Dutton, 1907.

RavenWolf, Silver. *Angels: Companions in Magick*. St. Paul, MN: Llewellyn Worldwide, 1996.

Raymond of Penafort. "Dominican Documents: Primitive Constitutions." *Dominican Central Province*. 2008. Online: http://www.domcentral.org/trad/domdocs/0011.htm.

Rendtorff, Rolf, ed. *Problem of the Process of Transmission in the Pentateuch*. JSOT Supplement Series 89. Sheffield, UK: Sheffield Academic, 1990.

Reymond, Robert L. *A New Systematic Theology of the Christian Faith*. Nashville: Thomas Nelson, 1998.

Rhodes, Ron. *Angels among Us*. Eugene, OR: Harvest House, 2008.

Riordan, William. *Divine Light: Theology of Denys the Areopagite*. San Francisco: Ignatius, 2008.

Rohl, David. *From Eden to Exile*. London: Arrow, 2003.

Rorem, Paul. *Biblical and Liturgical Symbols within the Pseudo-Dionysian Synthesis*. Toronto: Pontifical Institute of Mediaeval Studies, 1984.

———. "Martin Luther's Christocentric Critique of Pseudo-Dionysian Spirituality." *Lutheran Quarterly* 11 (1997) 291–307.

———. *Pseudo-Dionysius: A Commentary on the Texts and an Introduction to Their Influence*. New York: Oxford University Press, 1993.

Rubenstein, Jeffrey L. *The Culture of the Babylonian Talmud*. Baltimore: Johns Hopkins University Press, 2005.

Ruether, Rosemary Radford. *Gaia & God: An Ecofeminist Theology of Earth Healing*. San Francisco: Harper, 1992.

Ryan, Thomas. *Thomas Aquinas as Reader of the Psalms*. Notre Dame, IN: University of Notre Dame Press, 2000.

Schemm Jr, Peter R. "The Agents of God: Angels." In *A Theology for the Church*, edited by Daniel L. Akin. 293–339. Nashville: B. & H., 2007.

Schleiermacher, Friedrich. *The Christian Faith*. Edited by H. R. Mackintosh and J. S. Stewart. Edinburgh: T. & T. Clark, 1928.

Schoot, Henk. *Christ the "Name" of God: Thomas Aquinas on Naming Christ*. Vol. 59. Leuven: Peeters, 1993.

Serres, Michel. *Angels: A Modern Myth*. New York: Flammarion, 1995.

Shalom, Shin. "Fifteenth of Shevat." In *Seder Tu B'shevat: The Festival of Trees*, edited by Adam Fisher, 5. New York: Central Conference of American Rabbis, 1989.

Sheets, R. J. "The Scriptural Dimension of St. Thomas." *American Ecclesiastical Review* 144 (1961) 172–73.

Smith, William Stevenson. *Ancient Egypt, as Represented in the Museum of Fine Arts, Boston*. Boston: Metcalf , 1960.

Sorabji, Richard. *The Philosophy of the Commentators, 200–600 AD: Logic and Metaphysics*. Ithaca, NY: Cornell University Press, 2005.

Smith, Mark S. *The Origins of Biblical Monotheism*. Oxford: Oxford University Press, 2003.

Speiser, A. E. "The Creation Epic." In *Ancient Near Eastern Texts Relating to the Old Testament*, edited by James B. Pritchard, 60–71. Princeton: Princeton University Press, 1950.

"State Membership Report: Denominational Groups, 2000." *The Association of Religion Data Archives*, 2010. Online: http://www.thearda.com/mapsReports/reports/state/48_2000.asp.

Stern, Chaim. *Paths of Faith: The New Jewish Prayer Book for Synagogue and Home*. New York: SP, 2002.

Stern, Ephraim. *What Happened to the Cult Figurines? Israelite Religion Purified after the Exile*. Washington, DC: Biblical Archaeology Society, 1989.

Stevens, Wallace. "Angels Surrounded Paysans." In *Collected Poems*, 496–97. New York: Random House, 1951.

Strauss, David. *The Life of Jesus, Critically Examined*. New York: Blanchard, 1860.

Stuckenbruck, Loren T. "'Angels' and 'God': Exploring the Limits of Early Jewish Monotheism." In *Early Jewish and Christian Monotheism*, edited by Wendy E. Sproston North and Loren T. Stuckenbruck, 45–70. London: T. & T. Clark, 2004.

Sullivan, Kevin Patrick. *Wrestling with Angels: A Study of the Relationship between Angels and Humans in Ancient Jewish Literature and the New Testament*. Leiden: Brill, 2004.

Tamburello, Dennis. *Union with Christ: John Calvin and the Mysticism of St. Bernard*. Louisville: Westminster John Knox, 1994.

Taylor, Terry Lynn. *Creating with the Angels*. Novato, CA: Kramer, 1993.

———. *Messengers of Love, Light and Grace: Getting to Know Your Personal Angels*. Novato, CA: New World Library, 2005.

Teixidor, Javier. "Review of The Genesis Apocryphon of Qumran Cave I. A Commentary." *Journal of the American Oriental Society* 87 (1967) 633–36.

The Episcopal Church. *The Book of Common Prayer*. New York: Church, 1979.

Thiessen, Henry Clarence, and Vernon D. Doerksen. *Lectures in Systematic Theology*. Grand Rapids: Eerdmans, 1979.

Thomas, Dylan. "All That I Owe the Fellows of the Grave." In *The Poems of Dylan Thomas*, Rev. ed., 93–94. New York: New Directions, 2003.

Tigchelaar, Eibert J. C. *Prophets of Old and The Day of the End: Zechariah, the Book of Watchers and Apocalyptic*. Leiden: Brill, 1996.

Torevell, David. *Liturgy and the Beauty of the Unknown*. Farnham, UK: Ashgate, 2007.

Torrance, Alan. *Persons in Communion*. Edinburgh: T. & T. Clark, 1996.

Torrance, Thomas F. "The Spiritual Relevance of Angels." In *Alive to God*, edited by J. I. Packer, 122–39. Vancouver, BC: Regent College, 1992.

Torrell, Jean-Pierre. *Saint Thomas Aquinas*. Vol. 1. Washington, DC: Catholic University of America Press, 2005.

Towner, Wayne Sibley. *Daniel*. Interpretation. Atlanta: Westminster John Knox, 1984.

Trevelyan, George. *Exploration into God*. Bath, UK: Gateway, 1991.

Tugwell, Simon, ed. *Albert and Thomas: Selected Writings*. New York: Paulist, 1988.

———. *Early Dominicans: Selected Writings*. Mahwah, NJ: Paulist, 1982.

Tuschling, R. *Angels and Orthodoxy: A Study in Their Development in Syria and Palestine from the Qumran Texts to Ephrem the Syrian*. Tübingen: Mohr Siebeck, 2007.

Valkenberg, Wilhelmus. *Words of the Living God: Place and Function of Holy Scripture in the Theology of St. Thomas Aquinas*. Leuven: Peeters, 2000.

VanSeters, John. *The Pentateuch: A Social-Science Commentary*. Sheffield, UK: Sheffield Academic Press, 1999.

Van Wieringen, Archibald L. H. M. *The Implied Reader in Isaiah 6–12*. Leiden: Brill, 1998.

Virtue, Doreen, and Charles Virtue. *Signs from Above: Your Angels' Messages about Your Life Purpose, Relationships, Health, and More*. Carlsbad, CA: Hay House, 2009.

Von Balthasar, Hans Urs. *Cosmic Liturgy: The Universe according to Maximus the Confessor*. San Francisco: Ignatius, 2003.

Von Harnack, Adolf. *Lehrbuch Der Dogmengeschichte*. Vol. 2. Tübingen: Mohr, 1990.

Von Rad, Gerhard. *Genesis: A Commentary*. Philadelphia: Westminster John Knox, 1972.

Waldstein, Michael. "On Scripture in the Summa Theologiae." *Aquinas Review* 96 (1996) 73–94.

Warren, Rick. *The Purpose-Driven Life*. Grand Rapids: Zondervan, 2002.

Wear, Sarah Klitenic, and John M. Dillon. *Dionysius the Areopagite and the Neoplatonist Tradition: Despoiling the Hellenes.* Farnham, UK: Ashgate, 2007.

Weil, Simone. *Waiting for God.* London: Fontana, 1959.

Weinandy, Thomas, ed. *Aquinas on Scripture: An Introduction to His Biblical Commentaries.* London: Continuum, 2005.

Weisheipl, James. "Mystic on Campus: Friar Thomas." In *An Introduction to the Medieval Mystics of Europe*, edited by Paul E. Szarmach, 135–94. Albany, NY: SUNY, 1984.

Weisheipl, James, and Fabian Larcher, trans. *Commentary on the Gospel of John*, n.d. Online: www.diafrica.org/kenny/CDtexts/SSJohn.htm.

Westermann, Claus. *God's Angels Need No Wings.* Philadelphia: Fortress, 1979.

Wevers, John William. *Notes on the Greek Text of Deuteronomy.* Atlanta: Scholars, 1995.

White, Lynn. "The Historical Roots of Our Ecological Crisis." *Science*, March 1967, 1203–7.

White, Stephen L. "Angel of the Lord: Messenger or Euphemism?" *Tyndale Bulletin* 50 (1999) 299–305.

Widmer, Michael. *Moses, God, and the Dynamics of Intercessory Prayer.* Tübingen: Mohr Siebeck, 2004.

Wink, Walter. *Naming the Powers: The Language of Power in the New Testament.* Minneapolis: Augsburg Fortress, 1983.

Williams, Rowan. *The Poems of Rowan Williams.* Grand Rapids: Eerdmans, 2004.

Wiseman, D. J. "Babylonia 605–539 B.C." In *The Assyrian and Babylonian Empires and Other States of the Near East, from the Eighth to the Sixth Centuries B.C.*, edited by John Boardman, Vol. III/2. The Cambridge Ancient History, 229–51. Cambridge: Cambridge University Press, 1991.

# Index

Made in the USA
Columbia, SC
09 August 2023

21456991R00138